REVOLUTION & EVOLUTION
Gorbachev and Soviet Politics

Martin Crouch
University of Bristol

PHILIP ALLAN
NEW YORK   LONDON   TORONTO   SYDNEY   TOKYO

First published 1989 by
Philip Allan
66 Wood Lane End, Hemel Hempstead
Hertfordshire HP2 4RG
A division of
Simon & Schuster International Group

Printed and bound in Great Britain
by Billing & Sons Ltd, Worcester

British Library Cataloguing in Publication Data

Crouch, Martin
  Revolution and evolution: Gorbachev and Soviet politics
  1. Soviet Union. Political development. Role of
  Gorbachev, M. S. (Mikhail Sergeevich), 1931-
  I. Title
  320.9'47'0924

    ISBN 0-86003-408-9
    ISBN 0-86003-708-8 Pbk

Library of Congress Cataloging-in-Publication Data

Crouch, Martin
  Revolution and evolution: Gorbachev and Soviet politics/
  Martin Crouch.
  ISBN 0-86003-408-9
  ISBN 0-86003-708-8 Pbk

  1. Soviet Union – Politics and government – 1917
  2. Gorbachev, Mikhail Sergeevich, 1931-. I. Title.
  DK288.C76   1989
  947.084 – dc20   89-6567
                                                        CIP

Contents

Preface   vi

1 The Revolutionary Era Under Lenin and Stalin   1

The Russian Historical Tradition – Russia before the
Revolution – Radical and Revolutionary Movements – The 1917
Revolution – Lenin and the Origins of the Monolithic Party –
The New Economic Policy of 1921 – Stalin and the Revolution
from Above – The Achievements and the Costs of the Stalin
Revolution – The Political Revolution – The Great Patriotic
War, 1941–45 – The Stalin Era and its Controversies – Further
Reading

2 Continuity and Change from Stalin to Gorbachev   36

The Khrushchev Era, 1953–64 – Economic and Foreign Policy –
De-Stalinisation and Political Reform – Khrushchev's
Overthrow – The Brezhnev Era, 1964–82 – Early Consolidation
– Brezhnev in the Ascendant: the Détente Era – The Years of
Stagnation – From Brezhnev to Gorbachev, 1982–85 –
Gorbachev's Rise to Power – Gorbachev's Reform Programme
– Continuity and Change Since Stalin – Further Reading

3 Ideology, Political Culture, and Dissent   72

The Official Ideology – From Marx to Stalin – Ideological
Change after Stalin – Ideology under Gorbachev – The
Effectiveness of Official Ideology – The Wider Political Culture
– Soviet 'Socialist Patriotism' – Ideology, Political Culture, and

Change – The Rise of the Dissident Movement – The Limits of the Dissident Movement – Dissident Thought: Medvedev, Sakharov and Solzhenitsyn – *Perestroika* and the Dissident Achievement – Conclusion – Further Reading

**4 The Communist Party of the Soviet Union
The Politics of Power** 106

The Mass Party Membership – The Party Elite: The *Apparat* and the *Nomenklatura* – Party Structure and the Leading Party Bodies – The Party Congress – The Central Committee – The Politburo and the Secretariat – The General Secretary – How the Party Rules: The Theory and the Practice – The Effectiveness of the Party: I. The Party and the Military: Who Rules? – II. Leadership Recruitment: The Brightest and the Best? – III. The Party's Internal *Perestroika*: Can the Party Reform Itself? – Further Reading

5 Modern Society: Tensions and Inequalities 143

The Official View – Town versus Country – The Skilled versus the Unskilled – *Perestroika* and the Problems of Economic Inequality – The Technical Elites versus the Party *Apparat* –The Writers and the State: A Case Study – Stalin and the Rise of Socialist Realism – The Post-Stalin Era and the Decline of Socialist Realism – Gorbachev and the Writers – The Soviet Nationalities Question – Anatomy of a Problem – Mitigating Factors – Gorbachev, *Glasnost* and the Nationalities – Conclusion – Further Reading

6 The Economic and Environmental Record 179

Soviet Economic Performance – The Stalin Command Economy – The Reform Debates – Gorbachev and Economic *Perestroika* – Economic Problems and Prospects – The Environmental Record: I. The Chernobyl Disaster, 1986 – II. The Case of Lake Baikal – III. The Diversion of Siberian Rivers – Conclusion – Further Reading

7 Models and Overviews of Soviet Politics   **204**

Stability through Power – I. The Totalitarian Model – II. The
State Capitalist Model – III. The Neo-Traditionalist Model –
Stability through Consensus: I. The Modernisation Model – II.
The Institutional Pluralism Model – III. The State Corporatist
Model – The Uncertain Future – Further Reading

8 *Perestroika* and the Prospects for the 1990s   **214**

Perestroika: The Optimist's View – *Perestroika*: The Pessimist's
View – Conclusion

A Selected Chronology of Soviet Politics, 1985–89   **224**

Bibliography   **233**

Index   **241**

Preface

There is an old Chinese curse: 'may you live in interesting times'.
Such a thought must weigh heavily on anyone attempting to write
or make sense of the Soviet Union today. We do undeniably live in
interesting times. *Perestroika, glasnost* and Gorbachev have not
just caught the imagination of the world, but have profound
implications for politics both East and West. The changes taking
place, however, are so rapid and momentous that it is more than
usually difficult to encapsulate Soviet politics at present. This book
is therefore written with some trepidation but in the belief that, for
introductory purposes, even an interim assessment is better than
none.

After many years of apparent enchantment the Soviet political
world is now in ferment. Long established traditions and assumptions are being challenged almost daily – disorienting and yet
exhilarating both for many Soviet citizens and for Western
students. The hitherto monolithic and secretive Soviet Communist
Party has set in motion the most ambitious attempt yet at political
democratisation since the 1917 Revolution. Its leaders have called
for an unambiguous end to the 'monotonous regimentation' of
economic and political life which has for so long characterised the
Soviet system. In an echo of the Prague Spring of 1968, Gorbachev
has called for a degree of political pluralism and for giving
'a human face to socialism'. The Stalinist command economy
which has sat upon society for sixty years is in the process of giving
way to a far more lively and competitive – if confusing – market
system. Nationalist upheavals have occurred, notably in the Baltic
states and the southern republics, on a scale unheard of for seventy
years. Open political and intellectual questioning about the past –
particularly the Stalin era – has finally resulted in an official

commitment to build a national memorial to the millions of innocent victims of those times.

Meanwhile – to take somewhat less momentous matters – the first Soviet MacDonalds hamburger restaurants have opened in Moscow and the Leningrad headquarters of the Communist Party at Smolny – a revered symbol of the original Bolshevik seizure of power in 1917 – have been the setting for officially tolerated rock concerts, developments that must seem almost sacrilegious to many older Soviet citizens.

What are we to make of all this? Is the Soviet Union finally emerging into a new era of economic affluence and social and political tolerance? On one reading, Gorbachev's *perestroika* is after all a logical and evolutionary development. It can be interpreted as an irresistible product of a genuinely new and far-sighted leadership, which is determined to achieve an economic transformation domestically and an end to the Cold War between East and West. It is also having to respond to significant long-term changes in Soviet society, which is now much more articulate and demanding than ever before. But, taking another view, the problems that *perestroika* faces are daunting. The Russian tradition has been noted more for its drama and violence, for occasional revolutionary upheavals followed by long periods of repression, than it has for any qualities of long-term evolutionary development. Will the Gorbachev years prove to be an all too easily reversible phase, merely a brief thaw that soon freezes over again?

There are as yet no final answers to these questions. This book, however, is an attempt to provide some introductory perspective, by placing contemporary developments in a wider historical and political context. In order to do this we start with two propositions. The first is that, whatever the outcome may be, *perestroika* is the product of both evolutionary and revolutionary forces, and is best interpreted in this light. It is an evolutionary process with potentially revolutionary consequences. In many respects *perestroika* is a remarkable break with the Soviet past. Yet it can only be fully understood in relation to it, for the continuities are still striking amidst all the changes.

The second proposition that informs this book is that the questions we should ask about Soviet politics today should be essentially the same as those we ask when thinking about political systems elsewhere. Any judgements we make should be tempered by an awareness that all political systems have strengths and weaknesses and have to contend with pressures for change. Many of the problems that face Soviet leaders are, to a greater or lesser extent, present elsewhere.

The structure of this book seeks to reflect such concerns. There are eight chapters, each tackling a particular theme. Chapter 1 deals with the origins of the Soviet political system and its formative years. How and why did the one-party state under Lenin come about? What were the achievements and the costs of the Stalin era? How should we assess the endless controversies about this period? In Chapter 2 we seek to consider how effective the Soviet system has been at adapting to and coping with pressures for change. The entire post-Stalin era from Khrushchev to Brezhnev and Gorbachev is here considered, complete with its uneven record of reform and reaction. Was the situation Gorbachev inherited in 1985 as bleak as he subsequently maintained? Did the political system essentially fail to make the appropriate adaptations in those years?

These two chapters, though geared to particular themes, are complementary and broadly chronological for they are intended to provide, among other things, a concise assessment of the historical and political background to *perestroika*.

The remaining chapters take specific themes. Chapter 3 looks at ideology and political culture. How important are ideas in shaping a nation's politics? What are the principal characteristics of Soviet ideology and how Russian rather than Soviet are its roots? How has it evolved over time? Has Soviet society as a whole now started to outgrow any single imposed official dogma, the dissidents having paved the way for a more open and pluralist society that can no longer be instructed what to think?

Chapter 4 then looks at political institutions and their role, particularly that of the Communist Party itself. Who wields political power? At what cost has the party preserved its status as the 'leading and guiding force in Soviet society'? Has this cost been too great, the party itself increasingly the cause of the very stagnation *perestroika* seeks to eliminate? How far do current reforms go?

Chapter 5 considers the principal social, cultural and ethnic divisions within the USSR and the political responses to them.

Chapter 6 takes the theme of system performance, notably on the economy and on environmental matters, significant pointers to ingrained political strengths and weaknesses. How effective have Soviet politics and administration been in these crucial areas? In Chapter 7 we then stand back a little and examine the range of basic models or approaches to Soviet politics that now exist. What light do they throw on the nature of the system overall?

Finally, in Chapter 8, we attempt an interim assessment of *perestroika*, its achievements and its problems. Will the evolutionary strand this time prove stronger and more enduring than in the past?

These main chapter themes involve questions that are similar to those asked about political systems elsewhere but, given the quite severe constraints of length, this book necessarily has omissions. As the above outline indicates, it is essentially an introduction to Soviet domestic politics and has relatively little on foreign policy and international relations. This is a conscious choice, for domestic concerns are unusually paramount in Soviet political life at present. Meanwhile, because of the length of time that occurs between writing and publication, events will have unavoidably overtaken at least some of the judgements that appear on the following pages. This shortcoming at least is one beyond the author's control.

I should like to thank the publishers Croom Helm, Hutchinson, and George Allen and Unwin for permission to reproduce certain tables in this text. I should also like to acknowledge the stimulation and advice that I have received from David Lane, Gerry Segal, Robert Porter, George Sanford and Philip Cross and the long hours spent typing by Anne Dempsey and Mary Woods. My family, Zuzana, Katherine and Daniel, gave me continuous support and encouragement. Needless to say, surviving errors of fact and judgement are all my own work.

Martin Crouch
University of Bristol
March 1989

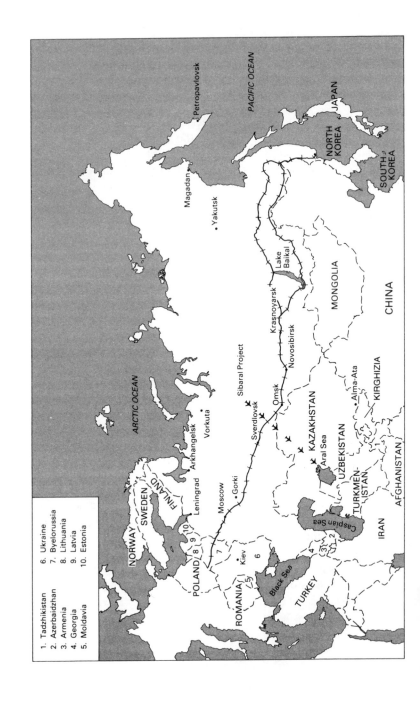

1. Tadzhikistan	6. Ukraine
2. Azerbaidzhan	7. Byelorussia
3. Armenia	8. Lithuania
4. Georgia	9. Latvia
5. Moldavia	10. Estonia

ARCTIC OCEAN

PACIFIC OCEAN

Petropavlovsk

Magadan
• Yakutsk

Lake
Baikal

MONGOLIA

CHINA

NORTH
KOREA

SOUTH
KOREA

JAPAN

Krasnoyarsk

Novosibirsk

Omsk

Sibaral Project

Sverdlovsk

Vorkuta

Arkhangelsk

KAZAKHSTAN

Aral Sea

Alma-Ata

KIRGHIZIA

UZBEKISTAN

TURKMEN-
ISTAN

Caspian Sea

IRAN

AFGHANISTAN

NORWAY

SWEDEN

FINLAND

Leningrad

Moscow

• Gorki

POLAND

Kiev

Black Sea

ROMANIA

TURKEY

1

The Revolutionary Era Under Lenin and Stalin

In this chapter we are essentially considering how and why the Soviet political system came into being and took the form it did under Lenin and Stalin. In order to do this we shall look briefly at the wider Russian tradition, and then at the specific pressures that eventually led to revolution in 1917, what part Lenin and the revolutionary movement played, and what it was that they sought to achieve. Was Lenin's legacy of the monolithic one-party state quite what he had intended? Where did Stalin's subsequent 'revolution from above' come from, and what were the achievements and the costs of that extraordinary era, the legacy of which continues to shape Soviet politics to this day?

The Russian Historical Tradition

The Russian historical tradition can be said to have been dominated by three distinctive characteristics, all of which have persisted into modern times. First, there has been the repeated scourge of foreign invasion and a consequent sense of insecurity. This has fuelled a drive for territorial expansion that has lasted several centuries. The origins of the Russian state can be traced back to the small principality of Kiev in the tenth century. Kiev was to become a considerable feudal state extending east across the steppe and north into the forest zone. It developed a relatively close relationship with the Byzantine Empire from whence, in about 988, it adopted Orthodox Christianity and the Cyrillic rather than the Latin alphabet. These moves effectively distanced the Slav peoples culturally and politically both from Catholicism to the west and Islam to the south and east. They did not, however, avoid damaging internal quarrels and eventual foreign invasion, when Kiev and the whole of the Slav lands fell prey to the Tatar Mongols in the mid-thirteenth century.

Russia was to remain under the Tatar yoke for nearly 250 years, not strictly occupied, but with her princes paying humiliating tribute to their Tatar overlords on the Volga. Russian culture and identity survived, but completely isolated from the European Renaissance and the Reformation, leaving Russia a psychologically beleaguered nation. The princes of Muscovy (Moscow and the surrounding territories) gradually emerged to prominence as the main tribute collectors and, under Ivan III, finally drove out the by now enfeebled Tatars in 1480. Ivan the Terrible (1533–1584) began the long process of 'defensive expansionism' based on the heartland of which Moscow is the centre, breaking up the Tatar khanates on the Volga, and opening the way for a rapid and more or less unimpeded Russian advance across the Urals into Siberia. Ivan had himself symbolically crowned Tsar (or Caesar) in 1547, for Moscow was now not merely a powerful state but beginning to see itself as the 'Third Rome' (after Rome and Byzantium) with a claim to dominion over the whole of Christendom.

Expansion eastwards was replaced, particularly in the seventeenth and eighteenth centuries, by expansion westwards under Peter the Great (1682–1725) and Catherine (1762–96). Wars against the Swedes, the Poles and the Turks saw the Russian frontier move west to incorporate – or reincorporate – the Baltic, Poland, the Ukraine, Belorussia and the Crimea. The nineteenth century saw the annexation of Finland, Georgia and Armenia, the conquest of the rest of the Caucasus, the colonisation of Central Asia, and the acquisition from China of fresh territory in the Far East. With some exceptions, notably Poland, Finland and the small but highly prized Baltic States, this vast empire came under the control of the Soviet regime either in 1917 or in the ensuing Civil War of 1918–20, as Soviet power was consolidated. The Baltic States and eastern Poland were re-annexed in 1940. The Soviet Union's territory today is therefore almost the same as that of the pre-revolutionary Russian Empire. By far the largest nation in the world, as it has been since the seventeenth century, its territory covers one sixth of the entire land surface on earth: as much as Canada, the United States and Mexico combined, nearly as much as the whole continent of Africa, and some ninety times the size of Great Britain.

After expansionism, a second key characteristic of Russian history has been the long tradition of centralisation and autocracy: the almost complete absence of any constructive interplay between the rulers and the ruled (Pipes 1977, p. 22). There are many explanatory strands to this, not least the long Tatar influence and the belief in discipline and unity in the face of an often self-evidently hostile surrounding world. The Soviet Union borders directly on twelve states many of which have been traditionally antagonistic to Russian or Soviet interests. Unity in the face of such circumstances has often been prized. Significantly, Russia's 'time of troubles' in the early seventeenth century was precisely an era of unusually weakened central state power, ending only with the accession of the powerful Romanov dynasty.

However, the sheer size and geography of the nation have also played a part. The Soviet state possesses vast natural resources: perhaps half the world's known coal reserves, one quarter of its forest area, oil and gas in abundance, and huge rivers for hydro-electric power, as well as valuable mineral wealth such as iron-ore and manganese deposits, gold, silver, diamonds, platinum, uranium and other vital industrial minerals. But they have often been located in the most remote and difficult regions. The enormous distances inherent in Russia's geography have been overcome historically only by relatively strong and centralised state direction. An old Russian proverb, 'God is in his heaven and the Tsar far away', reflects the fact that it has never been easy for the centre to impose its writ on far distant regions. This still applies: for example, the mismatch between natural and human resources is as marked as ever. Today, 75 per cent of the Soviet population live west of the Urals, where only about 30 per cent of the national energy reserves are to be found. 88 per cent of water resources are in the north and east, but are increasingly needed in the south where the Islamic population in particular has tripled within the past thirty years and could well double again within the next generation (Micklin 1987, p. 67).

The third distinctive characteristic of Russian history and culture is that they have been markedly isolated from world developments throughout much of their existence. This has in part been due to the abundance and variety of Russia's natural resources, but it has also been a response to the repeated history of cultural and political invasion. A marked consequence of this has been that Russian history, from at least the sixteenth century, can be seen as a recurrent pattern. Periods of isolationist stagnation have been followed by a fresh realisation of Russia's relative social and economic backwardness, leading to crash programmes of modernisation imposed from above. Thus Ivan the Terrible attempted to reform the system of government in the sixteenth century by breaking the power of the *boyars*, the landed aristocracy. Peter the Great, in the early eighteenth century, influenced by his travels to England and Holland, sought to develop Russia as a great European power, with an industrial economy and a navy to match those in particular of the Swedes. Peter created obligatory taxation and state service for all and brought the Orthodox church under much more direct state control. He also created a new Europeanised capital, the 'window on the West' of St Petersburg (now Leningrad), on the Gulf of Finland. This pattern of strategic reform from above, in order to catch up with or overtake the West, continued under later Tsars and, in effect, under modern Soviet leaders, not least Stalin in the 1930s and Gorbachev in the 1980s.

Russian history and tradition, then, have been dominated for a millenium by foreign invasion and territorial expansion, by the centralisation and relative strength of the state over society, and by isolation from an outside world which they nonetheless seek to emulate, if not surpass. We shall have occasion to refer to these characteristics in more depth at later stages; but bearing this background in mind, let us now consider the revolutionary era itself. Why was there a revolution in 1917? What did the revolutionaries want?

Russia before the Revolution

Given the scale and violence of post-revolutionary change in Russia, it is tempting in retrospect to portray the latter-day Tsarist

Empire as timelessly languid. But the reality was different. The 1917 Russian Revolution germinated as a consequence of unprecedently rapid economic and social change after 1861, but change that was unmatched by effective political modernisation and development. The consequent tensions encouraged a revolutionary movement and destroyed the old regime.

In 1861 Alexander II, 'the Tsar Liberator', as he came to be called, inaugurated a vigorous series of reforms from above, starting with the emancipation of the peasants from serfdom. Alexander was in that pattern of modernising autocrats who have punctuated Russian history. In 1837, when only nineteen, nearly twenty years before his accession, Alexander had undertaken an eye-opening tour of the Empire, visiting isolated and wretched villages in the Urals, convict settlements and political exiles in Siberia. It made a profound impact on him, as did the more immediate humiliation of Russian military defeat at the hands of the British and the French in the Crimea in 1854–6. The Crimean War was much needed proof once more that Russia was no match for those European powers she wished to emulate. The Tsar thus embarked, though not without court and gentry opposition, on a programme of radical restructuring which embraced not merely the abolition of serfdom, but significant legal, military and educational reforms, arguing that the old order was not only morally unacceptable but thoroughly inefficient and would sooner or later lead to social turbulence unless tackled.

Emancipation was a bold and revolutionary move, but it was no panacea. The peasants were given the freedom that the majority had undoubtedly yearned for since it was taken away in the sixteenth century, but it was very conditional freedom. In practice it often substituted for the old bondage to the landowner a new bondage to the village commune, or *mir*. The *mir* was, in the Russian context, a peculiar institution, a village democracy with elected elders, which every few years redistributed the land under its control in such a way as to give every household equal treatment, thus fostering a sense of communal ownership. After 1861 the peasants still had to get commune permission to leave their native villages but, above all, now had to pay the landowners compensation via the commune for the land they had previously tilled as serfs. In practice this eventually forced millions to leave the villages and seek waged labouring employment in the towns and cities in order to pay their debts. Emancipation provided the human raw material for industrialisation, but did very little to solve the endemic problems of a poverty-ridden and unproductive peasant colossus.

Russia's industrialisation drive, meanwhile, gathered pace particularly with the large-scale development of railways from the 1870s onwards. Significant strides were made in the 1890s and, after a brief slump, in the decade before the First World War. The Trans-Siberian railway, between Moscow and Vladivostock, first proposed in the 1850s, was finally completed in 1905. Industrial production increased five-fold between 1885 and 1913. A modern industrial base was created, though much of it was state planned and directed, minimising the growth of an independent entrepreneurial class. It relied heavily on foreign capital, not least because the landowners had little financial capital to invest. Its development was also very uneven geographically and in terms of scale. Much of the industrialisation drive was geared to small-scale light industry, but there were some very large-scale heavy industrial projects too. These were overwhelmingly concentrated in a small number of swollen towns and cities, with much consequent overcrowding and squalor. Moreover, the rate of industrial growth overall was not sufficient to ensure Russia a high place in the international league table; there remained an important discrepancy between her economic backwardness and her aspirations as a Great Power on the European model (Nove 1969, p. 13).

As a consequence, two distinct strategies for industrial modernisation were to emerge, the products of successive Prime Ministers. The first, identified with Count Witte in the 1890s, used protective tariffs to pursue a deliberate strategy of industrialisation which would enable Russia to catch up with the West. Foreign capital investment was encouraged and so were greater tax burdens on the peasantry to restrict domestic consumption. Naturally, such a strategy could not fail to be disliked by the peasantry, who comprised over 80 per cent of the population. In contrast, the second strategy, that of Pyotr Stolypin after 1905, was a 'wager on the strong' peasant, and was intended to promote peasant endeavour by rewarding energy and initiative. Stolypin's aim was to create a class of better-off peasants whose spending on industrial goods would provide the driving force for further industrialisation. Whether these reforms would in the long run have laid the foundations for solid peasant support of the regime, or merely created greater differentiation and bitterness in the countryside, is unclear, for the First World War intervened. What is instructive, however, is that although both strategies had their successes, they also contained dangers for the stability of the regime, for neither could avoid serious social tensions or provide painless solutions.

Meanwhile, the fundamentally unreformed Tsarist political system was increasingly unable to guarantee continued social stability. Alexander II had been assassinated in 1881 by Populist terrorists who advocated a form of agrarian socialism and saw selective assassination as a means of weakening the existing state and achieving their goal. His successors naturally enough retreated into cautious conservatism, heeding the arguments that autocracy was nothing if not absolute and that reform only led to further social changes beyond the government's control. As a consequence, there was a continuing and growing division between state and society with the state able to rely on the support of only a dangerously narrow stratum of officialdom, notably the civil service, the police, the military, and the clergy. Ranged against the state in attitudes varying from sheer inertia to violent opposition were the peasants, the new urban proletariat, many of the new technical and professional classes created by Alexander II's reforms, the critical intelligentsia and most of the non-Russian minorities, particularly the Jews and the Poles. Any major military disaster, as in the Crimea, could well threaten the absolutist structure. This was exactly what happened in the 1905 revolution, the competence of the autocracy having been found wanting in the 1904 war with Japan. A whole series of resentments, from peasant land hunger and urban living conditions to middle-class resentment at the absence of political freedoms, all coalesced to produce a spontaneous revolt against absolutism. In October 1905 Nicholas II was forced to issue a Manifesto granting a constitution. This conceded some popular rights and led to the setting-up of an elected, though admittedly very unrepresentative, national assembly, the Duma.

Even at this late stage moderate reformism might have regained the initiative. There were many men of liberal views in public life who expected such an outcome and there were good grounds for their optimism. The last decades of the Russian Empire witnessed a great flowering of literature, science and the arts. There was greater emphasis on the due process of law, with trial by jury including peasant jurors; elected county councils (*zemstva*) were set up; there was improved literacy and health care and much greater freedom to travel. The social and economic upheavals since 1861, in other words, had contained some very positive features. But Nicholas II, an unimaginative man mystically wedded to the principle of autocracy, let the reformist chance slip. Little was done to encourage any peaceful resolution of the nation's tensions. After 1905 the autocracy fought intransigently to regain its lost authority, once again creating a situation in which few could be expected to come to its aid when the next crisis arose. Thus it played into the hands of the vigorous revolutionary movement now at work in Russia.

Radical and Revolutionary Movements

Radical opposition to Tsarism spanned more than a century. The first protest had occurred as long ago as 1790 when a nobleman, Alexander Radishchev, published his bleak and damning work, *A Journey from St Petersburg to Moscow*. For his pains Radishchev was exiled to Siberia, a fate that has befallen countless dissidents in later generations. A second and more dramatic affair was the 1825 Decembrists revolt. The Decembrists were a group of army officers, radicalised by their experience of driving Napoleon out of Russia into Europe. They returned determined to over-throw Tsar Nicholas I and institute republican reforms. Their coup, however, was abortive and provoked a strong reaction from the Tsar who imposed a police state and strict censorship. This in turn fomented a major intellectual debate that occupied much of the century, the Slavophile–Westerniser dispute. This controversy was itself a product of Russia's geography, and it has absorbed many Russian dissidents even well into the late twentieth century. But it was fully formulated and most fervently pursued during the mid-nineteenth century. Was Russia a part of Europe, or was she separate, perhaps even Asiatic?

In a sense, this question represented unfinished business from the time of Peter the Great. His legacy of forced Europeanisation had for many people not gone deeper than the Baroque and Classical façades of St Petersburg, or the French spoken as the language of the Russian court. It had left a profound split in the national consciousness, encapsulated for instance in the ambiguity about St Petersburg in Alexander Pushkin's poem, *The Bronze Horseman* (the title referred to an equestrian statue of Peter in the city that was his 'window on the West'). Pushkin's admiration for the Tsar's achievements was counterbalanced by an awareness of the human and spiritual cost of such forced development.

The Slavophiles, or pro-Slav traditionalists, broadly wanted to undo what they saw as the damage done by Peter the Great. They stressed the merits of the ancient Slav traditions of collectivity and Orthodoxy as well as the need to find distinctive Russian paths of development. The West was seen as rootless, spiritually shallow and excessively materialist. This tradition produced radicals such as Alexander Herzen who advocated in the 1850s a rural socialism based on the village commune. In the 1870s a mass educative movement known as Populism took hold, as urban radicals sought to persuade the peasantry that the village commune was an instinctive form of socialism that could be used to achieve radical reforms. By the early twentieth century, and particularly after the 1905 Revolution when organised political parties came into the open, the Populist tradition had spawned a peasant party known as the Socialist Revolutionaries (SRs). It advocated a decentralised form of economy with only small-scale industrial manufacture.

However, the SRs suffered from a number of divisions which eventually weakened their political impact. While many SRs wanted a form of cooperative socialist agriculture, the majority favoured the creation of an independent yeomanry with small holdings. Meanwhile, some SRs supported terrorist tactics (assassination and bomb throwing), while others disapproved, not least because, after the Tsar himself had been assassinated in 1881, it simply led to further repression from above, which made it even more difficult for reformers to operate. The gulf between leaders and led, too, was very great. The Populism of the 1870s had foundered on a misplaced urban idealisation of the peasant as a noble savage, and the SRs were themselves always an awkward alliance of urban lawyers and illiterate peasants. Above all, by the

1890s the Slavophiles had lost much of the argument as well as a number of their leaders to the westernising Marxists, whose arguments were now in the ascendant.

Although Karl Marx's writings had been familiar to some radicals from the 1850s onwards, it was not until 1883 that the first Russian Marxist group was set up, and then in exile in Geneva by former Populists such as Georgi Plekhanov (1857–1918). From afar they began to look at Russia with fresh eyes. Plekhanov and later, in the 1890s, Vladmimir Ilyich Ulyanov (Lenin, 1870–1924) spearheaded a polemical attack on the Populists, essentially establishing two points. The first was that the pace and scale of industrialisation in Russia had now rendered irrelevant the Slavophile vision of an essentially rural economy. Capitalism was inevitable, argued Lenin, and the new industrial working class, not the peasantry, was the real vanguard of the future (Harding 1977). The second was that a socialist revolution was inevitable, for not only was Marx's analysis of the inexorable laws of history correct (feudalism, capitalism, socialism and ultimately communism succeeding each other), but this very process had been occurring in Russia during their lifetime. Feudalism had been abolished in 1861; capitalism was now flourishing; socialism had to follow: the historical process was only too clear.

There were, however, central dilemmas for Russian Marxists. How long would the capitalist epoch last? By the end of the nineteenth century there were still barely 3 million workers in a population of more than 125 million. Capitalism had only just begun and therefore, ironically, it looked as if the lifetime task of the revolutionaries should be to further the cause of capitalism, no less, because, as Marx had argued, socialism could only follow when capitalism collapsed under the weight of its own (advanced) contradictions. Meanwhile, on whose side were the peasants? Marx, towards the end of his life, had been prevailed upon to state that a rural revolution in Russia was a possibility, but Russian Marxists were essentially unimpressed and remained instinctively distrustful of the peasantry.

These dilemmas, as well as other tensions produced in the intense atmosphere of an underground revolutionary movement, led to a major split within the growing Russian Social Democratic Labour Party (the RSDLP) in 1902 into the majority (Bolshevik) and minority (Menshevik) factions. The Mensheviks, led by Julius

Martov, argued that history could not be telescoped and that the task of the revolutionaries therefore was to pursue a long-term strategy of education and trade union work among the working class. Lenin and the Bolsheviks, by contrast, developed a strategy for seizing power in the foreseeable future.

Lenin had initially broken with the RSDLP in 1902 over the question of organisation. In *What is to be Done?* (1902) Lenin argued with some passion not only about the need to create a new social order, but also that this could come about in a police state only if revolutionaries were totally committed and seriously organised like a military élite. Then, in *Two Tactics of Social Democracy* (1905), Lenin tackled the question of the peasantry arguing that, although their interests differed from the urban proletariat, their hunger for land had radicalised them sufficiently for the Bolsheviks to make common cause with them. This was the only way forward, for Russia's middle class was politically weak and a relatively new creation. It could not therefore be relied on to instigate independently the sort of liberal reformism found in European capitalist societies. Third, in *Imperialism, the Highest Stage of Capitalism* (1916), Lenin argued that, however inappropriate it might seem for the vanguard of the working class to lead a revolution in an essentially peasant society, the Russian revolution would be the spark that would soon start a genuine world-wide conflagration of worker-led revolutions. The workers of the world would unite to bring down capitalism and pave the way for the communist utopia, as Marx had envisaged.

Just how creative a disciple Lenin was of Marx has been the subject of much debate. Suffice it to say that, in the short run, Lenin proved to be a powerful and effective translator of Marx's ideas into a Russian context. He drew on the earlier Populist tradition of élitist activity and organisation, harnessing it to a vision of a revolution in which the urban proletariat would be the vanguard. Moreover, as industrialisation progressed, the Bolsheviks' natural constituency of the urban exploited grew in number and came to be influenced by the radical ideas put forward in Bolshevik newssheets such as *Iskra* (The Spark) and, from 1912, *Pravda* (Truth).

Even so, it is easy in retrospect to exaggerate the strength of the revolutionary movement. The Bolsheviks were an illegal underground minority some of whose supporters were not entirely

convinced that the Mensheviks were wrong (Lane 1968). In 1912
Lenin himself, when only 42 years old, gloomily predicted that the
revolution would not come within his lifetime. There were many
other political groupings which, at least on the surface, appeared
much more significant, such as the peasant-based SRs, the middle-
class liberal Constitutional Democrats (Kadets) and the right-wing
and monarchist Octobrists who supported the Tsar's 1905 October
Manifesto. The Russian Empire arguably might still have evolved
peacefully into a modern democratic state. The precipitant that
finally destroyed that dwindling hope was the First World War
of 1914–18.

To Russia's long-standing weaknesses, especially the inability to
adapt the political system to cope with industrial and social
change, the war now added a host of short-term disasters. Russian
military unpreparedness and backwardness were once again
revealed. The peasantry, much of it in army uniform, the urban
proletariat, and the technical and professional classes were all, for
different reasons, increasingly radicalised. A 'dual polarisation'
developed (Haimson 1964). Not only were relations between Tsar
and people sharply divided, but there was also a new alienation
between the Romanov court and the traditional defenders of the
regime, notably the police, the military and the influential
moderate leaders. This left Nicholas dangerously isolated, and the
Tsarist order finally collapsed as a consequence in the face of
domestic, military and economic crisis and because of a lack of
international support in the winter of 1916–17. Nicholas abdicated
his powers in February 1917, humiliatingly stranded by the
workers on a railway siding some distance from the capital.

The 1917 Revolution

The Russian Revolution was an historic watershed, unleashing
powerful forces. It has been to the twentieth century what the
French Revolution was to the late eighteenth and nineteenth
centuries: at one and the same time a beacon of hope to some, and
a fateful warning to others. It has given rise to major controversies
both about its nature and its aims, and its long-term consequences
are still with us.

The events of 1917 itself can be interpreted in more than one way. Both Soviet and Western historians have argued that there were two revolutions: the bourgeois February revolution and the subsequent socialist October one. Others have suggested that there were really three revolutions, each operating to a different time scale: the revolution of the cities, of the military front, and of the countryside (Ferro 1980). Alternatively, the revolution can be seen simply as one deepening crisis of authority which spanned the entire period from 1914 – a comprehensive breakdown of the old order in war and revolution, best viewed as a single span.

The collapse of Tsarism in February was not unexpected. There had been repeated military disasters in the war with Germany, there were food shortages in the capital, St Petersburg (whose Germanic name had been Russified to Petrograd in 1914), frequent and widespread strikes, demonstrations and bread riots. Accusations of treason were levelled openly at the German-born Empress. Finally, troops in Petrograd mutinied, the government panicked and the Tsar abdicated. Three hundred years of the Romanov dynasty had come to an end in a few days. In its place, the liberals of the Duma formed a Provisional Government to pick up the pieces, and the workers and soldiers, whose revolutionary actions had helped to precipitate the fall, organised their own *soviets* (the Russian word for councils), which assumed responsibility for the day-to-day running of the cities – bread, light, trams and so forth.

This phase of 'dual power' soon collapsed into what Leon Trotsky (1879–1940) called 'dual powerlessness' (Trotsky 1959, p. 199). The Provisional Government, inheritor of the liberal reformist tradition , believed firmly that Russia's potential as a Great Power had been held back only by the outdated and incompetent yoke of Tsarism. It had therefore misread the initial pro-war patriotism of 1914 and consequently believed that February had given it a popular mandate to prosecute the war anew, this time successfully. It also supported land reform but, because it consisted of moderates many of whom were lawyers, it argued that redistribution needed to be handled within a legal framework devised only after proper discussion in a new national assembly. This would have to wait until after the war when the peasants were out of uniform and back in their villages. Such procrastination over land reform, coupled with ambitious further military offensives, proved to be a fatal miscalculation by the

Provisional Government, losing it vital credibility and support, which instead passed to the increasingly impatient and radical Soviets.

The crisis of authority deepened during the summer, the peasants increasingly seizing land on their own initiative. Meanwhile, mass desertions from the army became commonplace, the worker and peasant conscripts voting with their feet. The dilemma for the Provisional Government was that the central questions of land and peace were completely entwined. The land could not be redistributed while the peasants were at war, and yet the peasants would not fight without land redistribution. What authority the Provisional Government retained was rapidly dissipated, particularly after an abortive coup attempt in August by the military under General Kornilov. Kornilov sought to destroy 'this rabble' of soviets and shore up the Government, but was thwarted by the Government itself, now headed by the socialist lawyer, Alexander Kerensky. The end result was that by the autumn Kerensky was politically isolated both from the military on the right and from the soviets on the left. The beneficiaries were the Bolsheviks.

Lenin and the Bolsheviks had played little part in February. Lenin had at the time still been in exile in Switzerland. On his return to Petrograd in April, Lenin had proclaimed that the Bolsheviks should on no account support the bourgeois Provisional Government or the war. 'All power to the soviets' was his slogan. At the time even many Bolsheviks thought Lenin was too extreme and out of touch. But events were to prove them wrong. Lenin had argued in April that the bourgeois revolution should now proceed to its second, socialist stage and he committed the Bolsheviks to that cause. By the autumn this strategy seemed to be working. The party was claiming 200,000 members, and was increasingly dominant in urban soviets. Moreover, only the Bolsheviks had refused to back the war effort, the Mensheviks and the SRs having gone so far as to join the Provisional Government in May, which had lost them much popular support. Bolshevik organisational and propaganda skills were also beginning to pay off: their simple slogans, 'all power to the soviets' and 'bread, peace, land' caught the public mood. In September, in a move of considerable flair, Lenin quietly dropped the Bolshevik principle of land nationalisation, and adopted the SR policy that land should pass to the peasants with redistribution being carried out locally. This neutralised the peasantry politically at a crucial time, in the sense that they did not actively oppose the Bolshevik takeover when it occurred.

By now it was an open secret that the Bolsheviks aimed to seize power in the name of the revolution. Kerensky's reaction was to attack ('far from welcoming the soviets, I regret their very existence'). In October he closed down the Bolshevik printing presses and imprisoned some of their leaders. Paradoxically, this helped trigger the eventual Bolshevik coup. Lenin appears to have had no doubts about the wisdom of seizing power at this point, but his Central Committee was less sure, several prominent members including Lev Kamenev and Grigori Zinoviev arguing that they lacked sufficient support in the country (Daniels 1967, p. 94). Lenin argued that it was now or never. The Second All-Russia Congress of Workers' and Soldiers' Deputies was due to meet in Petrograd on October 26th, with the Bolsheviks happily in a majority. Elections to the long awaited Constituent Assembly, which would legitimise a Kerensky-backed constitution, were due in November. The soviets would then become somewhat irrelevant. A coup timed so as to defend the soviets was therefore necessary. On the night of October 25th Bolshevik detachments under the command of Trotsky and the Petrograd Soviet took over key positions in the capital, notably the communications centres, railway stations, post and telegraph offices, bridges, garrisons. The operation was virtually bloodless, despite the subsequent Bolshevik mythology of the 'storming of the Winter Palace'. The great operatic star Fyodor Chaliapin sang as usual at the Petrograd Opera House that evening, and the Bolsheviks who did get inside the Winter Palace were politely relieved of their coats by the footmen. The Provisional Government, like the Romanov dynasty, put up little resistance at the end. The next day Lenin announced to the Congress of Soviets that they would now 'proceed to construct the socialist order', and Bolshevik decrees on land and on peace were duly passed.

However, it was one thing to seize power in the heavily industrialised capital city where Bolshevik support was relatively strong, but another matter to transform that into a nationwide revolution. The extent to which the Bolsheviks were in a minority was revealed a few weeks later when the elections to the

Constituent Assembly were duly held – Lenin having previously castigated the Provisional Government for repeated delays was now in no position to abandon them. In this general election the Bolsheviks received only 25 per cent of the vote, whereas the peasant-based SRs had 38 per cent and, because of the electoral system, an absolute majority of the seats. The Constituent Assembly met only once, in January 1918, and was then forcibly disbanded by detachments of Bolshevik Red Guards. The Bolsheviks regarded this parliament as a form of bourgeois élitism, inferior to the spontaneous democracy of the soviets. But most non-Bolsheviks were outraged. The episode helped precipitate the Civil War which broke out soon afterwards.

Although the Bolsheviks were a minority who had seized power by force and were led by men many of whom had only recently returned from exile abroad or in Siberia, it would be misleading to see October simply as an alien imposition. A genuine revolutionary wave was engulfing Russia, radicalising all sections of society, spreading anarchy and social upheaval everywhere (Pethybridge 1972, p. 199). Bolshevik support was limited but it was growing and to many, not least the peasantry, the alternatives were worse – military rule, a return of the old regime, or a complete break-up of the Empire in further chaos and war.

In retrospect it is clear that the Provisional Government had been dealt an almost impossible hand. Parliamentary democracy cannot be created overnight and in Russia the social and cultural base for such a development was extremely weak. The deep crisis of authority triggered by the war had produced by October what Ferro has called 'a state without a government, a government without a state', a situation beyond the competence of the Provisional Government. Nonetheless, the Bolshevik coup was not inevitable. It owed a lot specifically to Lenin's leadership and persistence, to Trotsky's oratory and organisational skills and to the miscalculations of their opponents.

Nor did the Bolshevik coup, because it was successful, necessarily prove that Lenin's longer term analysis was right. The world revolution did not follow, to the disillusion of many. This left the Bolsheviks open to the charge that, by 'telescoping' history and rushing prematurely into the socialist revolution, they had come to power in a nation that crucially lacked a solid industrial base and therefore adequate working-class support. Consequently, the

Bolsheviks were fulfilling the old prophecy of Marx's collaborator, Friedrich Engels, and running the risk of succumbing politically to the predominant class – the peasantry. They would thus, said their critics, either lose their way, or be violently overthrown. The necessary pre-conditions for the creation of a socialist society – a firm industrial base, international security, social harmony and tolerance – were simply not there: hence many of the Bolsheviks' subsequent difficulties.

Lenin and the Origins of the Monolithic Party

The October coup was neither the beginning nor the end of the Russian Revolution. It took three more years and a Civil War before the Bolsheviks had effective control over not just the cities but the vast bulk of the Russian Empire, and it was not until the 1920s that the centralised one-party state, the most significant consequence of Lenin's revolution, finally emerged.

Despite Lenin's insistence that the Bolsheviks should be a disciplined and united organisation it was in fact, even after 1917, often an unruly alliance of 'groups, groupings, factions and tendencies' (Cohen 1971, p. 5). This was in part a product of long years in opposition and in part a reflection of the chaos of the times, not least the physical difficulties in welding together over such vast distances a unified movement. But there were basic disagreements, the rows over war and peace being symptomatic. The Bolsheviks had been opposed to continuing the war and by 1918 had no army with which to fight, anyway. Some Bolsheviks, notably those on the left such as Nikolai Bukharin, favoured what amounted to a revolutionary war with the Germans; Trotsky, now Commissar for Foreign Affairs, successfully argued that the Bolsheviks should adopt a policy of masterly inactivity and wait for the imminent collapse of the German regime. The Germans, however, fought on and forced the Bolsheviks to a humiliating peace treaty at Brest-Litovsk in which they had to cede Poland, Lithuania and the Ukraine, territory incorporating one third of the population of the Empire, half of its industrial plant, and 90 per cent of its coalfields. Only the overall peace of 1918 saved the Bolsheviks from the full implementation of this treaty.

More fundamentally, there were really two distinct political strands to the Bolshevik heritage, though they often became entwined. One was 'proletarian democracy', embodied in the belief that the revolution should lead to workers' control, freedom and spontaneity, with an emphasis on the 'withering away of the state' and all coercive organs of power. Such sentiments bulked large in the popular Bolshevik bible of the day, the *ABC of Communism*, jointly authored by Bukharin and the economist Preobrazhensky. Set against this was a centralising tendency which emphasised that Utopia could best be achieved by planning and state control and by collective economic rather than bourgeois individual rights. The basic economic strategy after 1917 illustrated this dichotomy. Until 1921 economic policy was, in effect, to centralise. Banks were nationalised, as were other key sectors of the industrial economy. There was forcible requisitioning and rationing of food. Attempts were made to devise a long-term national economic plan. But there were also serious attempts at workers' control and at dispensing with high wages for 'specialists' whose work could be undertaken by 'any literate person', and there were many attacks on the bureaucracy that came with central planning. Was all this 'Communism', as it was called at the time, or merely 'War Communism', as it subsequently became known – a series of temporary and not always co-ordinated responses to the circumstances of the Civil War? It was unclear, and consequently there were periodic waves of dissatisfaction within the party over basic policy.

Amidst all this, it was the Civil War that was to prove the great unifier creating a continuing need for strong party discipline. The Bolshevik takeover of power took some months for the ordinary population to digest, particularly in the provinces, for news travelled slowly. By the spring and summer of 1918, relatively well organised anti-Bolshevik forces had been assembled and started to fight back. By the winter of 1918–19, at its peak, the Civil War involved no less than eighteen separate armies each claiming control of at least some territory, many supported by the foreign intervention forces of fourteen allied powers. The Bolsheviks were driven back into the old Russian heartland around Moscow and Petrograd. Opposition forces were, at one time, within a few hundred kilometres of Moscow – since 1918 once more the capital city.

Bolshevik victory in the Civil War was finally achieved in

October 1920, partly because the allied powers lost interest and the German war had ended, thus relieving some pressure, and partly because the anti-Bolshevik forces were by 1919 disunited and in collapse. These forces were ravaged by typhus, their supply lines were overextended and inadequate, and they were receiving little local support from the peasantry. Above all, however, the Bolsheviks won because under Lenin and Trotsky an effective and committed Red Army was created that could not only claim to be fighting for political supremacy but was also able to wrap the flag of national liberation around itself.

The most important long-run consequence of the Civil War was the impetus it gave to the creation not just of the one-party state but to the character of that single party. The one-party state itself flowed directly from Lenin's belief, expressed in *State and Revolution* (1917), that the socialist revolution could only survive if it smashed the old ruling apparatus and replaced it with the dictatorship of the proletariat, exercised in practice by the Bolshevik vanguard. Thus freedom of the press was curtailed and class enemies imprisoned or shot by the Cheka, the Bolshevik secret police. Mensheviks, SRs and other political groups were driven out of existence in Russia by 1922. The ends justified the means, it was argued, for the alternatives were seen as chaos or counter-revolution. The intolerance and brutality of the Civil War speeded up the process, but the goal had never really been in doubt.

There is much more room for debate, however, about the transformation of the Bolsheviks into a strictly centralised and disciplined party between 1917 and 1921. Some of Lenin's critics, notably the Polish revolutionary Rosa Luxembourg and Trotsky himself, who only joined the Bolsheviks in 1917, had prophesied from the outset that the logic of *What is to be Done?* would lead to isolated and dictatorial party rule. At first this was not clear. For all his intolerance towards non-Bolsheviks, Lenin's leadership was based on enormous prestige, not personal dictatorship. He was relatively punctilious about debate and discussion within the party, even under the multiple pressures of revolution, civil war and economic chaos. The party press was lively, well-informed and frank about most issues. But decisive change came about in the winter of 1920–21. For the first time the leaders, who at least had held together during the Civil War, were in open dispute. The major issue was the place of trade unions under socialism. Trotsky, fired by his success in the Civil War, called for the workers to be brought under military style discipline. Zinoviev and a rather formidable coalition within the party known as the Workers' Opposition dissented, as did external critics such as the Mensheviks who argued that a planned economy could not be built by slaves 'in the way the Pharaohs built the pyramids'.

Meanwhile, seven years of war and revolution had left the economy in ruins, with industrial production by 1921 only 15 per cent of that of 1914. There was rebellion on the naval island base of Kronstadt, in the Gulf of Finland a few miles from Petrograd. In the countryside there were major peasant revolts, and in the towns hunger, inflation and cold. The leaders, tense and worried, decided enough was enough and secured, at the 10th Party Congress in March 1921, the banning of 'factions and groups' within the party. Discussion and criticism of policies was still to be allowed, but no coherent presentation of rival programmes was to be permitted and, once a decision was taken, it was to be carried out with disciplined unity.

Initially this ban remained on paper only, and for some years opposition groups continued to function within the party. But whether it represented simply an emergency response to specific circumstances, or whether it was the 'true nature' of Bolshevism which finally emerged, is much disputed for it is a matter of considerable importance (Schapiro 1965; Service 1979). The events of 1921 provided the foundation on which the monolithic party of Stalin was to be built, this party being the most enduring legacy of the Lenin era.

The immediate effect was for power to be increasingly con-centrated in the hands of the rapidly expanding party machine at the expense of the rank and file. This 'bureaucratisation' seemed to result not only in inefficient and arbitrary rule, but threatened a gradual decline in independent debate and criticism, going well beyond what had been envisaged in the no-factionalism rule of 1921. Trotsky was a particular critic of bureaucratisation but so, too, eventually was Lenin himself. Lenin had fallen seriously ill in 1922 and never fully recovered. Isolated and frustrated, he began to view the regime in a new light and penned a series of attacks on the leadership which came to be known as his Testament. Lenin was particularly critical of Stalin, the party's General Secretary, for his oppressive and ignorant methods, and at the end of his life was determined that Stalin should be removed from office. His Testament was also a partial acknowledgement of failure: that the Bolsheviks had tried to do too much too soon without the appropriate cultural and administrative base. It is possible, as some have argued, that had Lenin lived, a more rational and humane system would have evolved (Lewin 1973, p. 129). But Lenin's Testament never acknowledged the extent to which his own anti-factionalism rule had undermined real democracy and debate. For all his political flair, Lenin was a revolutionary first and last and had never really thought clearly about the institutionalising of political power or about the virtues of responsible and responsive government.

The New Economic Policy of 1921

A further reason for Lenin battening down the hatches in 1921 was that, in order to stave off complete economic collapse, the Bolsheviks were about to embark on a New Economic Policy of great controversy. The NEP was, according to Lenin, a 'temporary retreat' in order to placate the peasantry and rebuild the economy to pre-1914 levels, but many saw it simply as a capitulation, the 'peasant Brest-Litovsk'. NEP confirmed the private ownership of agriculture and abolished the hated grain requisitioning of War Communism. A free market in agriculture was re-established, peasants being able to sell independently all produce over and above their set quotas. Private enterprise was encouraged in light industry, consumer goods and services, the state retaining control of what Lenin called the 'commanding heights' of the economy: banking, heavy industry, transport and communications and foreign trade. Wage differentials were increased and gradually higher payments to specialists became the norm. In order to encourage efficiency, profit and loss criteria were introduced and all undertakings managed commercially.

In the short run NEP was a success. By 1926 industrial and agricultural production had returned to roughly pre-war levels, the Stolypin-like 'wager on the strong' having apparently worked. It was accompanied by much social and cultural brilliance, too, as the energies unleashed by revolution were given their head. There were conductorless orchestras, trees painted red, divorce by postcard and much salon talk of the 'withering away of the school'. The arts flourished, not least painting, design and architecture and the new medium of film.

NEP had its darker side, though: urban overcrowding, rising crime and alcoholism, profiteering middlemen, the continuing repression of political opponents. Many pre-revolutionary non-Bolshevik socialists and anarchists ended up in the same cells with the same jailors as they had had under Tsarism. In particular, there was a political price to pay for this 'temporary retreat'. To the urban proletariat, in whose name the Bolsheviks were ruling, the real beneficiaries, as Engels had warned, were the demographically dominant peasantry, who still formed 80 per cent of the population. The proletariat, meanwhile, suffering from unemployment and disillusionment, took to describing NEP as the New Exploitation of the Proletariat. As a consequence, NEP undermined much of the remaining idealism of the Bolsheviks, creating an increasingly divided party, unsure of where it was going (Narkiewicz 1970, p. 14). The ultimate beneficiary of all this was Stalin.

Stalin and the Revolution from Above

Stalin's 'revolution from above' after 1928 was arguably more important than 1917, for it transformed the Soviet Union, creating a modern military and industrial superpower. To understand the Soviet Union of today it is still necessary to grasp the essentials of the Stalin era. In this section we shall consider first how Stalin rose to power, second what the achievements and the costs were, and third the controversies that this period of history still evokes. The wider and continuing legacy of Stalin on Soviet politics will be examined in the next chapter.

Joseph Stalin (1879–1953) was born in Georgia, the son of a poor cobbler. He joined the revolutionary movement at the age of eighteen, and was imprisoned and exiled to Siberia before becoming a member of the Bolshevik Central Committee in 1912. He was noted not as an intellectual but as one of the ruthless men of action of the Bolshevik underground. He did not play a very prominent part in 1917, but did act – disastrously as it turned out –

as a military leader in an ill-fated Bolshevik attempt to recapture Poland in 1920. He ignored Trotsky's commands, contributing to the failure to capture Warsaw. Hence the early antipathy between Stalin and Trotsky, summarised in Trotsky's contemptuous description of Stalin as an 'outstanding mediocrity'. Stalin, as the well-known contemporary journalist Sukhanov put it, was something of a 'grey blur', but this did not prevent his being appointed General Secretary of the party in 1922. On the contrary, it was thought that Stalin, as a useful but unimaginative workhorse, might bring some order into the rather chaotic party organs (R. Medvedev 1971, p. 17).

This appointment was to provide the vital springboard for Stalin's rise to power. The party apparatus grew apace from the early 1920s as routine and administration took over from revolution and war. It was a development that was crucially underestimated by many in the Bolshevik leadership for whom politics meant oratory and argument and dramatic action. Stalin the mere technician soon became a shaper of events, as the party apparatus wrested men, money and decision making from the soviets including Lenin's own preferred instrument of rule, the Sovnarkom, or Council of Peoples' Commissars (Lenin's 'cabinet') (Rigby 1979). These institutions had been dominated by the Bolsheviks from 1917, but they were technically products of the wider revolution, not party bodies as such. A new caste of party officials appointed by Stalin from the centre rather than, as with the soviets, elected locally, soon came to dominate. Stalin, who among other things was also Commissar for Nationalities, sat at the centre of the web, his initial power very dependent on control of a political machine.

Stalin's ascendancy was also dependent on two other key matters. One was victory in the factional disputes over policy which beset the leadership on the death of Lenin in 1924. NEP was at best a retreat, a hated necessity. Which was the correct way forward now for the socialist revolution? At first Trotsky and then Zinoviev and Kamenev threatened party unity from the left, arguing against NEP in favour of an industrialisation programme paid for by 'squeezing' the peasantry. Trotsky was already politically isolated even before Lenin's death, partly because of his attacks on the Workers' Opposition in 1920, partly because many feared his ambition and – with the French Revolution as their object lesson – saw in him a new Napoleon. Zinoviev and Kamenev who, with Stalin, formed the ruling triumvirate for a time after Lenin's death, were effectively defeated by the Fifteenth Party Congress in 1927. The no-factionalism ruling of 1921 was the left's undoing. Stalin as General Secretary was able to command automatically loyal majorities within the party, and gradually tightened the noose, denouncing such critics as 'factionalists' and removing them from the leadership. The same method was used to destroy the right, now led by Bukharin, in 1929 when Stalin finally did abandon NEP and switch to a programme of rapid industrialisation. Bukharin publicly denounced this switch, but was immediately trapped by the same 'factionalist' logic.

These factional victories of Stalin between 1924 and 1929 did not necessarily prove that his arguments were superior, but they did reveal a mastery of timing and tactics as well as the power inherent in controlling the apparatus. Moreover, they demonstrated certain weaknesses in the opposition: a conspiratorial and élitist tradition that resulted in last-minute and hence futile attempts to gain wider public support; an unwillingness to organise independently of the historic Marxist party, encapsulated in Trotsky's tortured commitment to 'my party right or wrong'; and a degree of personal virulence towards each other that had marked the revolutionary movement from its earliest days.

The other key factor in Stalin's rise to power was his sheer persuasive skill. Stalin's abandonment of NEP was not simply tactical, for there was a genuine enough debate about industrialisation at the time and both circumstances and opinions did shift. Bukharin, for example, had moved from the far left to the right wing of the party within ten years. More to the point, however, Stalin said what the party faithful wanted to hear, and in words of one syllable that were plain to all (Tucker 1973, p. 303). The party tripled in size between 1924 and 1928, recruiting large numbers of young, malleable urban 'workers from the bench' who had little formal education and were instinctively hostile to the peasantry. Stalin addressed these people in simple, often liturgically repetitive, speeches and writings, conveying a message of optimism: socialism in one country. The world revolution had not come to pass and was unlikely to do so in the near future. They were on their own, but if they drove out 'Oblomovism' from

Russia and used the energy and discipline of the Bolshevik tradition there was still nothing they could not achieve. (Oblomov, a figure from nineteenth-century Russian literature, had come to personify all that was lazy and disorganised in national life.) Stalin's success thus lay in harnessing Russian nationalism to a great drive for industrialisation and modernisation. Both the optimism and the directness of the appeal could be seen in the much quoted landmark speech Stalin made in 1931 (Stalin in Fitzpatrick 1982, p. 119):

> To slacken the tempo would mean falling behind. And those who fall behind get beaten. But we do not want to be beaten. No, we refuse to be beaten . . . . We are fifty to a hundred years behind the advanced countries. We must make good this distance in ten years. Either we do it or we shall go under.

This combination of apparatus power, factional victory and political skill put Stalin in undisputed control of Soviet politics by the end of the 1920s. It was to remain so for a quarter of a century.

The Achievements and the Costs of the Stalin Revolution

The Stalin era began with a casualty, the collapse of the *smychka,* or social harmony, between town and country that, at least in theory, had underpinned NEP. By 1928 the latent tensions behind NEP proved uncontrollable. Bukharin and the right had exhorted the peasantry: 'enrich yourselves' and, most importantly, 'do not fear the consequences'. But tragically, although some in the party could see how essential a prosperous agriculture was, most disliked and distrusted the actual phenomenon of prosperous peasants, and the peasants knew this. The Bolsheviks had never been able to decide whether the peasants were on their side, but by the late 1920s were increasingly treating the *kulaks*, or better-off peasants, as their class enemy, though these were precisely the more industrious and entrepreneurial types the regime needed. This contributed to a fatal undermining of peasant confidence so that in 1928–29 a major crisis arose, the peasantry ceasing to provide the towns and cities with adequate food. In April 1929, as an answer to this, Stalin launched a nation-wide programme of forcible requisitioning as in the Civil War, the *smychka* was broken and NEP died. This was followed by forced collectivisation (i.e. nationalisation without compensation) of agriculture from October 1929. Millions of peasants were persuaded, cajoled or bullied into new collective farms, private farming being destroyed. From January 1930 the *kulaks* – maybe as many as one in five families – were summarily and brutally expelled from their villages, often being deported to labour camps to provide the 'squeezed' raw material for the industrialisation drive that was the rationale of the entire 'revolution from above'.

After 1928 Stalin presided over the most rapid and extensive industrialisation drive imaginable. The party had been committed in principle since 1925 to an industrial leap forward based in part on a squeezing of the peasantry, but only with Stalin's political supremacy did it come about.

The achievements of the first two Five-Year-Plan periods from 1928 were quite extraordinary. Industrial output roughly quadrupled. Whole new industries were developed including chemicals, cars, machine tools and tractors. There were major hydro-electric schemes and a Moscow Metro. What was known as a 'command economy' evolved. This, in essence, has survived into the modern era, the most enduring and distinctive of all Stalin's achievements. It abolished the market economy of NEP, substituting what was seen as a basically socialist system of centralised control. Prices were set bureaucratically, and enterprises were ordered to maximise output at almost any cost, and to fulfill the plans laid down from on high by Gosplan, the state planning committee, and by the central ministries. Unemployment disappeared. Whole new cities arose such as Magnitogorsk in the Urals, a Stalinist showpiece. Geographically, industrialisation spread very wide, bringing development to hitherto entirely rural areas. Quite apart from anything else it is difficult if not impossible to visualise Soviet victory in the subsequent 1941–5 war without this preceding decade of rapid, forced industrialisation. No recognisable continuation of NEP could have achieved as much (Wheatcroft *et al.* 1986).

But the costs were at least as great as the achievements. Industrialisation at this pace was inevitably a form of organised chaos, and at the expense not only of the peasantry but of the urban population. Wage rates doubled, but prices tripled, taxation was increased, and living conditions deteriorated. Bread and many other daily necessities were rationed. The urban population doubled between 1928 and 1939, from one in six to one in three of the population. Chaos, overcrowding, an 'attrition in human relations' set in (Lewin 1985, p. 229). For many the country seemed to resemble one vast nomadic labour camp. The Stakhanovite movement named after a record-breaking Donbas coal miner, Alexei Stakhanov, was symptomatic of the problems of forced development. It was part of a fundamentally irrational 'rush to build' mentality which characterised the era. Problems were not 'solved' but 'attacked' or 'stormed' in campaigns and often destructively. As Bukharin had argued, 'you can't build today's factories with tomorrow's bricks'. Stakhanovite overfulfill-ment was properly speaking the antithesis of coordination and planning. Overfulfillment should have been as heinous as under-fulfillment, but typically the one was lauded, the other damned as sabotage. Characteristically, the 1928 Five Year Plan was actually completed in four years. Admittedly, the second Five Year Plan was less chaotic, with far fewer unrealistic targets, but it was hampered by the purges and the need increasingly to divert resources into a rearmament programme. The third Five Year Plan was cut short by the outbreak of war in 1941 but so, too, was any proper debate about whether the quite real decline in growth in the late 1930s and early 1940s was due to Hitler or to structural defects in the command economy that only became more apparent much later. Overall, it added up to an industrialisation drive that was better described as *forced* rather than *planned*.

Collectivisation of agriculture meanwhile achieved nothing, and at truly appalling cost. A peasant culture and economy were destroyed. Output fell dramatically, recovering only to 1927 levels by 1941. The party had launched what amounted to a civil war on the peasantry and the latter retaliated by slaughtering – and often eating – their livestock rather than see it put into the common pool. The growth of the Soviet tractor industry was a desperate official response to the wholesale peasant slaughtering of horses: an odd sort of progress at best. The coercion and brutality created a stunted agricultural sector that was to haunt the regime for decades. The 1939 census revealed a shortfall of some ten million people, mainly Russian and Ukrainian peasants. This was a moral, ethnic and economic disaster that did much to weaken support for the regime, particularly in 1941–2 – German rule being at first considered preferable. Collectivisation also brutalised the urban party workers who were despatched to carry it out, such people no doubt finding it easier than might otherwise have been the case to enforce the subsequent Stalin purges.

The Political Revolution

A political revolution also occurred after 1928. The party developed into a monolithic vehicle for Stalin's industrialisation and collectivisation drive, and after 1928 simply ceased to tolerate any dissent. Moreover, a semi-religious cult grew up around Stalin ('the beloved father and teacher – saviour of the Soviet people'), which bestowed on him an aura of authority and infallibility. Many came to be persuaded that the chaos and the brutality were despite rather than because of the dictator. At the peak of the cult in 1949 *Pravda* devoted three-quarters of its pages for a whole nine months to 70th birthday greetings to Stalin. Meanwhile, the party ceased to be a mass revolutionary movement, becoming merely one of a number of bureaucratic empire *apparats* through which Stalin ruled. No party congresses were held from 1939 to 1952; under Lenin they had occurred annually. Correspondingly the central ministries and, above all, the secret police were allowed to wield vast economic and political power. Stalin, in time-honoured tradition, divided and ruled over the party rather than through it.

After the assassination of the Leningrad party leader Sergei Kirov in 1934 (Petrograd having been renamed again after Lenin's death), an era of show trials and purges swept the nation, culminating in what was known as the Great Purge or *Yezhovshchina* (after the police chief Nikolai Yezhov) in 1937. Anguish and death became commonplace as the Old Bolsheviks of 1917 were arrested, put on show trial and imprisoned or shot, hundreds of thousands of lesser party members following in their wake. Many were accused of seeking to overthrow the regime, or spying for the British, or charged with other fantastic crimes. As with the *kulaks*, so now other people were arrested by quota and by category rather than through any due process of law. Most damagingly of all, the military leadership was senselessly destroyed: three out of five marshals, all eight admirals of the fleet and half of all the officer corps were shot or imprisoned. This had incalculable consequences in the 1941–45 war.

Stalin's political system survived in large measure through terror and perhaps because of a traditional national servility towards despotism. But it must not be overlooked that it was also supported by a formidable combination of vested interests and genuine belief in what was seen as Progress. Some 400,000 'red specialists', newly trained technical cadres, were 'thrust forward' after 1928. Many of the abler and more ambitious members of the newly activated social groups – the working class, and middle peasants – seized their chance, often fully committed to this historic transformation. Not only were they prepared to accept the costs, arguing, in the revolutionary cliché, that the ends justified the means, but they were persuaded that such costs were a necessary and inevitable part of the process, the Marxist dialectic of history at work. Progress required destruction. As one survivor from the times, Lev Kopelev, put it:

> With the rest of my generation I firmly believed that the ends justified the means. Our great goal was the universal triumph of Communism and for the sake of that goal everything was permissible – to lie, to steal, to destroy hundreds of thousands and even millions of people.
>
> (Kopelev 1977, p. 11)

This point was corroborated by others. John Scott, an American working at the Magnitogorsk steel mills in the 1930s, later described how the 'guarantee of employment coupled with high wages for specialists' was potent enough to create a willing body of students who came to night schools after as much as twelve hours' work in the daytime 'sometimes on an empty stomach . . . on a backless wooden bench . . . and studied mathematics for four hours straight' (Scott 1973, p. 49). Moreover, most people acquired at least a basic literacy in these years. The Stalin literacy programme was a classic example of the virtues that could flow from a centralised mobilisation regime committed to clear priorities.

As well as the terror then, there was also a degree of social and political support for Stalin and a widespread belief in the attainability of a qualitatively different society – an industrialised urban one. Hence the revealing mixture of relief, bewilderment and even sorrow that variously affected most people on hearing of the dictator's death in 1953.

The Great Patriotic War, 1941–45

The German invasion in June 1941 was an unmitigated disaster for the Soviet Union. Within weeks nearly half the Soviet people and a third of the nation's productive capacity were lost or threatened. A long and cruel war ensued as a direct result of which nearly 20 million Soviet people died. Whether the war itself could have been avoided is an open question, for Hitler's aggressive ambitions were not readily amenable to diplomacy or compromise. Stalin was certainly aware of the threat and sought to construct an anti-German alliance with other European powers after 1933. When this strategy collapsed, Stalin finally entered into a Non-Agression Pact with Hitler in 1939, a move that was deeply shocking at the time to many both inside and outside the Soviet Union, but which at least sought to buy time and thus postpone any war.

It was all the more remarkable then that Stalin was caught completely unawares by the eventual invasion, having clearly decided to distrust or ignore all the evidence laid before him by Soviet military and intelligence specialists. Moreover, the senseless military purges of 1937 now exacted a further price, for the army was poorly led and ill-equipped, despite the breathing space of 1939–41. The shock of invasion was compounded by Stalin's instructions to the army to defend every centimetre of territory right up to the borders, resulting in hundreds of thousands of troops being easily surrounded and killed or captured by the Germans.

After this disastrous start and at a terrible human price, victory was eventually achieved by 1945. Stalin, as Supreme Commander of the Soviet Armed Forces, led what became a popular war of national liberation that ended only with the Soviet army in occupation of much of Eastern and Central Europe as far as Berlin. This victory in war and the national struggle it required has subsequently contributed greatly to the legitimacy and mythology of the Soviet system, as we shall explore further in Chapter 3.

The Stalin Era and Its Controversies

The sheer scale and drama of the Stalin era was enormous and still raises fundamental controversy. In drawing this chapter to a conclusion, it is worth considering some of the central debates.

First, there are the questions about the inevitability or otherwise of the Stalin revolution. Collectivisation and industrialisation had profound and lasting consequences, but NEP was not pre-ordained to end in 1928. Indeed, Lenin for one had envisaged NEP as a policy for at least a generation. Why therefore did it end when it did? Nove has argued that, although there was nothing inevitable about 1928, it was in a sense a 'necessary' development if the Bolsheviks were to survive politically. Their whole *raison d'être* was under threat the longer NEP continued: some break-through into an industrialisation drive was essential if socialism as they understood it was to be achieved. Others are less sure. Cohen, Bidelux and others consider that Bukharin and the right had a coherent alternative programme that, had it been implemented, would have produced a more gradual, less destructive and thus ultimately more productive end result (Cohen 1971; Bidelux 1985). Nove's point is that, while this might have been an intellectually acceptable way forward, it did not command adequate political support (Nove 1964). Bukharin's prescription that 'we shall move forward at a snail's pace, but at the same time we shall be building socialism' sounded at best rather dreary. Meanwhile some historians, such as Lewin, have stressed that, whatever the alternatives were, what actually occurred in 1928 was not so much the implementation of a clear strategy, as a muddled and panicky reaction to immediate events, a disaster stemming from the fundamental inability of the regime to control food supplies (Lewin 1968).

Then there are disputes about the costs and the achievements. Much is still unknown about this era: remarkably, the statistics for cattle deaths under Stalin are more comprehensive than those for human loss. Irrespective of the figures, though, there are arguments about whether the Stalin revolution was justified, whether the ends did indeed justify the means. For many the view that human loss can in some way be measured against economic gain is unacceptable. Carr, however, writing in the 1960s, suggested that there was a prevailing squeamishness among historians about handling the terror and that the brutality of the Stalin industrialisation drive was rarely put into any comparative context: human history, he argued, has been harsh and all industrialisation processes dreadfully cruel and uprooting (Carr 1964, p. 80). In that sense the Soviet experience is different only in degree, not in kind. Von Laue, writing in the 1980s, similarly argued that we are often quick to moralise about the Stalin era but slow to develop any imaginative understanding of the problems Stalin faced (Von Laue 1981, p. 181). The essential context in which Stalin has to be placed, argued Von Laue, is one of national encirclement and underdevelopment. Only a strong and ruthless leader could have held the Soviet Union together, let alone turned it into a nuclear superpower. Liberal democracy was an unaffordable luxury in a Hobbesian world of struggle for sheer survival.

The debate about ends and means is unlikely to be resolved, however much it is reformulated. But there has been significant and probably lasting rethinking in recent years about the whole concept of totalitarianism as applied to the Stalin era. The totalitarian regime, it has been argued, has six basic features: a single mass party led by a dictatorial leader, an official ideology, state control of the economy, state control of propaganda and communications, monopoly control of the armed forces, and police terror (Schapiro 1972). These combine to create an almost unbreakable syndrome of absolute power and terror that have characterised certain regimes, notably those of Stalin and Hitler. They are different in kind from 'normal' regimes. This view, which is examined in more detail in Chapter 7, has had an enormous impact in shaping our ideas about the Stalin era, and it remains tenaciously alive, not least because it has some truth in it. But, even as applied to the Stalin era, it also raises many questions.

First, it is an approach that does not easily accommodate the facts of political change, and assumes an internal regime coherence and consistency that can be quite misleading. The Stalin era was at least two quite discontinuous phases. Up to 1941 the regime was revolutionary and innovative: after 1941 essentially conservative and nationalist. Meanwhile the original industrialis-ation drive was politically and economically progressive, but the social policies of the time were by contrast a retreat into

Victorianism after the radicalism of the 1920s. Stalinism did not all point in the same direction, as it were.

Second, whilst no-one claims that Stalin was literally all powerful, the use of the term 'totalitarian' has created an enduring tendency to downplay or ignore the often Gogolian inefficiency of the Soviet state at the time (Nikolai Gogol's play *The Government Inspector* (1836) was a timeless masterpiece about provincial sycophancy and corruption). The Stalin system was in fact ramshackle enough to absorb a lot of 'report padding', corruption and incompetence both by officials and ordinary citizens (Fainsod 1959). The German occupation proved in contrast to be a much more efficient and brutal form of despotism. Many in the Ukraine, who had at first welcomed the Nazis as liberators, soon changed their minds. The Stalin political system was in fact a much more complex phenomenon than just a single dictator imposing his will from above by force. Even the Great Purge of 1937 can be seen in this light. This was less a master plot by a megalomanic dictator than a form of political civil war between leaders and led, both sides being divided, with Stalin among other things desperately trying to create an efficient and responsive political machine in the provinces (Getty 1985). In other words terror may well have been a product of weakness as much as strength. None of this alters the fact that Stalin was a ruthless leader who ruled in part through sheer terror, but the politics of the era were in retrospect much too complex to be described as simply 'totalitarian'.

There are two other general questions about the Stalin era that need to be briefly considered, both of which refer back to the 1917 Revolution itself. First, in what way was Lenin 'responsible' for Stalin? In one sense it can be argued that he was crucial. Lenin paved the way for the disciplined and centralised single party, and Stalin to a degree can be seen simply as a faithful heir to the spirit of Lenin's teaching. But it is unrealistic to assume that Stalin's dictatorship was an inevitable outcome of Lenin's rule. The Bolshevik tradition contained democratic strands, as well as centralist and authoritarian ones. Moreover, the discontinuities between Lenin and Stalin are at least as striking as the continuities (Cohen 1977). The isolationism inherent in the strategy of socialism in one country, the sheer lying (Stalin announced that the country was 'dizzy with success' at the time of the collectivisation disaster in 1930), the changed role of the party, the personality cult, the vast scale of the industrialisation drive, the 'excesses' or purges, are all fundamentally unLeninist and amount to a difference of kind between Lenin and Stalin. Indeed, the discontinuities in a sense were unavoidable. The Bolsheviks were seeking to create the first socialist state on earth. They had no blueprints and little turned out as they had expected. They were increasingly overwhelmed in the first few years by the sheer backwardness of the country. So, to a degree, experimentation took over, War Communism, NEP, and the command economy following in quick succession.

The second question to consider concerns the associated debate about how to define the Russian Revolution. When did it end? Was it one deepening crisis of authority spanning 1917 to 1921, for example, as suggested earlier? On this reading 1921, with the end of the Civil War and the 10th Party Congress, was the real watershed. Basic physical control of the old Empire was now assured and the outlines of the monolithic party were already apparent (Chamberlin 1935). What followed were discontinuous phases of rule. Or, conversely, was the Stalin 'revolution from above' an integral part of a single revolutionary process, spanning the years from 1917 well into the 1930s? Fitzpatrick and Skocpol have both argued the latter view, stressing that the revolution could not be considered to be complete until a stable structure of authority and power had been rebuilt. This took until the 1930s to achieve, and the intervening years of Civil War, NEP and the collectivisation drives were 'successive stages in a single process of terror, progress, and upward mobility' (Fitzpatrick 1982, p. 3). The revolution was not fulfilled until the Bolsheviks had achieved a modern industrial economy in the Stalin era. In this sense the Lenin and Stalin eras were inseparable and continuous.

The whole period, then, like any in history, can be interpreted in many different ways if only because, in the end, there is little agreement about whether the Stalin era did represent a fulfillment of the aims of the 1917 Revolution or a fundamental betrayal of its hopes. What is particularly striking, however, is the extent to which this piece of history has always been not simply a matter for academic debate, but a focus for powerful political controversy both in the Soviet Union and abroad. The costs and the achievements of this dramatic period have still to be fully assimilated, even under conditions of *glasnost* and *perestroika*.

Indeed, the whole revolutionary era of Lenin and Stalin has never lost its immediacy for Soviet politics, as we shall see in the next chapter.

Further Reading

There is a vast literature on revolutionary and pre-revolutionary Russia. Crankshaw (1976) provides an introductory overview of the years from 1835 to 1917. Pipes (1977) traces the growth meanwhile of the Russian state and its role in managing society from as far back as the ninth century.

On 1917 itself Ferro (1980) provides a wide-ranging social, economic and political analysis. Daniels (1967) focuses on the Bolshevik takeover of power itself. Harding (1977) considers Lenin's contribution to the revolutionary movement. The subsequent growth of the one-party state after 1917, and its reasons, are discussed by Schapiro (1965) and Service (1979). Lenin's methods of government are examined by Rigby (1979) and his eventual forebodings about Stalin by Lewin (1973). The complexities of transforming a Leningrad coup into a nationwide revolution are revealed by Pethybridge (1972), Narkiewicz (1970) and Fainsod (1959).

The Stalin revolution from above after 1928 is discussed by Lewin (1968) and Nove (1964, 1969). Its deeper social roots are considered by Pethybridge (1974). The alternatives to Stalinism are examined by Bidelux (1985) and by Cohen (1971) in his biography of Bukharin. Full-length studies of Stalin include Medvedev (1971), Tucker (1973), and McNeal (1988). Contemporary memoir material such as Ginsberg (1967), Mandelstam (1975), Solzhenitsyn (1975) and Kopelev (1977) provides another set of perspectives, as do some recent Western studies, notably Getty (1985) on the Great Purges of the 1930s, Von Laue (1981) and Fitzpatrick (1982).

2

Continuity and Change from Stalin to Gorbachev

All political systems have to adapt over time and respond to pressures for change. Failure to do so, as the Romanovs discovered in 1917, can be fatal. In the Soviet case the whole period since 1953 has seen a continuing political struggle about how to cope with the Stalinist legacy and adapt its institutions and values to modern requirements. The consequence has been a continuing split within Soviet politics between reformers and conservatives. Both tendencies have been aware of the need for change, but have differed markedly in their views. Conservatives have been broadly suspicious, seeing change as at best something to be controlled slowly from above; reformers by contrast have been increasingly sceptical of the effectiveness of the old ways, particularly of the Stalinist command economy and the habits of fear and authoritarianism that it encouraged.

This split has in a sense been personified by successive Soviet leaders, and in this chapter we shall consider their very different characters and strategies. But despite the apparently regular swing of the pendulum from reformism to conservatism, significant and lasting changes have occurred in Soviet politics since Stalin. In this chapter we shall consider not only these changes but also the continuities that have persisted under Khrushchev, Brezhnev and Gorbachev. We start with Khrushchev and his tackling of the Stalin legacy. How radical a reformer was he and what did he achieve? Then we shall consider the subsequent Brezhnev era. Was it simply a conservative reaction or something more complex in its own right? Finally, we look at the succession crisis of the 1980s and the emergence of the Gorbachev reforms. What overall assessment can be made about the ability of the post-Stalin Soviet system to handle the pressures for change?

The Khrushchev Era, 1953–64

Khrushchev was General Secretary of the Soviet Communist Party for eleven years, from 1953 to 1964, but his power and authority were never those of Stalin. He was, however, the key figure in Soviet politics at a time of great and often unsettling change and one who sought to carry through such change essentially without coercion, relying instead on persuasion and argument. The Khrushchev years are thus not only important in themselves but still of relevance today, for his vision, his methods and his eventual failure all have continuing implications for further attempts at reform in the Soviet Union.

Nikita Khrushchev (1894–1971) was a true beneficiary of the revolution. Born into an illiterate peasant family in the Ukraine, Khrushchev joined the Bolsheviks in the Civil War, subsequently receiving a basic technical education in the new party schools as one of the 'thrust forward' young generation, coming to power under Stalin. He was responsible for running the city of Moscow in the 1930s at a time of rapid industrialisation and growth and, among other things, oversaw the construction of the Moscow Metro, one of the showcase 'hero projects' of the time. (Though Stalin was never far away – in his memoirs Khrushchev described how Stalin personally vetoed his attempt to run British double-deckers on Moscow's streets: he was afraid they would topple over.) (Khrushchev 1971, p. 52) Khrushchev was a major political leader on the Ukrainian front during the 1941–5 war, subsequently running the Ukraine as the republic's First Secretary. He was intelligent and energetic with much native shrewdness and garrulity, one of the more independent minded leaders in Stalin's entourage. His career was essentially that of a practical achiever, largely in the provinces, rather than as a Kremlin *apparatchik*. All of this made Khrushchev a force to be reckoned with, but by no means the most obvious man to succeed Stalin.

There were, however, no established traditions of institutional political power on which Stalin's successors could call. Any such rules had been suspended by Stalin for more than a generation. The police chief Lavrenti Beria, who appears to have attempted a coup, was arrested and shot in 1953. The other leaders then divided the principal party and state jobs among themselves and declared the result 'collective leadership'. Khrushchev became General Secretary of the party and Georgi Malenkov, whom many regarded as the heir apparent, the Chairman of the Council of Ministers, or government leader. It was symptomatic of the fluidity in Soviet politics that it was far from clear at that time who would benefit most from this outcome. Not only were individual leaders jockeying for position but so too were entire *apparats*, notably the party, the economic ministries, the military and the secret police. Malenkov for a time sought to use the central economic ministries as an effective power base. He and other rivals for power, including Vyacheslav Molotov, were eventually routed by Khrushchev, and the latter finally consolidated his powers as both General Secretary of the party and Chairman of the Council of Ministers in 1957.

Like Stalin thirty years earlier, Khrushchev rose to political supremacy through his patronage control of the party apparatus, which in turn now closely controlled the secret police. After the fall of Beria, the party took direct supervisory control of the KGB at each level, integrating what had become an autonomous political and economic empire into the party. Moreover, Khrushchev, like Stalin before him, rose to power by a judicious handling of a range of policy questions that then confronted the leaders. The parallels are risky, however. Terror, in the sense of arbitrary arrest, was abolished in 1953, partly because the leadership itself feared the consequences of a further purge, partly because it was increasingly clear that a modern industrial economy could not be run efficiently by half-starved slave labour. This ending of terror was a major psychological change in Soviet politics, and it meant that neither Khrushchev nor his successors were the arbitrary and feared autocrats that Stalin had been. Indeed, Khrushchev in particular was never able to establish more than a limited ability to turn his formal powers into genuine political authority.

Economic and Foreign Policy

Nonetheless, Khrushchev's rule did tackle some fundamental questions that had built up in the latter Stalin years. Four key areas can be identified: the economy, the party and ideology, foreign policy and, above all, Stalin himself.

Under Stalin the Soviet economy had completed the first stages of an industrial revolution but, as even Stalin had conceded in his last years, the economic system could not stand still. It was overcentralised and insufficiently flexible in the face of a more complex environment. Khrushchev was to develop this theme. In 1957 he pushed through some decentralising of economic power from the central ministries to newly created *sovnarkhozy* (Regional Economic Planning Councils) in order to improve the system's ability to coordinate for quality and productivity locally rather than focus simply on national mobilisation for quantity. The *sovnarkhozy* reforms also, and deliberately, benefited Khrushchev's own patronage network of local party officials at the expense of Moscow planners, but Khrushchev's awareness that the economy had some systemic flaws was real enough. He increasingly railed against its 'uneven development', symbolised by a world lead in space technology but a chronically backward agriculture. It was the Soviet cosmonaut Yuri Gagarin who in 1961 became the first man in space. Meanwhile, Soviet peasants were still having to be told what fertiliser was. The resulting campaign in favour of a shift of national resources into chemicals, light industry and consumer goods became a significant part of Khrushchev's rule.

In no area was Khrushchev more active than in agriculture. The Stalin legacy was a crisis of underinvestment, low productivity and even lower morale. Khrushchev, with his peasant roots, prided himself on some expertise in this area – a controversial claim in the opinion of his critics. He argued successfully for a grand 'hero project' to place agriculture at the top of the political agenda for the first time since the 1920s. This was the Virgin Lands scheme introduced in 1954. The Virgin Lands, mainly in Kazakhstan, comprised a vast acreage now brought under cultivation for the first time. Like many Soviet hero projects, the Virgin Lands scheme was rushed and chaotic. In the short run it encountered

major and predictable problems with soil erosion, as well as lack of
housing and other facilities for the hundreds of thousands of newly
recruited Russian workers, but as a morale-building enterprise it
had considerable success and it did raise grain output at a critical
time (McCauley 1976).

A second key area of change was in foreign policy. Khrushchev
was effectively the first Soviet leader to travel abroad. Stalin had
only ventured outside the Soviet Union twice, to Potsdam (Berlin)
and Teheran for Allied conferences in 1944–45. Khrushchev
travelled extensively, not least in Europe, Asia and the Middle
East, and in 1959 visited the United States. The Soviet delegation
was invited by President Eisenhower to stay at his retreat of Camp
David in Maryland.

> I couldn't for the life of me find out what this Camp David was . . . we
> had to make special inquiries and get someone to research the
> problem. Finally we were informed that Camp David was what we
> would call a *dacha*, a country retreat . . . [not] the sort of place where
> people who were mistrusted could be kept in quarantine . . . I'm a
> little bit ashamed. It shows how ignorant we were in some respects.
> (Khrushchev 1977, p. 428)

Such travels helped to encourage some new thinking on
questions of war and peace in the nuclear age. From 1956
Khrushchev argued repeatedly that nuclear weapons made war
inappropriate: capitalism therefore could not now be defeated
militarily. The socialist states would have to coexist peacefully
with capitalism until it collapsed as a result of its own internal
contradictions. This doctrine of 'peaceful coexistence' was
attacked by many communists, not least Mao Tse-Tung, who
argued that nuclear weapons were 'paper tigers' and fear of war
ought not to circumscribe one's actions (and that, as he put it to
Khrushchev, even if 300 million Chinese died in a nuclear
holocaust, many would still remain).

The doctrine of peaceful coexistence exacerbated a growing
feud with China. Meanwhile, despite another doctrinal revision by
Khrushchev, that 'different roads to socialism' were permissible,
and that the Soviet model did not necessarily apply globally
(initially formulated in 1955 with Yugoslavia in mind), relations
with other communist parties were often complex and fraught.
Moreover, 'peaceful coexistence' did not pave the way for great
improvements in East–West relations. Unlike the subsequent

Brezhnev policy of 'détente', it did not presuppose a lessening of international tension. On the contrary, East–West relations in Khrushchev's time on each side were based on assumptions about the virtues of tension and brinkmanship, which Khrushchev proved only too ready to exploit. Hence the nuclear brinkmanship of the Cuban crisis in October 1962. This stemmed from Khrushchev's determination to see the Soviet Union accorded global strategic parity by the United States, something that he failed to gain although Brezhnev was to achieve it before the decade was out. Superpower parity was, for the Soviet leaders, not just a requirement of the nuclear age, but part of an older dream to cast off a national and cultural inferiority complex. Khrushchev's memoirs painted a very revealing picture of this concern with status for its own sake. On his journey to Washington in 1959 he knew 'it would make a better impression if we took one of our own planes', not a foreign plane, particularly if they flew in the new Tupolev 114, which had a

> larger passenger capacity, longer range, greater thrust, and faster cruising speed than any other . . . we could see the wonder in [the Americans'] eyes . . . they'd never seen anything like it . . . We felt pride in our country, our Party, our people and the victories they had achieved . . . If the President of the United States himself invites [Khrushchev] then you know, conditions have changed. We'd come a long way from the time when the United States wouldn't even grant us diplomatic immunity.
>
> (Khrushchev 1977, p. 429)

De-Stalinisation and Political Reform

The most significant of all Khrushchev's reforms was his de-Stalinisation campaign. At the 20th Party Congress in March 1956 he launched a politically explosive attack on Stalin in a 'secret speech' – the contents of which were very soon revealed to the world by Western communist party delegates in Moscow. For good measure, Khrushchev also read to the assembled party élite Lenin's Testament, which had never before been given even as limited a hearing as this. Essentially, Khrushchev attacked Stalin's 'cult of personality', the 'illegal repressions' of honest party comrades, and the consequent decline in authority of the party itself. Stalin's misconduct of the war, particularly in 1941, was also singled out. Khrushchev was not alone in wanting to tackle Stalin's legacy and, as he admitted in his memoirs, 'we could not just do nothing'. The *gulag* or prison camp system, as the writer Alexander Solzhenitsyn showed very clearly in *The Gulag Archipelago*, was starting to break down through sheer overweight and growing internal tensions. Many victims, their sentences completed or lifted, were returning from the dead as it were, and questions that would simply not go away were beginning to take shape about Stalin's rule. Khrushchev's critique was a very limited one, and probably a compromise, confined only to failings from 1934. There were no words at all for non-party victims, and no rehabilitation for any of the major leaders such as Trotsky or Bukharin. But the effect of the speech was almost revolutionary. Stalin's rule, for all the suffering it had imposed on the Soviet people, had formed deep roots. The suffering had often been rationalised away as an historically necessary process. Now both the perpetrators and the victims of that cruelty were being told that much of it had simply been a mistake. It was difficult to avoid the conclusion that the ruling party, which prided itself on its infallibility, had been misled.

Why did Khrushchev do what he did? It is never easy to unravel motives. Whether even Politburo leaders had been kept ignorant of the full details of what was happening under Stalin, or whether they had known but, as the writer Ilya Ehrenburg put it, just 'gritted their teeth and kept silent' is unclear, although, in Khrushchev's case, there did seem to be some real moral indignation behind his de-Stalinisation campaign. There is no denying that it was also politically expedient. He absolved the party from blame, even suggesting that the party had retained some precarious independent existence as a Leninist organisation under Stalin. It pleased some Western communist leaders who had independently been pressing hard for such a campaign: the Italians, for instance, were to fight, though unsuccessfully, for the rehabilitation of Bukharin. Above all, the secret speech put Khrushchev's critics within the party leadership on the defensive. Those such as Malenkov and Molotov who had worked closely with Stalin in Moscow were much more easily tarred with complicity in the purges than a basically provincial figure like Khrushchev himself.

The consequences of Khrushchev's secret speech were not quite as expected. There was a limited rehabilitation of victims, and the continuation of a wider cultural thaw. But then, in October 1956, there was a violent reaction in Poland and Hungary. Stalin's system of rule had much shallower roots in Eastern and Central Europe and Khrushchev's doctrine of different roads to socialism, coupled with his de-Stalinisation campaign, produced anti-Russian uprisings that required brutal Soviet military intervention. This in turn led to a concerted attempt to overthrow Khrushchev himself in June 1957. In an unprecedented move, a majority of the Politburo coalesced on a range of issues to vote him out of office. Khrushchev was to survive this affair, branding his opponents for their 'anti-party factional methods', but he did so only with the support of the military (Pethybridge 1962).

Although on the surface this 1957 crisis consolidated his political position, in reality it appears to have simply meant the redrawing of the battle lines more clearly than before, with the conservatives arguing that further reforms threatened the authority and control of the Communist Party itself. The U2 Affair in 1960, when an American U2 reconnaissance plane was shot down deep inside Soviet territory, marked a critical turning point (Tatu 1969). The military now joined the critics, contending that such planes penetrated so far only because of Khrushchev's cuts in military procurements. By the 22nd Party Congress in 1961, Khrushchev was on the defensive. No doubt on the grounds that attack is the best form of defence, he used the occasion to launch a series of particularly damning revelations about the personal complicity of prominent Soviet leaders in Stalin's purges. These culminated in a macabre and histrionic episode when an Old Bolshevik, that is to say one of the revered number who had been party members since before the Revolution, told the Congress that she had had a vision the previous night in which Lenin had come to her. He complained at having to lie side by side with Stalin in the mausoleum on Moscow's Red Square (Linden 1966, p. 123). The Congress drew to a climax with Khrushchev having Stalin's body removed from the mausoleum and buried in a newly dug Kremlin grave. Khrushchev no doubt hoped to inter more than just a mummified corpse in the process.

Khrushchev's final attempt to tackle the unsavoury aspects of the Stalin era was his approval of the publication of Solzhenitsyn's *One Day in the Life of Ivan Denisovitch* in 1962. This tale of the *gulag* was by far the most explicit account yet published, but it split the nation to the extent that, for a time, there was a saying in the Soviet Union: 'tell me what you think of *One Day* and I'll tell you who you are'. De-Stalinisation stirred up powerful and sometimes unpredictable passions, the victims of the purges often no more eager to rake over painful memories than the perpetrators.

Meanwhile, there was a fourth key area of change to which Khrushchev addressed himself, namely the role of the party itself and the need to revitalise the revolutionary tradition. Khrushchev was a utopian in the sense that he believed that the creation of a perfect communist society, a society of abundance and equality, was an attainable practical proposition; indeed, in the 1961 Party Programme he put a date on it. The Soviet Union would overtake the United States economically by 1970 and attain the ideal society of communism 'in the main' by 1980. In so doing he sought to recreate a sense of forward movement in what he saw as a still unfinished revolution, while at the same time proposing something in place of the dethroned image of Stalin. Khrushchev returned increasingly to the need for Leninism and 'Leninist norms'. In practical terms this was to be seen in the 1958 legal reforms which reintroduced an element of legal due process: no longer were people to be arrested by category and sentenced by quota, but only as a result of individual trial and judgement. The wider idealism was present in Khrushchev's educational reforms of 1958, which tried to attack what he saw as a slowing down of the revolutionary impulse in society, namely the increasingly hereditary and stratified nature of the social system. Entry to higher education should follow only after everyone had worked either in industry or in agriculture for a spell, argued Khrushchev, though with only limited success.

Khrushchev's style was populist in the modern sense of the term: he appealed over the heads of the political establishment and the bureaucracy to ordinary people. Thus the death penalty for economic crimes was reintroduced in 1961, a move aimed particularly at officials. The Ministry of Agriculture was moved out bodily from Moscow to makeshift premises in the mud of the countryside, a punishment for years of falsifying the statistics. The party, he declared in 1961, was not just a vanguard Leninist party but a 'party of the whole people', peasants included. After 1961 Khrushchev sought to impose a quota system for the regular renewal of the political élite: no-one could serve more than 16 years in the Party Central Committee, nor more than 12 years in the Politburo (unless their 'generally acknowledged prestige' led to an overwhelming vote in their favour). More dramatically still, in 1962 he split the party apparatus nationally into two separate but parallel hierarchies, one specialising in agriculture, one in industry, all on the grounds that the apparatus had become excessively dominated by dogmatic Marxist timeservers. ('What kind of communism is it that can't produce a good sausage?')

In this whole area of party and ideology Khrushchev did raise fundamental questions about what constituted relevant expertise in the modern world, about whether Stalinist centralisation of the economy had not hindered local initiative and responsibility, and about whether the building of real trust between leaders and led was crucial to continued success. However, other party leaders were not sure that he had the right answers. Khrushchev was unceremoniously retired in October 1964 in a unique Politburo and Central Committee revolt that shook the entire communist world.

Khrushchev's Overthrow

It is plausible to see Khrushchev's fall as a product of élite opposition to his reformism, not least deep resentment at his 1962 restructuring of the party apparatus. The subsequent conservatism of the Brezhnev era lends credence to this view. But when *Pravda* attacked Khrushchev as a 'hare-brained schemer with half-baked conclusions, hasty decisions and unrealistic actions', who indulged in 'bragging, phrase-mongering and bossiness' they were not entirely wide of the mark. Khrushchev's reformism, outlined above, had rarely connected up into a coherent programme. De-Stalinisation was seen by many as having outlived its usefulness, increasingly jeopardising the party's leading role instead by setting party members against each other. Decentralisation of the economy had in practice created as many problems as it had solved. The 1957 *sovnarkhozy* reforms had created powerful regional and republican party barons whose authority Khrushchev had then attempted to curtail when he split the apparatus in 1962. Khrushchev never successfully squared the circle of decentralising economic power while at the same time preserving central political control. Moreover, he did tend to operate erratically and without consultation. Typically, a plan to merge all five Central Asian republics into one was announced by Khrushchev on a visit to Tashkent in 1962, a statement that the Politburo forced him to withdraw almost before his plane had returned to Moscow. In addition there were real policy failures. The Cuban crisis of 1962 was a serious miscalculation. The domestic economy began to slow down, and Khrushchev humiliatingly had to import grain in 1963.

Oddly, by 1964 he had no real constituency of support, having alienated almost every group on whom he might have relied. The party apparatus disliked his frequent restructuring, the military his attempts to dictate strategic policy, and the intelligentsia increasingly scorned his philistinism. Khrushchev's vigorous programme of religious persecution lost him further support, not least amongst the peasantry.

Admittedly, the pressures on Khrushchev were immense and contradictory. The task of steering the Soviet Union through the first years after the death of Stalin was never going to be easy, as the one-party state attempted to rule without the use of terror for the first time in a generation. Moreover, the fact that Khrushchev did not undertake any more fundamental rethinking is not entirely odd. The Soviet economy at that time, unlike the 1980s, was not widely perceived as one in almost irreversible decline. Annual growth rates were still as high as 6 per cent. When the Conservative British Prime Minister Harold Macmillan, visiting the Soviet Union in 1959, said in the context of the Soviet economy that 'the rate and quality of your progress is indeed extraordinary and – so far as I know – unparalleled in history', he was echoing a sentiment then remarkably widespread both East and West (Wells and Northedge 1982, p. 148).

In retrospect Khrushchev has had a low reputation. The Brezhnev leadership simply ignored him, and many western historians have accepted the thrust of the Politburo's 1964 criticisms, viewing him as at best a 'premature de-Staliniser' who miscalculated and thus damaged the opportunities for real reform for a further generation. Others, not least the Russian intelligentsia, developed in the 1970s a nostalgia for Khrushchev's thaw era. The sculptor Ernst Neizvestny, whom Khrushchev had

much in common. All had sprung from peasant or working-class backgrounds, had joined the party in the 1920s or early 1930s and had received a technical education in those years, becoming part of the generation that acquired high office relatively early because of the rapid turnover of personnel during the purges. All three, in this respect, were typical of an entire generation of Soviet leaders. Unlike Khrushchev, who was a beneficiary of the Revolution itself, so to speak, this generation was the beneficiary of Stalin's 'revolution from above'. Their formative early career years were the 1930s and perhaps even more the war years 1941–45.

Brezhnev had joined the party in 1931 and had been one of the thousands of young urban party workers sent out to assist in the collectivisation drives. Later, he built a career as a competent party apparatus official, becoming First Secretary in the Republic of Moldavia from 1950 to 52 and in Kazakhstan from 1954 to 56 at the time of Khrushchev's Virgin Lands scheme. Then he returned to Moscow as a Central Committee Secretary and Politburo member. Kosygin had been People's Commissar for Light Industry in 1939, and a Deputy Chairman of the Council of People's Commissars (the predecessor of the Council of Ministers) from 1940, building a considerable reputation in the years that followed as a 'technocrat', an able economic administrator, rather than as a party apparatus official. Podgorny had built his career in the Ukraine, rising to become First Secretary of the Republic in 1957. By 1964, therefore, all three, and many thousands of other officials, had already had lengthy careers stretching back to Stalin. By now they were in most respects deeply conservative – if they had not been from the outset – and some of their earliest decisions confirmed this.

At the outset Brezhnev enunciated the rule that officials' jobs were secure, in effect for life, barring gross incompetence or corruption. This principle of 'trust in the cadres; stability of cadres' became one of the most enduring and significant characteristics of the entire Brezhnev era, with considerable longer-term consequences, and confirmed a growing sense of safety among the political élite. In addition the unpopular and, in practice, confusing 1962 bifurcation of the party *apparat* into separate agricultural and industrial hierarchies was scrapped, as were the *sovnarkhozy* disliked by Kosygin's central planners. This all amounted to a package of changes aimed at satisfying both party and state *apparats* and was a clear reaction to Khrushchev's tinkering. It was also a reminder that collective leadership was not just a cliché but a response to a growing reality in Soviet politics, namely the existence of relatively distinct and powerful *apparats*, each with its own political agenda. There was no longer a Stalin who subjugated by force. Furthermore, no-one could take away the knowledge that one General Secretary had already been overthrown for excessive 'bossiness'. The Politburo leadership under Brezhnev thus increasingly became a co-ordinating and stabilising body, seeking to rule through compromise and consensus, rather than a mobilising agency for social and economic change.

In practice, as in the past, the General Secretary gradually came to dominate the leadership. Two issues in particular encouraged this trend, both underlining the ultimate party virtues of central control and authority. The first was the rise of dissent, triggered very largely by the trial and sentencing in 1966 of two writers, Yuri Daniel and Andrei Sinyavsky, for publishing their works abroad. The growing dissident movement was rapidly interpreted by the party as a challenge to its very authority and the party responded accordingly with repeated campaigns for vigilance and unity.

The second issue, that of economic reform, was a reminder that the post-Khrushchev leadership was initially somewhat equivocal. The case for economic reform had been gathering pace both in the Soviet Union and in Eastern and Central Europe since the early 1960s. There was increasing evidence that the Stalin command economy was simply an inappropriate mechanism for the more complex and technologically advanced circumstances of even the 1960s. Country by country, reform measures were introduced including eventually some in the Soviet Union. Kosygin, unlike Brezhnev, was an economic reformer and in 1965 managed to introduce a package of measures which were intended to boost productivity and innovation by making profit rather than quantitative output the principal goal for enterprise managers, who were granted much more latitude than before.

Economic reformers differed in their prescriptions but were united in their analysis that change was necessary. The party apparatus, broadly speaking, both in the Soviet Union and elsewhere, remained fundamentally suspicious. Reform meant decentralisation and managerial power, a rethinking about the

priority accorded to the military sector, a reintroduction of
the market, greater competitiveness and real uncertainty as to
whether all this might not threaten the power and authority of the
party itself. All such conservative doubts were vindicated in 1968
by events in Czechoslovakia, in the so-called Prague Spring. In the
view of Brezhnev and the Soviet leadership as a whole, this was a
reform movement that ran out of control and would have led to
the eventual loss of communist power in Czechoslovakia. The
result was a Warsaw Pact military invasion in August 1968. This
was justified at the time by the so-called 'Brezhnev Doctrine' of
limited sovereignty: that the security of the socialist states is
indivisible and if one state is undermined or attacked by
'anti-socialist forces' it is the fraternal 'right and duty' of the others
to 'intervene and curtail' such counter-revolution.

The international repercussions of uninvited Soviet tanks in
Prague were immense and, for the Soviet Union, very damaging
politically and ideologically. The domestic consequences for
Brezhnev were rather different. The party apparatus had never
been happy with the Kosygin reforms, being sensitive to the fact
that a majority of the working class was opposed to them – on the
grounds that it might mean new working practices, higher prices,
a more competitive life. Soviet leaders at that time were well
aware that such discontents could turn violent, for the unsettling
experience of Novocherkassk had occurred only six years
previously. In the summer of 1962 Khrushchev raised meat and
dairy prices by about one third. Simultaneously, a locomotive
works in the city of Novocherkassk on the Don River in Southern
Russia chose to lower wages. Spontaneous rioting and violence
followed in which at least 70 people were killed, and far more
according to unofficial accounts. This event undoubtedly shook
the Soviet leadership considerably and made it subsequently ultra-
cautious about provoking industrial workers again. The Prague
Spring thus confirmed in the minds of the party *apparat* the
dangers of reform and the absolute necessity of party authority
and discipline. As a consequence it destroyed any possibility of
radical economic and political reform in the Soviet Union for a
generation. The Kosygin reforms were never formally rescinded,
but they ran into the sands, openly ignored or sabotaged by many
party *apparatchiks*. Brezhnev meanwhile rose to become indisput-
ably first among equals in the collective leadership.

Brezhnev in the Ascendant: the Détente Era

Brezhnev's acquisition of real political authority in areas other
than that of the party itself can be traced back to about 1968. By
1970 it was he, not Kosygin, who was clearly in command of the
Soviet Union's basic economic and foreign policy. Only Brezhnev
signed the decree promulgating the next Five-Year Plan in 1971
and the Strategic Arms Limitation (SALT) treaties with the
United States; and from 1972 the Politburo was described as being
'headed by Brezhnev'. An accumulation of medals and titles
followed. In 1976 Brezhnev, on his 70th birthday, was referred to
as the *vozhd* – a highly resonant term in the Soviet context,
implying a national chieftain and hitherto used only to describe
Stalin. Brezhnev awarded himself the title of Marshal of the Soviet
Union in 1976, by which time he was also Supreme Commander of
the Armed Forces and Chairman of the Defence Council. In 1977
he assumed the Presidency, ousting Podgorny. By 1978 his war
memoirs had been set to music and had earned the author, among
other plaudits, the Lenin Prize for Literature.

Much of this could be seen as the display of a vain and insecure
man. The secret visit of President Nixon's National Security
Adviser Henry Kissinger in 1972 was a case in point. Kissinger had
flown secretly to China in 1971, lost to the world's media for four
days while he negotiated a new Sino–US rapprochement that
effectively ended a quarter of a century of diplomatic non-
recognition. This move appeared to upset Brezhnev, not so much
because it created a new power relationship that would greatly
complicate the Soviet Union's own strategic and diplomatic
thinking, but because Brezhnev had never been dignified with an
equally secret mission. Propriety was in due course saved, but only
by Kissinger making an (entirely unnecessary) secret visit to
Moscow in 1972 (Kissinger 1979, p. 1124).

Despite all this, however, the Brezhnev leadership always
remained a collective to a far greater degree than Khrushchev's.
Brezhnev at least sought to take his Politburo with him on all
major matters, and even at the height of the virtual cult of the
1970s, the essentials of collective leadership remained intact.
Brezhnev's leadership was also, in this middle period, that of a
decisive man. He translated his formal powers and titles into real

political authority by developing what was at the time in many respects a successful overall strategy. No Soviet leader can simply 'do nothing', for continuation in power, as elsewhere, requires authority based on policy achievement (Breslauer 1982). In Brezhnev's case the cornerstone to this authority was ultimately the policy of détente.

The détente process evolved in the 1970s and was rooted in three preconditions. The first was an acceptance by the United States under President Nixon from 1969 that there was 'rough parity' in nuclear matters between the two superpowers. The doctrine of peaceful coexistence on the Soviet side was now matched by the doctrine of Mutually Assured Destruction (MAD) on the Western side. Both accepted that nuclear war would inflict unacceptable damage. The second precondition was a common recognition of the Soviet Union's continuing concern about the security of her position in Europe. The third precondition was a Soviet awareness that economic reform had petered out and that the best way of maintaining momentum short of launching a potentially destabilising new reform was to gain wider access to Western technology, grain and credits – in other words, that there was an essentially conservative alternative to economic reform.

Détente was thus a powerful diplomatic drive, launched by Brezhnev, to lessen East–West tensions and thereby attain an interrelated set of domestic and foreign policy goals. It appealed to the United States and the Western powers under Nixon and Kissinger, for whom MAD implied an imperial 'spheres of influence' view of the globe, and who were also persuaded that by enmeshing the Soviet Union into the capitalist world economy, the very nature of the Soviet system might thereby be changed ('victory without war', said Nixon). Meanwhile, the Soviet Union took the view that détente had a strictly European context and did not in any way limit Soviet strategy and tactics in the Third World, for in the Soviet phrase the true 'correlation of forces' globally still pointed to an eventual, albeit peaceful, victory for the progressive forces of socialism. History was still on the side of Moscow. The conceptual and political frameworks assembled in Moscow and in Washington therefore fitted together only in places and the subsequent collapse of the détente edifice was not altogether surprising (Edmonds 1983, p. 137). Nonetheless, for a time this highly ambitious process appeared to succeed.

The symbolic climax of détente was the Conference on Security and Cooperation in Europe held in Helsinki in 1975. This resulted in 35 nations signing a series of agreements recognising the 1945 borders of Soviet power in Central and Eastern Europe as legitimate, and encouraging wider economic, scientific and technical exchange and cooperation, as well as seeking to guarantee certain measures on human rights. The first two components represented a considerable diplomatic achievement for the Soviet Union; the third, however, came largely from the West and raised more questions than it solved. Specifically, the Helsinki human rights clauses envisaged greater freedom of movement for people and ideas, including 'freedom of thought, of conscience, of religion or belief for all'. In the absence of positive Soviet moves to implement this agreement, however, it merely fuelled dissident unrest and contributed greatly to the Czechoslovak Charter 77 and the Polish Solidarity movements of the next few years.

Brezhnev claimed at one point that he had had to 'sweat political blood' to get détente. There were certainly various critics within the leadership (Gelman 1984). Some, like the Ukrainian First Secretary Pyotr Shelest, as well as other party leaders in the western borderlands, had originally had doubts in the early 1970s about whether Soviet security interests would really be served by opening up the borders to trade, technology, culture and tourism, with all the attendant risks of 'bourgeois' ideas and practices. In any case, it was never clear whether the existing series of bilateral treaties signed with European powers, notably the non-aggression treaty with Germany in 1970, was not a perfectly adequate security guarantee. And Kosygin returned to the offensive in 1976 with public criticism that détente had not obviated the ever more pressing need for domestic economic reform.

Generally, however, détente was seen at the time as a successful achievement, a recognition of Soviet superpower parity and a major contribution to that greater sense of security which many Soviet people now felt they had. On the surface, too, the Soviet economy was satisfactory. The Brezhnev détente years were marked by an unprecedented rise in Soviet living standards. There were dramatic pay increases for most people, outstripping price increases (average personal savings rose from 50 to nearly 1,000 rubles per head between 1960 and 1982). There were new hero projects, notably the Baikal–Amur Railway (BAM) which was to be a second Trans-Siberian line, the Kama River truck factory, and the Togliatti car factory (the latter a specific outcome of détente with Fiat), as well as the Siberian gas pipeline which was to produce substantial hard currency earnings, notably from West Germany. Meanwhile, vast new oil fields in Siberia guaranteed cheap energy for the Soviet bloc, while OPEC price rises enabled the Soviet Union – the world's second largest oil exporter – to increase her prices on world markets and thereby reap enormous dividends. Agricultural investment and output increased and private plots were again encouraged after Khrushchev had latterly tightened up on them.

Soviet society itself was by now hierarchical, stable and conservative, the dissidents an isolated minority. For most people the 1970s saw a slow but gradual widening of the bounds of debate and discussion, the élites in particular being allowed some discretion (Malcolm 1984; Hill 1980). The most significant social change was perhaps the rise of a sense of nationalism coupled with some nostalgia for the rural past on the part of ethnic Russians themselves. This was a development which found expression in film and literature during the 1970s, and with which the Brezhnev leadership was very much in tune (Bialer 1980a, p. 54). Khrushchev had demolished ancient churches and cathedrals: Brezhnev restored many of those that were left, even on occasion getting UNESCO grants to do so.

Politically, the Brezhnev heyday often involved a successful balancing act. This could be seen in Brezhnev's handling of the institutions of power, such as the military. Khrushchev had sought to dictate military appropriations policy arguing that large armies, navies and air forces were obsolete in the nuclear age. Brezhnev stood back from such involvement, allowing the military much greater professional latitude. The effect of this, coupled with an overall increase of 4 per cent per annum in real terms in military expenditure until 1976, was to leave the military politically quiescent to a degree that had not been the case under Khrushchev.

In all this there was an important lesson collectively learnt from the Stalin and Khrushchev years: that political and technical authority ought not to be confused. Khrushchev had combined both party and government posts. This meant that, in principle, he was responsible not only for the broad directives of policy but also for their specific implementation. He was thus in practice vulnerable in the event of policy failures. Brezhnev turned the complexities of collective leadership to his advantage. Thus, when the harvest was successful he took the credit, and when it failed his Minister of Agriculture was dismissed, as happened twice in the 1970s.

The political balance which Brezhnev struck was nowhere more clear than on the Stalin question. Further de-Stalinisation was ruled out, but so were attempts to re-glorify him by Brezhnev's younger Politburo challengers Alexander Shelepin and Vladimir Semichastny after 1964. The party issued an authoritative pronouncement on the centenary of Stalin's birth in 1979 which confirmed this. Stalin had been a 'very complex and contradictory historical figure' who had both achievements and grave errors to his name, but the glorious party and people had together won great victories both in peace and in war. In 1956 there had been 'an exhaustive appraisal' of the era, including a recognition of the very difficult conditions in which the 'struggle for socialism' had taken place. The party had 'swiftly overcome' the legacy of the cult and 'thoroughly disclosed the factors behind its emergence and the damage it had done to Soviet society'. As a reaction to the alarums of Khrushchev this was for many a welcome and soothing formula. Critics such as the poet Yevgeni Yevtushenko, who wrote to Brezhnev in 1974 saying that 'the truth has been replaced by silence', seemed to strike few chords.

A final affirmation of the stability of the period was the promulgation of a new Soviet Constitution in 1977, with its emphasis on the Brezhnev years as an ideologically distinct phase known as the era of 'developed socialism'. Developed socialism, which is discussed more fully in the next chapter, implied social stability and harmony, and dwelt on the virtues of the status quo, as opposed to the impatient and unrealistic utopianism of Khrushchev and the social disharmony of the Stalin era.

Brezhnev had once hinted to Western journalists that it was his ambition to retire voluntarily at the age of 70 (the age at which, incidentally, Khrushchev had been pensioned off ostensibly suffering from 'old age and ill health'). Had he done so, he might well have been accorded some considerable credit as a leader who fashioned a successful conservative consensus at home and a vigorous détente strategy abroad. In fact, Brezhnev continued in power long enough to see many of his policy achievements turn sour.

The Years of Stagnation

Mikhail Gorbachev's criticism at the 27th Party Congress in 1986 that the last years of Brezhnev's life were a time of stagnation, complacency and missed opportunity is hard to avoid. New thinking was at a premium if only because a generation that had survived the purges and the war to rule a stable and respected superpower was understandably proud of this achievement and not inclined to undertake any real self-criticism.

One by one, however, cracks appeared in the façade. Brezhnev himself was ageing and often ill, working less and less and increasingly unable to provide the dynamism needed to lead the Soviet Union. A classic instance occurred, less than two months before his death, when he was seen live on Soviet television haltingly reading what turned out to be the wrong speech on Sino-Soviet relations. An aide took it from his hands and gave him the correct version, at which Brezhnev gamely started afresh, having been heard to say that it was 'not my fault' (Z. Medvedev 1983, p. 16).

Détente collapsed not least because of a Soviet failure to recognise that a simultaneous commitment both to lessen tensions on the one hand and to maintain a military build-up on the other simply did not work. There were many in the West determined to unravel détente in any case, but the Soviet occupation of Afghanistan completed their work for them. This collapse of détente appeared to catch the Soviet leadership quite unprepared, for they had no doubt persuaded themselves in their own words that détente was an 'historically irreversible' process. Indicative of the extent to which this collapse left Brezhnev adrift was the contrast between his keynote speeches to the 25th Congress in 1976, when he described 'how the world is changing before our very eyes and changing for the better', and to the 26th Congress in 1981, when he talked of how 'the period under review has been rough and complicated . . . [with] thunderclouds on the horizon'. The Polish Solidarity crisis of 1980–81, when popular protest nearly destroyed the Polish regime, was one such thundercloud. So, too, was the widespread evidence of declining Soviet influence in the communist world, with the Chinese and the Western Eurocommunists increasingly concerned to avoid the Soviet experience rather than adopt it for themselves. Paradoxically, by 1982 the Soviet Union was faced not only with capitalist encirclement but with a form of communist encirclement, too, relations with Poland and China being as troublesome as relations with any Western power (Bialer 1986, p. 173). Vast military power had not apparently gone hand in hand with economic, political or ideological power. Instead, over-extension abroad hid real economic and social decline at home.

Economic policy certainly ran into serious trouble in Brezhnev's last years, symbolised graphically by the importation of large quantities of grain, mainly from the United States. Between 1975 and 1982 about one quarter of all Soviet grain needs were met by imports. Despite an enormous investment programme, net agricultural output rose by only 0.9 per cent 1971–79, and declined far below plan levels in the years 1979 to 1982. Brezhnev's last major domestic initiative was a rather desperate Food Programme launched in 1982 aimed at making domestic food output the 'top economic priority' as an 'urgent socio-political task'. Economic growth overall was declining, apparently inexorably. National income growth rates fell from 41 per cent 1966–70 to only 16.5 per cent 1981–85, even on official figures (Aganbegyan 1988, p. 2) Expectations meanwhile were rising, partly fuelled by increasing numbers of Soviet people visiting Eastern and Central Europe as tourists and comparing Soviet reality with the noticeably more affluent Czechoslovakia, Hungary and East Germany (Bushnell 1980, p. 192). There is evidence that the leadership was aware of all this: indeed, Brezhnev spoke of the failure to make good on economic promises as a 'major political question'. But no concerted action ever followed.

In fact, there was much policy drift in later years, subsequently castigated by Gorbachev as 'muddling through'. Consensus politics appeared to degenerate into what Brezhnev himself repeatedly termed 'narrow departmentalism', as each bureaucracy defended its own territory. Even modest attempts at change were resisted lower down and Brezhnev, with his historic commitment to the stability of cadres, was in no position to fight back.

Corruption and the black economy flourished, morale and productivity declined. By 1982 Soviet society could be characterised without undue exaggeration as one in which the middle classes were essentially careerist, the working classes apathetic and anti-intellectual, the peasants alienated and youth remarkably cynical. 'We have turned into something between Gogol and Orwell – an animal farm of dead souls' (Schmidt-Hauer 1986, p. 123). Many of the brightest and best had been labelled as dissidents and imprisoned or driven into exile in the West. Alcohol sales had risen by 77 per cent between 1970 and 1980, with a consequently damaging effect on the nation's health. Though the exact figures are not clear, male life expectancy at birth appears to have declined from 67 years in 1964 to no more than 62 years by 1980, a startling drop (Colton 1986, p. 34).

Just why Brezhnev survived to die in office is not clear. There were efforts by Yuri Andropov and the KGB which might have succeeded before too long to undermine his position and possibly force him from office in 1982 over family corruption. Part of the answer must be that Brezhnev, to the end, was a canny politician who kept potential or real rivals isolated and successfully manoeuvred his own supporters into key posts. Many, and not just in his own immediate entourage, were also no doubt still grateful to Brezhnev: while he survived, real political change could be shelved. In addition, there were no rules about regular leadership renewal and few precedents to go on. Not least, as we shall see below, there were unresolved disagreements about the future direction of policy.

Judgement based on recent hindsight is often poor. Our views on the Brezhnev era, in both East and West, are on the whole considerably more critical now than they were at the time. Current Soviet reassessments in particular are unduly negative. In practice the consensus in favour of traditional authority and stability never really gave way, if only because, for all its failings, Soviet economic performance in the early 1980s could in some respects be contrasted favourably with that of capitalist states which were then going through a period of recession and mass unemployment. Nevertheless, it was clear even at the time that Brezhnev maintained all this at a considerable price, for he failed to tackle basic reform issues as well as the succession question, thus leaving a complex and troubling situation for his successors.

From Brezhnev to Gorbachev, 1982–85

In retrospect, the death of Brezhnev was not quite the end of the Brezhnev era. It did little to resolve a deep-rooted succession crisis, the interregnum from Brezhnev to Gorbachev being marked by serious drift, division and instability in the Soviet leadership. Symbolically perhaps, whereas the party had managed with only three General Secretaries in the sixty years from Stalin's appointment in 1922 to Brezhnev's death, it produced another three within just three years from 1982 (Brown 1985a, p. 1).

There were several strands to the Brezhnev succession crisis. The first was that of generational change, for it was not merely Brezhnev but a whole political generation that was coming to the end of its active life. The extraordinary longevity in office of this generation was a unique product first of Stalin's purges in the 1930s and then of the subsequent failure to devise any systematic method of leadership renewal in the post-Stalin era. It was compounded by the destruction in the 1941–45 war of the next generation, those just a few years younger. The resulting demographic gap was faithfully mirrored at the top of Soviet politics and it meant that, sooner or later, power was likely to skip a political generation and pass to men whose formative years as young *apparatchiks* were not those of the 1930s, nor even of the war, but of the reformist Khrushchev period (Hough 1980). There is no doubt that the old guard was aware of this and sought to postpone the changeover and the inevitable reappraisals it would bring. Rather than plan for an orderly transition, the Brezhnev leadership often sacked or downgraded ambitious younger leaders, increasingly surrounding itself with others of its kind.

Interwoven with this generational problem were personal rivalries and real divisions at the top about policy and the future direction of Soviet politics. The Brezhnev era had stifled but never quite silenced the voices of reform and by the early 1980s, with mounting evidence of economic disarray in particular, the leadership was increasingly polarised into conservative and reformist factions, the one often cancelling out the other. Nowhere was this more evident than in the successive leadership choice first of a reformer, Yuri Andropov, and then of a conservative, Konstantin Chernenko.

Brezhnev's immediate successor, Yuri Andropov, was only eight years younger than Brezhnev and for fifteen years had been chairman of the KGB as well as, since 1973, a full member of the Politburo. But he put in motion a series of measures that sought to revive the economy, notably tough new anti-corruption and anti-alcohol measures, and he took significant steps to renew the party apparatus. In little more than a year over one fifth of regional First Secretaries and over one fifth of the Moscow-based members of the Council of Ministers were replaced, as well as a third of the Central Committee Secretaries, psychologically breaking the Brezhnev tradition of 'stability of cadres'. Indeed, as if to emphasise the point, the Minister of Fisheries was shot in 1983 after having been found guilty of serious corruption.

There was considerable political logic to Andropov's moves. The KGB had earlier had a reputation as the guardian of revolutionary purity, and Andropov had no doubt continued to keep assiduous files on the Brezhnev era élites. Moreover, tighter discipline appealed to most people, though for differing reasons. Managers applauded the anti-alcohol drive; workers the anti-corruption measures. According to official figures output and productivity rose significantly during 1983.

Andropov, however, was a reformer in only a limited sense, on occasion speaking favourably of Brezhnev and, like him, appealing for tighter discipline rather than democracy. He sought, as Brezhnev had done, to improve the old mechanism of the command economy rather than transform it. Although Andropov encouraged greater public debate than before, particularly on economic questions, and admitted that the party 'did not have all the answers', he essentially treated economic reform as an isolated technical problem without wider social, cultural or political implications.

It is unclear how far Andropov would ever have taken reform, for he died only fifteen months after Brezhnev and was chronically ill almost from the start of his rule with kidney and heart disease. He was not seen in public at all for the last six months. His most lasting accomplishment was real enough, however, for he did consciously groom the next generation of leaders. He advanced Gorbachev's career at an unusually rapid pace, and brought several other younger men into the senior ranks of the leadership.

Gorbachev may have been Andropov's own preferred successor, but in practice, when the latter not unexpectedly died in February 1984, he was succeeded by a conservative member of the Brezhnev old guard, Konstantin Chernenko. Chernenko was 72 years old and already visibly ill with the emphysema that was to end his life in March 1985. His career had depended almost entirely on his long and close association with Brezhnev, with whom he had initially come into contact in 1950 when Brezhnev was First Secretary in Moldavia. Chernenko had served in effect as Brezhnev's personal political secretary from as early as 1960 although, despite this, his promotion to full Politburo rank had only occurred in 1978.

For the ruling leaders of a nuclear superpower to choose such an obviously limited and stop-gap figure requires some explanation. The most likely has to be that the Politburo was by now in chronic disagreement, split into conservative and reformist factions and further divided by personal rivalries, Chernenko being an acceptable compromise precisely because he was seen as a stop-gap figure. The result was a predictably brief and confused interregnum, all the important tensions remaining unresolved. On the one hand, a measure of stability returned to cadres policy, the clock even being turned back far enough to allow the symbolically important public rehabilitation and readmittance to the party of none other than Molotov, one of the least repentant survivors of the Stalin era and by now 94 years old. On the other hand, radical economists were officially published, reform debates continued, and a genuine shift of opinion amongst the party intelligentsia in favour of a major economic reform could be detected. Moreover, there was some evidence that Gorbachev was already the heir apparent, on occasion deputising at Politburo meetings for the absent Chernenko, and sometimes being officially described as the deputy General Secretary.

Chernenko himself clearly had relatively little power and even less authority, the bureaucratic pluralism of the recent past continuing unchecked. However, Chernenko's death, in finally ending the Brezhnev era and paving the way for Gorbachev, was a genuinely historic event, arguably more so than the mere death of Brezhnev himself.

Gorbachev's Rise to Power

In assessing the rise to power of Mikhail Gorbachev it is important not to lose sight of the fact that his success was by no means preordained. (Z. Medvedev, 1986) The Politburo remained split, this time between Gorbachev and the 71-year-old Victor Grishin, First Secretary of the Moscow city party machine and candidate of the conservative old guard. Half the Politburo were septuagenarians and the Central Committee consisted overwhelmingly of Brezhnev era appointees. In the circumstances, the choice of Gorbachev, the youngest member of the Politburo, as General Secretary was not only to have decisive and far-reaching consequences, but was a remarkable outcome in itself.

Gorbachev's claims to power, however, were good, and his achievement as the first of the new post-Stalin generation of leaders to become General Secretary was due to a remarkable combination of luck, judgement and sheer political ability. He was born into a peasant family in 1931, at the time of collectivisation and in the very year when the young Brezhnev had joined the party. From 1950 to 1955 he studied at the prestigious Moscow University Law Faculty, a relatively difficult occurrence at the time for one of his background. Later, he gained a second degree by part-time study as an agricultural economist.

His career as a Komsomol and party official in his native province of Stavropol in southern Russia prospered steadily, culminating in his highly successful tenure as First Secretary of the province from 1970, during which he achieved particularly good results in agriculture. He was promoted to Moscow in 1978 when he appropriately succeeded his predecessor in Stavropol, Fyodor Kulakov, as the Central Committee Secretary for agriculture. In 1980 he was further promoted to full membership of the Politburo, still only 49 and by a margin of five years its youngest member. (At the time only two other members were under 65.) He had clearly impressed at least some of the old guard: as the veteran Foreign Minister, Andrei Gromyko, remarked rather ambiguously to the Central Committee in 1985 when nominating Gorbachev for the leadership, 'comrades, this man has a winning smile, but I warn you he has iron teeth'.

Luck, too, seems to have played a part. Stavropol is a naturally warm and fertile land in the Black Earth region and a rewarding testing ground for ambitious leaders. By coincidence, at least three senior Politburo figures in the late 1970s had previous Stavropol links: the Agriculture Secretary Kulakov, whose death in 1978 propelled Gorbachev into the Politburo; Mikhail Suslov, the ideology Secretary and a Politburo member since Stalin's time who ran Stavropol from 1939 to 1944; and Andropov, who regularly vacationed in the province. Unusually and coincidentally, therefore, Gorbachev appears to have come to the attention of several Politburo members during the 1970s. Moreover, the increasingly rapid succession of Politburo funerals in the 1980s fortuitously advanced Gorbachev's seniority. It also diverted attention from the continuing national failures in agriculture which, at least theoretically, were now Gorbachev's responsibility. Other promising heirs had appeared before, but it was Gorbachev who was in position when, so to speak, the music stopped.

Gorbachev also had considerable experience to his credit by 1985. On one reading he was merely a recently elevated provincial party leader, his entire career based in his native region. Stavropol, however, is the size of Ireland and has a population of two million. Furthermore, Gorbachev had had seven years' experience of the Central Committee Secretariat and five years' full membership of the Politburo, a combination of experience possessed by few at that time. This had enabled him not only to build up his own network of political support, but to gain much wider expertise in both domestic and foreign affairs (Brown, 1985a). In short, there could have been few doubts about Gorbachev's credentials for the leadership. Such doubts as there were hinged on the fact that he was very clearly a radical reformer and with time on his side.

It is an open question whether either the Politburo or Gorbachev himself sensed in 1985 quite how radical and charismatic a leader he would prove to be. Gorbachev's own subsequent speeches implied a learning process ('the problems which have accumulated in society are more deep rooted than we at first thought' he said in 1987). But by 1985, in the vacuum caused by Chernenko's lack of leadership, Gorbachev had already established a reputation as a radical reformer who, like many others of his generation, had come to some fundamentally uncomfortable conclusions about the state of both the Soviet economy and society. In wide-ranging speeches in 1984 he had argued that what was needed was a new industrial revolution. At stake was 'nothing less than the ability of the Soviet Union to enter the new millenium in a manner worthy of a great and prosperous power'. With the economy slowing down and in 'disarray' at a time of rising expectations, he went so far as to argue that it might not even be possible 'to preserve what has been achieved', hinting at potential social and political instability. The issue was no longer when to overtake the United States, as Khrushchev had put it a generation earlier, but how to stop falling further behind the West technologically, a problem which had both strategic and economic implications. By the early 1990s Japan, not the Soviet Union, would be the world's second largest industrial economy and many hitherto unregarded states such as Taiwan and South Korea were now technologically far in advance of the Soviet Union in many key areas.

Gorbachev was thus in effect aware of the fundamental mismatch of the Brezhnev era between global power and influence, largely military, and an internal political and economic system beginning to exhibit unmistakeable signs of structural decline. Like other younger, well educated and more sophisticated members of the party intelligentsia, he had looked into the Soviet future and decided that it did not necessarily work. Anything less than a comprehensive and radical restructuring would render the archaic hammer and sickle on the Soviet flag ever more appropriate symbols for a great but backward nation.

Gorbachev's Reform Programme

Both the problems and the expectations facing Gorbachev in 1985 were therefore enormous. Subsequently he was to impress many domestic and foreign audiences as a visionary and charismatic leader, unleashing what at times seemed little short of a second revolution, with undeniably immense consequences for the Soviet Union and the world. As in the Russian past, at the time of Peter the Great, Alexander II or even Stalin, Gorbachev has sought to be a powerful moderniser determined to shock the nation out of old ways of thinking and acting.

To accomplish such a strategy, Gorbachev has essentially tried to do three things. One has been to promote new people and breathe new life into the party, and democratise political life to some degree (*demokratizatsia*); a second has been to put together a coherent reform programme of economic and social reconstruction (*perestroika*); the third to persuade people of its irreversible necessity and thus to implement it, not least through a policy of openness in public discussion (*glasnost*). We shall consider each of these briefly in turn.

A major priority from the outset, culminating in a special Party Conference in June 1988 – the first of its kind since 1941 – was the state of the party itself. Unprecedented personnel changes took place in the first year as the old and often – though not always – corrupt Brezhnev faction was weeded out. Gorbachev achieved in months a political ascendancy that had taken Brezhnev and Khrushchev several years. By the 27th Party Congress in February 1986 already half the Politburo and Secretariat leaders had been promoted within that previous year, major changes in military leadership had occurred, one third of the government ministers and one third of the republic and regional first secretaries had been replaced. Sweeping changes to all the crucial bureaucratic élites had taken place, particularly the Central Committee Secretariat. The power of any Soviet leader rests essentially on the efficient and responsive functioning of the party itself and a major priority for Gorbachev was the renewal of this group. No less than eight of the eleven Central Committee Secretaries were replaced in 1985–86 (Gustafson and Mann 1986). Nationally, tens of thousands of officials were transferred or dismissed.

Although the shake-out of cadres was a crucial early priority, and has continued to be of significance, it has been increasingly intertwined with a much deeper analysis, namely the absence of democracy within the party as such, and the need to conduct a political *perestroika*. In the view of Gorbachev and other reform leaders the party has become far too privileged, undemocratic and unrepresentative. It has become out of touch, caught up in the bureaucratic minutiae of decision making, and thus in danger of losing its ability to think and act strategically. In short, as Gorbachev spelt out in a major speech to the Central Committee in January 1987, the party has proved itself increasingly ineffective. Greater inner-party democracy and a clearer sense of political responsibility were essential if the brightest and best were to be encouraged, the economy restructured, and society regalvanised. 'We need little short of a revolution . . . those unwilling to make the change will have to go', Gorbachev had said rather earlier in this context in 1986.

Thus, at the 1988 Party Conference, far-reaching political reforms were finally approved. Party officials in future were to be limited to no more than two five-year terms of office, competitively elected rather than appointed from above. There was to be a new executive-style presidency at the top but, lower down, a major shift of power and responsibility from the party *apparat* to elected local soviets. 'For much too long', said Gorbachev, 'monotonous uniformity and mediocrity were made out to be the hallmarks of progress . . . the Soviet people want full-blooded and unconditional democracy.' For the reformers, however, *demokratizatsia*, though acutely desired, was also a means to an end – the achievement of a radical programme of economic *perestroika*. Let us now turn briefly to this.

Gorbachev's economic reconstruction required at the outset some preliminary demolition work, notably on the 'inertia and drift' of the Brezhnev era – or rather, more specifically the late 1970s and early 1980s. In an historic speech to the Central Committee in January 1987 Gorbachev launched a fully-fledged attack on those years when 'vigorous debates and creative ideas disappeared . . . when a strange psychology gripped the party, that matters could actually be improved without changing anything'. The result was a moribund economy in a 'pre-crisis situation', as Gorbachev characterised it at the next Central Committee meeting in June 1987. 'Taking it out of this state of affairs within the next two or three years . . . demands a truly revolutionary transformation.'

The outlines of Gorbachev's *perestroika* strategy, the success of which is crucial to his political survival, are now clear, but they have emerged piecemeal and not without debate at each stage. The basic strategy is dramatic in its implications. Gorbachev has called for an end to the Stalinist command economy, particularly in industry, a major scaling down of the role of the central planners and a managed shift to a mixed economy, a form of market socialism, with a combination of planning and market forces. The Central Committee agreed in June 1987 to follow this road, replacing the command economy with a form of self-management that involves elected plant managers and bankruptcy for unprofitable enterprises. Annual economic plans have been dropped in favour of strategic 5- and 15-year guidelines. The role of the central planners is being cut back so that, in principle, within a few years only about one third of the industrial economy would be centrally controlled, the remainder being replaced by enterprises trading directly with each other rather than through complex bureaucratic channels.

Central planning and public ownership remain key tenets of Soviet socialism, but private enterprise has been slowly though steadily encouraged in limited areas. In agriculture, meanwhile, a form of NEP has been under way since 1986, with state quotas and price levels but much greater freedom for the private sector. There are many ambiguities and problems involved in this economic restructuring – as indeed there are with political *demokratizatsia*. The basic strategy, however, is clear and is geared to the 1986 Party Congress commitment to double productivity by the year 2000 and achieve real and lasting improvements in personal living standards meanwhile.

Such reforms involve a recognition of a qualitative shift to a high wage–high output economy involving far more incentives and individual risks as well as increased inequalities. The 'new thinking' therefore has also led to a quite explicit debate about whether 'social justice' is not better achieved by encouraging individual effort and duly rewarding it, with no ceilings on what can be legally earned. The aim is to break the cycle of passivity and corruption and thus enable the rightful and long overdue integration of the Soviet economy into the global economy (Aganbegyan 1988, p. 154). This implies a convertible rouble and participation in the international trading system through membership of hitherto scorned capitalist organisations such as GATT and the IMF, for Gorbachev's *perestroika* also has an international dimension.

The 'new thinking' in foreign affairs involves several key propositions outlined at the 1986 Party Congress. First, there has to be much greater flexibility of thought in an ever more rapidly changing world. The concepts of the early revolutionary years are not appropriate at the end of the century. Secondly, international politics today is polycentric by nature rather than bi-polar and Soviet policy towards China and Japan, for example, should be given a much higher priority, the over-concentration on East–West relations, particularly with the United States in previous years, having proved self-defeating and inflexible. Thirdly, world capitalism, far from being in the terminal crisis that party ideologists had traditionally maintained, has a continuing vitality. Fourthly, the most significant problems facing mankind are not class warfare and revolution, but the threat of nuclear war, hunger and disease, environmental despoilation and the increasingly global and interdependent nature of all of these. Fifthly, it is counter-productive to maintain an isolationist fortress economy with the drawbridges to the outside world pulled up. Given the increasingly global nature of the economy, and the increasingly global division of labour and expertise involved, it is simply unrealistic to believe that the socialist states can be both self-sufficient and globally competitive. Sixthly, Gorbachev has argued bluntly that military power is expensive, often counter-productive and an inappropriate way of achieving real national power and influence. 'Pushing revolutions from outside is futile and inadmissible and doubly so when done by military means.' Reagan and the American arms build-up of the 1980s were not inevitable but in part a response to the Soviet military build-up of the 1970s. A less costly military strategy, but still one with a deterrent effect, would be 'reasonable sufficiency'of arms. National security could be better achieved not by an endless matching spiral of armaments but by a graduated decommissioning of the world's nuclear arsenals by the end of the century.

All of this involved a recognition of past failings including the self-deluding sophistry of policies based on the 1970s principle of the 'correlation of forces' that somehow, in the long run, history was effortlessly on the side of socialism. It also advanced to centre stage economic and technological questions and, in effect, the primacy of the domestic civilian economy, not a global military strategy.

How has Gorbachev sought to accomplish this *perestroika* and 'new thinking' in a country as vast as the Soviet Union, ruled by a party apparatus that has been notoriously opposed to reform and has destroyed reform measures in the past? In a country where change has normally come from above, leaders have traditionally imposed their visions with force. Modern Soviet leaders cannot or will not do this. Therefore, it is necessary for them to open the floodgates of debate and discussion just enough to persuade people by argument and example. To some extent this has to be done over the heads of a party apparatus that has become isolated and unpopular and, as one reader's letter published in *Pravda* in 1986 put it, is a 'sedentary, inert and viscous layer . . . that thwarts change at every step'. Thus, *glasnost* or openness.

Glasnost is not new: the term and the policy were used by Alexander II to describe his reforms in the 1860s. It was, in effect, the engine behind the Prague Spring reforms of 1968, although then called 'socialism with a human face'. But *glasnost* has been by far the most tangible evidence of *perestroika*, particularly since the 1986 Chernobyl disaster, which was a major precipitant for, as the reformers argued then and later, many problems arose precisely because of past unwillingness to be open. In effect, rumour, misinformation and secrecy are simply inefficient. Such views are ironically close to those of the Brezhnev era dissidents, a sign of how far the political pendulum has swung since 1985, and the reason why the staunchest supporters of reform include not only writers, journalists and film makers but, arguably, dissidents such as Academician Sakharov (released from internal exile and allowed to return to Moscow and circulate freely in 1986).

Glasnost has produced a remarkable upsurge in public debate, not least about the Stalin era, the war in Afghanistan, drug addiction, prostitution and homosexuality, the generation gap between young and old, and spectacular cases of official corruption and incompetence in both civilian and military life. Films and books banned for years, including Bukharin's *ABC of Communism*, Orwell's *1984* and *Animal Farm*, Pasternak's *Dr Zhivago* and the epic poem *Requiem* by Anna Akhmatova have been published, and the privileged zone of officialdom immune from criticism reduced almost to vanishing point.

The reform strategy taken in toto has shown Gorbachev to be a powerful, determined and ambitious leader. What has actually been implemented and achieved will be considered in more detail throughout later chapters, and a wider overview of reform prospects will form the conclusion to this study. But at this point, taking the whole sweep of post-Stalin political change, it is worth bearing in mind two propositions.

Continuity and Change Since Stalin

First, many changes occurred in the years before Gorbachev that were of considerable and lasting significance. An evolutionary strand to Soviet politics can be identified. Terror was abandoned in 1953; utopianism died a death with the fall of Khrushchev; even basic optimism at all levels about the continuing efficacy of the political and economic system had become seriously eroded by the end of the Brezhnev era, as the perception of relative decline began to take hold. Moreover, in society at large the post-Stalin era saw a revival of religion and nationalism accompanied by the growth of a more complex, educated and increasingly urbanised society.

Second, however, the ability of the political system to cope with even this evolutionary change was somewhat limited. The basic political battle lines between conservative and radical factions within the party stayed recognisably the same from the 1950s to the 1980s, merely alternating in power. Thus Gorbachev inherited a major dilemma. Could a one-party state find the resources to renew itself from within and recreate, at a later stage and in very different circumstances, the equivalent of the extraordinary modernisation achievements of the Stalin era? And could it do this in an evolutionary and non-violent manner?

The Gorbachev era has not yet produced any clear answers, but a precondition for success must be an ability both to build on – or learn from – the evolutionary experience of recent decades while at the same time reactivating that older Russian cycle of periodic revolution from above, discussed in the previous chapter.

Further Reading

Continuity and change over the entire post-Stalin era is discussed by Cohen (1980). McCauley provides an introductory overview of the Khrushchev period. R. Medvedev's biography of Khrushchev and Khrushchev's own memoirs (1971, 1977) provide many insights. Two Western Kremlinological accounts of the period are Linden (1966) and Tatu (1969).

On the Brezhnev years, Gelman (1984) considers the Politburo debates of the time and particularly the interweaving of domestic and foreign policy questions. Bialer (1980a) examines the Brezhnev generation in power, its aims and its record. Breslauer (1982) considers both Brezhnev and Khrushchev as leaders, and the importance of policy achievement to their political authority. Edmonds (1983) is an overview of foreign policy under Brezhnev.

Two studies of the Brezhnev era, its legacies and its paradoxes, are by Bialer (1986) and Colton (1986). Both highlight the problems that the post-Brezhnev leadership has had to tackle. There is a full-length study of Andropov by Z. Medvedev (1983) and his brief interregnum is also discussed in Frankland (1987) and Hazan (1987), who also considers Chernenko.

On the Gorbachev era, Walker (1988) provides many insights, having been a foreign correspondent in Moscow from 1984 to 1988. There are introductory biographies of Gorbachev by Z. Medvedev (1986) and Schmidt-Hauer (1986) and much further information in Brown (1985a). On *perestroika* and its ambitions see Gorbachev (1987) himself. Lewin (1988) considers the social changes that have partly created and now help to underpin the 'new thinking'.

3

Ideology, Political Culture, and Dissent

The Soviet Union's national borders have traditionally been not just geographical but also ideological boundaries. Ideas of course matter in any political system but nowhere has this been more palpably true than in the Soviet case. The political system itself grew directly out of Marxist revolutionary and ideological visions, and Soviet leaders attach particular importance to the sheer power of ideas to transform reality. Thus the Soviet Union, unlike the West, has to this day a single official ideology, in the sense of an authoritatively approved set of political doctrines to which all are supposed to subscribe. It remains one of the most distinctive characteristics of Soviet life.

In this chapter we shall examine first of all what this official ideology is and how it has evolved over time. Then we shall consider what importance should actually be attached to it, and the extent to which it has been absorbed by the Soviet people. What sort of wider political culture exists? Is Soviet politics 'Russian' as much as it is Soviet? Finally, we shall consider the extent to which Soviet society may now be outgrowing any single ideology. Has the dissident movement helped pave the way for a more open and pluralist society that can no longer be told what to think?

At the outset, however, it must be said that it is easier to pose such questions than to answer them. There are two particular difficulties here. First, it is notoriously problematic in any aspect of human life to establish clear links between belief and action. Do we act on our beliefs, or are our beliefs shaped by our actions? In the case of Soviet leaders, does ideology shape their policy, or policy their ideology? Official Soviet texts imply the former. 'The Marxist science of the laws of social development enables us not only to chart a correct path through the labyrinth of social contradictions, but to predict the course events will take' (Dutt 1961, p. 17). Ideology, in other words, is a guide to action. Thus all Soviet policies from the 1917 Revolution to Gorbachev's *perestroika* stem essentially from a pre-conceived ideological blueprint. Others have argued that the opposite is nearer the truth, namely that ideology serves merely as a convenient rationalisation after the event and is used as such more or less cynically by a leadership that has no particularly fixed set of beliefs other than the desire to stay in power (Bell 1965). Neither view can be empirically proved or disproved. In practice it is almost certainly more useful to see the relationship between ideas and actions as a complex and ambiguous one, with Soviet political leaders, like élites elsewhere, guided in part by preconceived ideas and in part by hard experience. But this too can only be assumed, not proven.

A second difficulty surrounds the use of the term 'ideology', over which there is much disagreement. There are essentially two ways, one broad and one narrow, of defining the term, but confusingly, both are commonly used in the context of Soviet politics. This is not merely an academic point. If we take ideology in its broad definition, then it means any belief system or value system, any more or less coherent set of ideas, however unsystematised or eclectic they might be. In this sense all political systems have ideologies, such as conservatism or liberalism, socialism, communism or nationalism. In this context it is worth recalling that even in Western democracies such as Britain or the United States the ideas that people hold have not necessarily been freely arrived at as a result of a competitive market in ideas, but have to some extent been shaped by dominant élite or media values. It follows from this that any differences between the role of ideas in the Soviet system and elsewhere can be seen as differences of degree, not of kind. Meanwhile, a second and more narrow definition of ideology is often used in the Soviet case, with the effect of emphasising just how different from Western societies the Soviet Union is. This is ideology defined as dogma, a single body of official doctrine with specific texts which set out a strategy for achieving a particular form of society. In this sense the Soviet Union, with its secular religion of Marxism–Leninism, is a dogmatic or ideological regime in a way that Western democracies are not, and the party leaders its high priests.

So, like the British Constitution, Soviet ideology and practice can mean different things to different people. Perhaps the key point to bear in mind at this stage is that, unlike in the West, there is a single official Soviet ideology and a substantial bureaucracy to implement it, but as in the West it is far from easy to be precise about the role that ideas play in shaping political practice, although the attempt has to be made.

The Official Ideology

The official ideology is normally described in Soviet texts simply as Marxism–Leninism. This implies that, whatever problems there might be in thinking about Soviet ideology, at least its content is clear and unchanging. Even this, however, is not the case. Soviet ideology is at one and the same time both more and less than Marxism–Leninism. It is less than Marxism–Leninism because in practice the writings of Marx, Engels and Lenin, which run to more than one hundred volumes in the official Soviet editions, provide at best a varied, ambiguous and at times contradictory core of doctrine which has been subject to a variety of interpretations by successive Soviet leaders. Not all of these writings have been acceptable at all times. (Indeed, the popular journal *Ogonyek* carried an article in 1988 entitled 'When should we rehabilitate Marx?') What they represent is an almost biblical storehouse of potentially useful materials that can be drawn on as the need arises. Meanwhile, Soviet ideology is more than Marxism–Leninism because those early ideas are now only the core, best seen today essentially as providing an historical explanation of the Revolution and a justification for the party's power, but offering little guidance on the running of the modern Soviet state. Successive leaders have not only selectively chosen and reinterpreted these ideas, but have added significant and often lasting formulae of their own, ever more frequently arguing that ideology must be a 'creative doctrine', drawing not from books but from 'practical experience'. The content of Soviet ideology is therefore more complex and more subject to change than the simple term Marxism–Leninism implies, as we shall now see.

From Marx to Stalin

Marxism as a social theory was designed to provide a framework for understanding human history as well as present and future developments. It also set forth an image of a better society to be attained in the future. The core elements in this theory were the ideas known as historical materialism and dialectical materialism. The first provided an economic interpretation of history based on the class struggle. As Marx put it, 'the history of all hitherto existing societies is the history of class struggle'. There were laws of historical development according to which societies moved through successive stages from primitive communalism and slavery, feudalism and capitalism to socialism, then ultimately culminating in the building of an ideal society known as communism. Under communism the means of production would belong to all and the labourer would work both for himself and for society as a whole in circumstances of material abundance and equality. Fear and oppression, not to mention the apparatus of state power, would wither away.

Each of these stages prior to communism contained inherent contradictions which would eventually lead to its destruction. This was the dialectical process, all successes containing within themselves the seeds of their own failure. Thus the rise of capitalism inescapably meant the exploitation of the proletariat by the capitalists. This would sow the seeds for an eventual socialist order, under which exploitation and class antagonism would cease. Socialism, however, was but a stage on the road to communism. Certain contradictions and survivals from the past would still need to be eliminated before utopia was achieved. Communism implied the final overcoming of such problems. Inherent in this analysis was a sense that change was inevitable and that there was a logic and inner meaning to history, founded on an optimistic belief in Progress.

Karl Marx (1818–83) and Friedrich Engels (1820–95) thus provided a basic theoretical framework, but had relatively little to say about the nature of a fully communist society, and even less about specific methods for its attainment. It was Lenin, by contrast, who sought to speed up the historically inevitable by providing much of the organisational basis and strategy for the Russian Revolution, and who was to lead the successful struggle to establish the Bolshevik regime, committed to the construction of communism. Lenin's most important doctrinal contributions, as discussed in the first chapter, were his ideas on party organisation and discipline (*What is to be Done?*); his strategy for a tactical alliance, given the Russian context, between the proletariat and the peasantry (*Two Tactics of Social Democracy*); his belief in the necessity of destroying the old bourgeois state and establishing a revolutionary dictatorship of the proletariat (*State and Revolution*); and his argument that the Russian Revolution would be merely the forerunner of a much wider European conflagration (*Imperialism the Highest State of Capitalism*). Lenin at least was confident that history was on his side. 'Now we shall proceed to construct the socialist order', he announced immediately after the takeover.

In practice, however, it soon became increasingly clear after 1917 that the implementation of socialism was a complex and difficult matter, the territory largely uncharted, the reality often at variance with the initial expectations. No wider European revolution followed. The industrial base for socialism was simply not there in Russia, and the state and its coercive organs, far from withering away as had been envisaged under socialism, instead showed every sign of becoming even more deeply entrenched than before. The Stalin era doctrinally came to terms with all this only at the cost of some remarkable paradoxes. On the one hand, Lenin was posthumously elevated to secular sainthood, and Stalin himself treated as the 'Lenin of today'. Power was deployed in the name of the Leninist dictatorship of the proletariat. Progress towards the original goal of communism was still proclaimed, the 1936 Stalin Constitution declaring that 'socialism, in the main, has been achieved'. Some continuities were therefore maintained.

Yet any connection between ideological doctrine and actual political practice is very difficult to trace. Stalin's most significant ideological contribution, the concept of socialism in one country (i.e. that a complete socialist economy could be established within the USSR) was a major turning inward from revolutionary internationalism, for it involved a shift away from Marxist visions to the more commonplace goals of nation building, modernisation and industrialisation. Concepts such as social justice were reinterpreted. Instead of wages being geared to the egalitarian revolutionary norm of 'from each according to his ability, to each according to his need', Stalin propounded the very different rule of 'from each according to his ability, to each according to his work', (i.e. his importance to the industrialisation programme, scarce skills being rewarded with high wages). Admittedly, as stressed in the first chapter, the doctrine of socialism in one country harnessed the powerful drive for revolution unleashed by 1917 to the widespread aspiration for domestic reconstruction and national achievement. But it culminated in 1941–45 in the virtual disappearance of Marxist–Leninist doctrine from official propaganda. By the end of the Stalin era there was little hint of any attachment to the basic Marxist principle of the dialectic of history. Far from change being encouraged and planned, the later years of Stalin were in practice increasingly concerned with the maintenance of order and stability both at home and abroad. Ideology became little more than stultifying dogma, with orthodoxy and fear reigning in the absence of any analytic vision.

Ideological Change After Stalin

The ideological legacy which Khrushchev inherited was therefore in need of fundamental revitalisation. In this respect Khrushchev did achieve something. At the 1956 Twentieth Congress Khrushchev had attacked Stalin's personality cult and the suppression of inner party democracy, calling for a return to 'Leninist norms' of leadership and party life. At the 1959 Twenty-First Congress, the current period of Soviet development was now defined as 'the full-scale construction of communist society' instead of the earlier and more modest designation of the period as 'the gradual transition to communism'. The dictatorship of the proletariat had ended with the victory of socialism in 1936. Since then an 'all-people's state' had come into existence, expressing the interests of the people as a whole. The state apparatus itself would wither away with the further development of socialist democracy although the party would not, for some central economic planning and control would always be required. The alternative was the anarchy of capitalist markets.

The most notable of Khrushchev's ideological innovations was the 1961 Party Programme, subtitled 'The Communist Manifesto of the Modern Era'. In this Programme, the first since 1919, Khrushchev set out a strategy for the transition from socialism to full communism, to be achieved 'in the main' by 1980. The strongest and richest capitalist country, the United States, was to be overtaken economically in 1970, and by 1980 abundance for the whole population would have been achieved. This timetable for utopia proved to be embarrassingly optimistic. After Khrushchev's fall it became unmentionable in print anywhere in the Soviet Union. In other respects, however, the Programme was relatively realistic. It advocated, for example, the doctrine of peaceful co-existence between communist and non-communist states. Military, and particularly thermonuclear, conflict was to be avoided in all international relations.

Khrushchev's optimistic perspectives did not long survive his downfall. However, it has never been politically feasible for Soviet leaders to ignore altogether basic questions about the progress or otherwise of the Revolution. Each leader has achieved authority at least in part by staking out his own period of rule as an ideologically distinct phase of the Soviet Union's development towards the ultimate communist goal.

For Brezhnev, the solution to all this emerged gradually, the outlines becoming clear only at the 24th Party Congress in 1971. Official theory now explicitly asserted that the Soviet Union was living under 'mature' or 'developed' socialism. The authoritative position was finally set out in the 1977 Constitution. A socialist society 'in the main' had indeed been constructed by 1936 with the rise of industrialisation and the elimination of the former exploiting classes. However, since that time, notably from about the late 1950s, the Soviet Union had advanced to a qualitatively higher level of social, economic and cultural development known as developed socialism (Evans 1977). In short, the socialist era was not one but two distinct historical phases. The early stages were now over, and the Soviet people lived in a more mature era that differed in at least three important respects from the past.

First, under Brezhnev the economy was not just technologically and materially more advanced but its development was now much more balanced. No longer was it a matter simply of steel or canals, as it had seemed to be at times under Stalin, but of modern agricultural and industrial development on the broadest front. Second, developed socialism was characterised by the social and political unity of all social groups. The dictatorship of the proletariat had given way to an all-people's state, in which the social antagonisms and destructiveness of an earlier era, notably the warfare conducted against much of the peasantry or the bourgeoisie, was now a thing of the past. Third, developed socialism was not just 'a natural and logical stage on the road to communism' but one whose features came into existence over an extended period. Progress would be 'long and gradual', a steady and orderly affair, implying something not to be rushed at brutally, as under Stalin, or haphazardly, as under Khrushchev.

These propositions, particularly the last, were subsequently refined further by Andropov and Chernenko. The official programme of developed socialism retreated still further from the optimistic and utopian perspectives of Khrushchev. Andropov emphasised in 1983 that the Soviet Union was only at the 'beginning' of this long historical stage of developed socialism and there should be no exaggeration of the rate of progress. Contradictions and difficulties inherited from the lower level of basic socialism remained. Chernenko went still further in 1984, warning that the perfection of developed socialism itself would require a 'whole historical epoch' and that the solution of contemporary problems was far more important than dwelling on some 'relatively distant, beautiful and rosy future'.

Ideology under Gorbachev

With Gorbachev's accession to power in 1985, the stately gradualism of developed socialism was rapidly buried. At the 27th Party Congress in 1986 and later, Gorbachev argued that the years up to the end of the century and possibly beyond would mark a 'new historical stage', the era of *perestroika*. The Brezhnev years had in practice degenerated into complacency and 'universal enchantment'. The concepts of socialism had in practice remained trapped 'to a large extent at the level of the 1930s and 1940s when society was tackling very different tasks'. It was no longer, if it ever was, a matter of smooth progress forward. 'History has not left us much time' to rescue socialism from a 'pre-crisis situation'; there was the possibility of real failure unless a fundamental reformation took place.

Gorbachev's ideological *perestroika* involved much new thinking. If real progress towards communism was to be resumed, argued Gorbachev, then this meant not just the 'intensification' and 'acceleration' of the economy, a degree of democratisation and openness in public life, but a renewed awareness of the 'human factor', and a preparedness to think afresh about virtually the entire range of inherited shibboleths. 'Ritually chanted' statements about an absence of social antagonisms under socialism, or about collective farming being on a higher ideological plane than the (much more productive) private agricultural plots, had merely erected dogmatic obstacles to reform and were, apart from anything else, self-defeating. If political and economic life were to be reinvigorated, there needed to be fresh thinking about quite fundamental matters. Was state ownership and control of the economy necessarily the only or the best form of socialism? Was a high-wage, high-output economy, with much greater differentials than hitherto, necessarily anti-socialist? Official ideology, Gorbachev conceded, had ceased to ask the right questions, let alone provide authoritative answers. Ultimately, therefore, even the role of the party needed to be considered. Unless the party dropped its 'infallibility complex' it would simply cease to have the expertise at its command that was needed to steer the Soviet Revolution into the next century, for official ideology did not and at present could not provide 'all the answers' in an ever more rapidly changing world.

In short, a more tolerant sense of 'socialist pluralism' had to be embraced. Neither society nor ideology could any longer be treated as monolithic. Since 1987 Gorbachev has authoritatively espoused this significant overarching concept being, as Brown has commented, 'the first leader in Soviet history to use the term "pluralism" – albeit qualified by the adjective "socialist" – other than as a term of abuse. Along with *glasnost* it represents a significant ideological innovation' (Brown 1988, p. 3).

Quite where the relative ferment of new thinking will eventually lead is still unclear. *Perestroika* itself has been compared both linguistically and politically to the Reformation in early modern

Europe, a fundamental reordering of the relationship between society and the state (Tucker 1987, p. 156). But there are still basic continuities with the past and these ought not to be underestimated. *Perestroika*, like all previous Soviet political programmes, is deemed to be historically irreversible. No alternatives can be envisaged. Real progress towards a higher stage of socialism is still the essence, with communism the ultimate goal. The sanctity of the party remains intact, as does the basic commitment to a socialist and therefore anti-capitalist economy. Meanwhile, this framework apart, as Gorbachev admitted when speaking in the Soviet Far East in 1986, *perestroika* is easier to proclaim than to define. 'Sometimes people ask, just what is this abstruse thing . . . what do you eat it with, as it were. We're all really in favour, but we don't know how to go about it.' Suffice it to say that the Gorbachev era has been marked by a concerted attempt to reinvigorate not just the content but also the effectiveness of the official ideology. Soviet politics without an effective official ideology would simply not be Soviet politics, for, in the words of an early Marxist, Nikolai Berdyaev, 'Russia is where the true belief is'.

What, then, constitutes official ideology today? It is probably best seen as three layers of ideas and beliefs. First, there are the precepts of *perestroika,* which provide the basic political programme and the main tasks to be accomplished between the 27th Party Congress in 1986 and the end of the century. These should be seen in practice both as longer-range visions and specific shorter-range policies that the party is committed to at any point in time. The latter in particular are at any one time in a state of gradual evolution. Second, there is a Marxist–Leninist core which is a limited but still significant 'scientific' component, for it explains and justifies the Soviet system, including the power and authority of the party, and its ultimate goals. Third, there is the very history of the Soviet Union itself, as reinterpreted by successive leaders. This is of independent significance, for what are seen as the main achievements of Soviet history have great resonance for many citizens. These include industrialisation and superpower status, victory over fascism in 1945 and, since 1985, even the ability to reassess the mistakes of the recent past and strike out afresh on the road to a major Reformation.

These three layers which constitute the official ideology have evolved over time as part of a recognisably political process. They are not simply, as it were, tablets of stone. The current party programme, Marxist–Leninist classics and speeches by party leaders all have their parts to play. Thus the speech given by Gorbachev on the 70th anniversary of the Revolution in November 1987 was itself a contribution to the ideological pronouncements of the *perestroika* era. In it Gorbachev, as previous leaders have done, laid down authoritative guidelines for interpreting the Soviet past, on this occasion condemning Stalin's 'unforgiveable' guilt over the purges, but reiterating the essential correctness of his industrialisation drive. This control of the past is as vital a component of the official ideology as are programmes for present and future development.

In many respects this is a long way from 1917. Marxism–Leninism itself is but a small and arguably declining part of the official ideology, which has been reworked and redefined quite often. But in an important sense the basic functions, the purpose and usefulness of ideology, have not altered at all. Official ideology, irrespective of its content at any one time, has three clear and unchanging functions. First, it provides some periodisation of the Revolution, defining the party as necessary and each leadership era as historically distinct. It thus imparts a sense of higher purpose and direction to the otherwise mundane business of politics. Second, it acts as a form of political manifesto, setting forth the main tasks of the regime and the people for the next few years. Third, in so doing it plays an important legitimising and integrating role, for an official ideology does help to unite the population of this vast and multi-national land, whether around relatively positive factors such as *perestroika* or the traditional negatives, such as opposition to other political systems in general, or capitalism in particular.

All of this can mean that this 'great science of society', as under Brezhnev, does little other than to justify the status quo. Developed socialism in practice stressed the permanence and the authority of political institutions. Nothing was likely to wither away in the foreseeable future. But, as under Khrushchev or Gorbachev, the official ideology can equally be a vehicle for galvanising the nation into fresh thinking and action. Its short- or medium-term rationale can vary considerably, and has done so, which is in part why there have been such differing views in the

West about whether Soviet ideology is a blueprint for action or merely a rather hollow justification for whatever decisions Soviet leaders take.

Either way, however, status quo or *perestroika,* the official ideology has one other distinct political attribute, particularly given its Marxist roots. It encourages within the élite a positive tendency to think in the long term and programmatically and at its best it sets some store by the dialectic of change. These are important virtues. Against this, however, has to be set the fact that in practice, as controlled by the party bureaucracy, Soviet ideology has repeatedly degenerated from bursts of creative thinking into long phases of essentially dogmatic orthodoxy in which repetition and fear have played far too large a part.

Just how damaging has that dogmatic tradition become? Is the power of an official ideology, however reformulated, losing its hold? Can the present Soviet leadership effectively underpin its authority with a reinvigorated set of ideas, or has what Gorbachev has called the 'pre-crisis situation' gone too far? It is to these questions that we now turn.

The Effectiveness of Official Ideology

Speaking to the Congress of the Komsomols, the youth wing of the party, in 1987, Gorbachev devastatingly criticised its inability to make a more positive impact on Soviet youth. 'One sometimes gets the impression that . . . it is as if young people are walking on one side of the street while the Komsomol activists are walking on the other side and moreover in the opposite direction!'

What Gorbachev highlighted was a deep-rooted problem. The effectiveness of any single ideology in shaping the behaviour of a nation is always necessarily limited, but the basic fact is that the effectiveness of Soviet official ideology, and therefore of the organisations that live by it, have declined significantly in recent years. Thus, Academician Sakharov, writing in 1975, commented on the way in which 'our society is characterised by ideological indifference and our regime by the pragmatic use of ideology as a convenient façade'. At the same time the historian Roy Medvedev wrote how the 'enormous and costly propaganda machine works in a vacuum' and Vladimir Bukovsky noted how 'from top to bottom no one believes in Marxist dogma any more'. (R. Medvedev 1975, p. 67; Bukovsky 1978, p. 62). All three, being dissidents, might be considered tainted sources, but what is striking is that a wealth of official evidence under Brezhnev suggested similar conclusions. As White has argued, the authorities failed to bring about a mass conversion to Marxism–Leninism (White 1979, p. 166). Attendance at political classes was at best generally unenthusiastic. Most people attended because they were expected to. Few took Marxism–Leninism very seriously. Typically, in 1973, in the southern Russian city of Rostov-on-Don, for instance, 80 per cent of party members admitted that they made little or no use of the Marxist–Leninist classics. At the same time a fifth of the surveyed workers at an aluminium plant near Irkutsk in Siberia said that their political education programme had encouraged them to read 'more fiction', a somewhat ambiguous compliment.

By the 1980s there was indeed little evidence of any New Soviet Man as envisaged in traditional propaganda over the decades. There had been early hopes that the very nature of Soviet socialist society would produce citizens who enthusiastically put the common good before all other considerations and do so as a result of a highly developed degree of political consciousness. To some extent these hopes were fulfilled. In the Stalinist era a major official hero was Pavlik Morozov, a Young Pioneer who, when he was thirteen, distinguished himself by denouncing his father to the security police as a *kulak*. Morozov, who was killed by enraged villagers as a result, thus symbolised for a generation the hope that ideology and community would come before even family loyalty. For several decades he was presented to children as a model figure and he certainly had his followers. Today he is hardly mentioned, such morality being widely and contemptuously rejected. *Yunost*, the literary monthly for young people, finally denounced Morozov in 1988 as a symbol not of 'resolution and class consciousness but . . . of legalised and romanticised treachery'. Meanwhile, and in contrast, as it were, a 1984 poll survey showed that, whereas virtually everyone agreed that domestic burglary was a punishable crime, only 16 per cent thought that theft from the workshop should even be reported to the authorities, let alone punished.

Furthermore, the evidence that Soviet people are often at best apathetic about politics can be multiplied almost endlessly. Most simply do not notice the vast mass of hortatory slogans and posters commonly festooned from buildings or in streets throughout the country, most frequently of all declaring 'Glory to the Soviet Communist Party' or quoting an economic slogan or marking a wartime or revolutionary anniversary. On May Day, for example, the flags and bunting go up in towns and villages as well as portraits of the trinity of Marx, Engels and Lenin, but it is hard to know what effect it all has. The collected works of Brezhnev, published in editions of 100,000 or more, generally sat idle on the shelves, even in his heyday.

Moreover, the party's ability to persuade people to take part in even the most perfunctory political activity declined. Although there are doubts about the exact figures, it is generally accepted in the West that turnout in Soviet elections under Brezhnev dropped significantly. It is a long way now from the 99 per cent of propaganda and myth: probably well under 90 per cent – still a formidable figure, but significantly down (Zaslavsky and Brym 1983, p. 70). Party and Komsomol propagandists meanwhile have faced growing problems in dealing with an increasingly educated and complex society. Attempting to instill a rigidly puritan work ethic while denouncing Western fashions, music and generally more permissive life styles has become a Canute-like task. Most striking of all, perhaps, is that many Soviet people have retained or found in religion an alternative morality to that of the regime, and one that has often been highly effective in actually shaping behaviour, as for example in encouraging greater sobriety.

The decline in political activity developed despite – or because of – a vast effort to control it. The Soviet regime runs a political education programme of remarkable scope and depth, with one and a half million full-time party propagandists to carry the party's message to every corner of the land. It has unrestricted access to the media, radio and television. Under *glasnost*, as intended, this has focused attention on a wide range of previously taboo issues, but traditionally party control has been very effective at deflecting discussion of such matters. Until 1985 the war in Afghanistan received virtually no Soviet television coverage, and the footage which did appear presented an essentially heroic picture. Controlling the political agenda, however, is not the same as influencing hearts and minds. In the end it is hard not to conclude that the often proclaimed Brezhnev era view that there was a new type of Soviet man and 'that Marxist–Leninist ideology has conquered the consciousness of the absolute majority of the Soviet people' was at best wishful thinking.

This increasing divergence under Brezhnev between 'the world of day-to-day realities and that of make-believe' as Gorbachev termed it in 1987, is now publicly acknowledged. 'Serious shortcomings in ideological and political education were in many cases disguised with ostentatious activities and campaigns and celebrations of numerous jubilees . . . and the mass distribution of awards, titles and prizes.' Gorbachev has suggested that such remoteness and self-delusion could eventually lead to political instability. 'Revolutionary parties which have hitherto perished have done so because they became too self-assured.' In other words, élite privilege and insouciance coupled with growing popular disbelief could eventually trigger real disruption.

Should we conclude from this that the Soviet Union's official ideology is, as Mao Tse Tung said of the nuclear threat, a 'paper tiger', a rather hollow construct inexorably losing its hold on an increasingly sophisticated society? Should Soviet ideology be seen as a declining force which is less and less able to legitimise and integrate, let alone act as a galvanising agent? In a sense such questions are unanswerable, for they involve generalising about the beliefs and values of over 280 million individuals. But, giving due weight to the sort of evidence already outlined, several important qualifications about ideology and its weaknesses need to be borne in mind.

First, the effectiveness and capacity of the ideology to influence people and shape reality has waxed and waned over time and is not necessarily in irreversible decline. It is possible that the Brezhnev years saw only a temporary decline. *Perestroika* could produce very different results, not least by enthusing the young, or by revitalising the Soviet economy and bringing some greater hope for the future. Political ideas after all are more persuasive if they can actually be shown to work or contribute to improving the perceived reality.

Second, grumbles about specific policies, or about the manner in which they or the wider ideology are propagandised, ought not to be equated with ideological opposition as such. Thus, there is a longstanding and widespread distrust of the KGB, and much hostility to the tradition of the closed border, evidence of which has surfaced very publicly in the Soviet press since 1985. There is also a lot of well-documented evidence of boredom with the repetitive and unimaginative nature of official ideological propaganda. These things do not necessarily imply, however, that the Soviet system itself is being rejected. Citizens grumble the world over.

Third, as in most political systems, the élites are more in tune with official values than non-élites. In recent years a large amount of both official and unofficial sociological evidence has shown that the better educated and more highly skilled – and rewarded – strata are not just more active and informed politically but also more supportive of regime values and policies (Zaslavsky 1982, p. 22).

Finally, some aspects of the official ideology are simply more effective than others. Much of the original Marxist–Leninist tradition understandably has less pulling power today than fifty to seventy years ago, but other aspects of the ideology are less easily written off, being widely acceptable to Soviet citizens. This is not least because there are many deep-rooted links between the official Soviet ideology and the older traditional political culture of the Russian people. This point about political culture is worth considering a little further. How 'Russian' are Soviet values?

The Wider Political Culture

The concept of political culture has been the subject of considerable academic debate in recent years. Put at its clearest it means, as Archie Brown has defined it, 'the subjective perception of history and politics, the fundamental beliefs and values, the foci of identification and loyalty, and the political knowledge and expectations which are the product of the specific historical experience of nations and groups' (Brown 1985b, p. 2).

Critics have contended that such generalisations are very close to the notoriously slippery concept of 'national character'. Every characteristic that is defined also has an opposite. It can be said that the Russian culture is autocratic and centralist, the opposite to that of the United States; but democratic, anarchist and libertarian traditions have also existed in Russia. The influence of writers such as Mikhail Bakunin and Leo Tolstoy in Tsarist times or some dissidents in modern times testifies to this. The key point to note, however, is that although there is some debate about the value of political culture as a concept, it does help focus attention on wider political traditions and values. These are often unspoken or uncodified but nonetheless are important in any assessment of the underlying strengths and weaknesses of a political system. Four particular elements of this wider Russian political culture are worth considering in a little detail here, for they contribute in significant if intangible ways to the overall acceptance of the Soviet system by its citizens.

First, there is the authoritarian tradition. This, at its most basic, implies an acceptance of order and discipline from above in the belief that the only alternative is anarchy and chaos from below. The widow of the poet Osip Mandelstam put this very effectively in her memoirs written in the Brezhnev years: 'this fear of chaos is perhaps the most permanent of our feelings.' A powerful hand was needed to stop 'the angry human river overflowing its banks' (Mandelstam 1975, p. 113). The dissident Andrei Amalrik at much the same time briskly dismissed 'the idea of self-government, of equality before the law and of personal freedom [as] . . . almost completely incomprehensible to the Russian people . . . To the majority of the people the very word "freedom" is synonymous with disorder' (Amalrik 1970, p. 32). These are almost timeless views. As a member of the editorial board of the leading monthly journal *Novy Mir* put it in 1987, 'our Russian misfortune . . . is an absence of democratic ideas and of self-confidence . . . [a tendency] to look up to the bosses to see whether they like it or not'.

The parallels between old Russia and the modern Soviet state are indeed considerable. The dissident movement in the 1960s and 1970s was lassoed by a Criminal Code that was very close in spirit to the so-called Iron Code of Tsar Nicholas I of 1845. Dissent and opposition essentially weakened the state and were thus punishable by long periods of imprisonment or administrative exile in Siberia. The historian Pipes has written about how the unchanging 'Russian problem' is the untrammelled nature of political power: Whatever the regime and its formal ideology, the system is, as Pipes characterises it, a patrimonial one, that is, one in which power, property and ownership are closely intertwined and controlled by a self-selected and enduring élite (Pipes 1977). As the dissident philosopher Boris Shragin put it in 1978, 'the old autocracy has gone but absolutism still prevails . . . the ancient landmarks of the past are increasingly visible behind the specifically Soviet features of our present stagnation' (Shragin 1978, p. 153).

The virtual deification of the leader as a remote and God-like, but nonetheless humble and understanding figure is also an enduring phenomenon associated with Gorbachev as much as with Lenin, even if it reached a unique apogee under Stalin. Political prisoners in the 1930s frequently believed that petitioning Stalin would solve their problems; that 'if only Stalin knew' how they had been framed by the obviously venal and scheming local officials he would right their wrongs. But, as Yevgenia Ginsberg eloquently showed in her memoirs, most continued to believe that the millions of *other* arrests made sense and that the general line was a correct one (Ginsberg 1967, p. 31). The tradition of what has been called a 'petition culture', not a 'rights culture', has continued into recent times. Many dissidents in the first instance petitioned higher authority rather than take to the streets demanding their rights, and this was not merely a matter of caution in the face of a traditionally powerful police state apparatus.

In this context the Gorbachev era of *perestroika* can arguably also be seen as part of the authoritarian tradition of reform from above. Demands for *perestroika, glasnost* and *demokratizatsia* have essentially come from above since 1985, rather than surging up from below. But the reality may now be irreversibly more complex, as modern society increasingly asserts itself against the state and the political culture itself is subject to change.

Second, there is the collectivist tradition. This is intrinsically bound up with the authoritarian heritage. A dominant popular Russian expectation is that citizens have communal and collective obligations (and rewards) which take precedence over any individual rights. This is not just a question of the closed borders or the tradition of individuals informing on other individuals, rooted in norms of group solidarity and intense suspicion of outsiders, particularly foreigners. It is also to be found permeating the whole area of the modern Soviet welfare state, many of the features of which are widely accepted. There is not only an older Russian, but also a modern Soviet, political culture at work here. Even among émigrés, Soviet health, education and welfare programmes are regarded as positive attributes. Similarly, many features of the traditional command economy such as its 'planned' (i.e. non-capitalist, non-strike-ridden) nature or its guarantee of full employment, reasserted in Article 40 of the 1977 Constitution, are broadly accepted. This may in part be because the party-controlled media have been sedulously effective in persuading individuals that Western capitalist alternatives are worse (unemployment, strikes, terrorism and violence, inflation). It is also derived from the traditional view that competitive individualism leads to a less just society.

A third traditional characteristic of Russian political culture is the sheer scope of government activity. As well as regulating legal and economic activity, the Russian state has traditionally held sway over religion and morals in the belief that a distinctive society could thereby be created, one in which both individual and social life should have some purpose other than mere physical survival. As the iconoclastic dissident philosopher and writer Alexander Zinoviev put it in his satire on Soviet life, *The Yawning Heights*, Russians don't just live like people elsewhere; they 'carry out epoch-making experiments' (Zinoviev 1978, p. 13). Thus, in medieval Russia a messianic belief flourished that Moscow should be a world centre of Christendom with an historic missionary role. Religious faith was never as independent of the state as elsewhere in Europe generally. The Romanov dynasty required its people to believe in what was known as Orthodoxy, Nationalism and Autocracy. This doctrine was one of the most distinctive attributes of the Tsarist political tradition. The Soviet regime, although a product of revolution in a secular age, continues that older tradition of the state and society serving a larger purpose. Commitment to *perestroika* is a civic duty, just as commitment to Stalin's industrialisation drive was in a previous generation.

Soviet 'Socialist Patriotism'

Finally, we should consider in this brief characterisation of Russian political culture and tradition the whole concept of nationalism, which is hardly exclusive to the Soviet Union, but is nonetheless as deeply embedded as any other set of values. The values of what the regime labels 'socialist patriotism' run right through the official ideology, but also have wider popular resonance.

The Soviet regime was from the outset highly nationalist, the early Civil War of 1918–20 establishing the pattern. Stalin's rule, despite the revolutionary and internationalist rhetoric, was at heart a traditional defence of national interests, at times expressed in quite xenophobic form, as with the ban from 1947 to 1954 on anyone marrying a foreigner. The very significant rise in popular Russian nationalism since the 1960s, discussed in Chapter 5, has been, as often as not, condoned and even encouraged by the regime. The Soviet army is typically seen in domestic terms as the defender of the motherland, a patriotic body, the 'school of the nation' as Brezhnev frequently termed it.

In a sense we are back with the theme of official Soviet history, one of the principal layers of official ideology, for traditional political culture and the official ideology are in the end inseparable. The memory of the millions of wartime dead in 1941–5 has been a major unifying trauma. Even today newly-weds visit their local war memorial to lay flowers in silent remembrance.

The extraordinary cult of Lenin, too, can be seen as in part a nationalist phenomenon, Lenin being deified as a great Russian leader as much as a revolutionary. The Lenin cult is not easy for foreigners to get to grips with, for, though it is endlessly fostered by the regime, it does have genuine depths to it. No Russian historical figure, other perhaps than the nineteenth-century poet Alexander Pushkin, is held in higher esteem. Lenin's influence is ubiquitous, from the 'little red corner' with books and pictures of a wise and fatherly Lenin in all children's kindergartens, to the basic political claim of all Soviet leaders, without exception, that their legitimacy is rooted in an ability to defend or restore 'Leninist norms'.

In short, if one takes these wider popular aspects of the political culture into account, a more complex picture can be drawn. The effectiveness of the official ideology may be limited, but it does have real strengths, and is to some extent reinforced by deeper national traditions.

Ideology, Political Culture, and Change

Some writers see this linkage as evidence that the Soviet system is fundamentally stable and historically 'normal'. David Lane, for instance, has written of the Soviet system in these terms (Lane

1985a, p. xiii). Others, such as Zinoviev, accept the linkage, but see it as evidence of the essential 'hopelessness' of the Soviet condition. Zinoviev, in several outrageously satirical works, has argued that the Soviet system is the logical and, in its own terms, successful outcome of the marriage between Marxism and the Russian national tradition. This is by no means an uncontested view. Many writers, not least Solzhenitsyn, have taken issue with it. For Solzhenitsyn, the legacy of 1917 was the destruction of a native tradition and the imposition of an alien, materialist philosophy. The result has been a totalitarian regime imposed upon a downtrodden people, a wholly avoidable national tragedy (Solzhenitsyn 1974, p. 34).

There can be no reconciling these divergent approaches. Nonetheless, it is difficult to avoid the conclusion that, although Russians are not in some biological sense incapable of sustaining a democracy, the sheer weight of their tradition makes it an uphill task (Brown 1985b).

Is *perestroika* therefore doomed in advance, because the authoritarian tradition is too strong? This is possible, but even though, in the case of political culture, we are essentially looking at dominant long-term national characteristics, these too, like the official ideology, can and do change with time. Many of the precepts of *perestroika* clearly do seek to achieve a reorientation not just of political policies but of the wider political culture too. People's behaviour actually has to change, it is said repeatedly. *Glasnost* and *demokratizatsia* even as practised under Gorbachev involve a serious challenge to traditional, even pre-Soviet, ways. Meanwhile, it may be that the slow but gradual rise of a 'civic culture', of a civil society, now threatens the authoritarian tradition from below in a manner that has simply not applied before. There has been a genuine growth in the power of society versus the state since Stalin. 'A no longer wholly regimented society has emerged, one still closely connected with the state but no longer its mere tool', as Tucker has put it.

'This phenomenon's early beginnings may be discerned in Khrushchev's time and its quiet continuation in Brezhnev's . . . But only under *[glasnost]* . . . has [it] become fully apparent . . . What we see now is no longer the Stalin-period's monologue of the state with itself . . . but the emergence of a dialogue between state and society.

(Tucker 1987, p. 170)

Arguably, the 'petition culture' is in decline, as are the collectivist traditions, not to mention the utopian urge. The political culture itself is changing, and *perestroika* is at least in part a recognition of this fact. But political culture, though malleable, is not infinitely elastic. Not only does any Soviet reform leadership have to contend with short-term political opposition of one kind or another, but with powerful and deep-rooted cultural norms. *Glasnost*, for all its evident attractions, does run counter to the belief of many that debate is best conducted behind closed doors. Economic *perestroika*, with its assertions of individualism and its expectations that income differentials should widen, runs counter to the collectivist tradition in many ways.

The relationship between belief and action, ideology and culture, is a complex one and generalisations often distort. The non-Russian nationalities, for instance, present a somewhat different story, as we shall see in Chapter 5. It is, however, worth bearing in mind at this point that, although Russian political culture and Soviet official ideology have been closely interlinked and that this has been a factor for basic system stability, the relatively fast-changing era of *perestroika* does raise new questions. *Perestroika* is at one and the same time a product of past limitations in official ideology and also a response to a political culture that is changing in significant ways. The rise of a civil society is an indication of the extent to which the regime simply has to respond ideologically if continued stability is to be maintained. This emergent civil society owes a considerable debt to the dissident movement of the Brezhnev era, a fact now openly acknowledged in the Soviet Union. It is to this movement, its values and its significance, that we now turn.

The Rise of the Dissident Movement

The Russian word for a dissident, *inakomislyashchiye*, means literally 'those who think differently', or, as Academician Sakharov has put it, 'one who thinks'. By definition, such people are few and far between in any society, but can have an impact wholly disproportionate to their numbers. Dissidence in itself is a natural enough concomitant of any relatively complex, urbanised, highly educated society. In the Soviet case, it is at one end of a spectrum that stretches from regime loyalists, through 'loyal oppositionists' (for example party members or officials who debated economic reform questions in the 1960s or who hold essentially Stalinist views in the 1980s) and informal groups (such as those concerned with environmental questions) to individual dissenters. Historically speaking, too, dissidence has been a common feature of the Russian civic landscape. The Tsars, like many Soviet leaders, were remote, paternalistic and rarely open to critical thinking, the result being among other things the flourishing literary, intellectual and eventually revolutionary debates of the nineteenth century.

The oddity in a sense was the virtual elimination of dissident activity under Stalin and its subsequent rebirth under Brezhnev. Stalin not only physically eliminated the critical intelligentsia but also rendered senseless any attempt at rational political dissent, for one of the hallmarks of the Stalinist terror was its arbitrary rounding up of people. Dissent was meaningless; 'if you're in for twenty-five years there must be a reason; you get ten years if you've done nothing' was a common cry.

The Khrushchev era was not free of dissidents. Khrushchev's own arbitrary and often illiberal instincts made sure of that, not least his anti-religious campaigns which led to the destruction of many Orthodox churches in the early 1960s. His downfall, however, was a major catalyst in the creation of the modern dissident phenomenon. It resulted in greater limitations on expression and ended the hopes of the many liberal or Marxist reform-minded members of the Soviet intelligentsia who had at least supported Khrushchev's de-Stalinisation campaigns.

The Brezhnev regime, by its relatively crude crushing of what was essentially 'loyal oppositionist' debate, greatly magnified the dissident problem, particularly by its early handling of the literary establishment. Literature and politics are often explosively linked in Russia, and writers have traditionally been amongst the most powerful critics of the state. This became markedly apparent after the extraordinary show trial in February 1966 of two writers, Yuli Daniel and Andrei Sinyavsky. Both had smuggled some of their work to the West where it was pseudonymously published in the knowledge that it was unpublishable in the Soviet Union. Both men were tried under Article 70 of the Criminal Code and accused of 'anti-Soviet agitation and propaganda . . . aimed at weakening the Soviet state', the first and only time in the history of the Soviet

Union when writers were put on trial for what they had written. The trial and subsequent sentencing of Daniel and Sinyavsky, to five and seven years' hard labour respectively, caused wide international outrage, not least amongst West European communist parties, and convinced many that the Soviet political system had reverted to a form of Stalinism.

Moreover, within the Soviet Union itself the trial triggered off a deepening politicisation amongst 'loyal oppositionists', turning many into dissidents. Typical of this more outspoken mood were young activists and demonstrators such as Pavel Litvinov and Yuli Galanskov, Alexander Ginsberg and Vladimir Bukovsky, many of whom were arrested and tried in the late 1960s as part of the snowballing consequence of the Daniel–Sinyavsky affair. Bukovsky publicly protested in Moscow about what he saw as the essential lawlessness of the regime itself, proclaiming in the Constitution that it adhered to the principles of free speech and association, but in practice using the Criminal Code, with its anti-Soviet-activity clauses, to destroy that spirit. What was the point, he protested at his trial, of being able to demonstrate 'for' if you could not also demonstrate 'against'.

Thus, by the late 1960s, not least in the wake of the traumatic Warsaw Pact invasion of Czechoslovakia in August 1968, crushing the Prague reforms, Soviet dissident life and activity reached a crescendo. Hundreds of citizens including many celebrated public figures were by now regularly prepared to demonstrate, sign open letters to the leaders or appeal to Western governments and public opinion in order, essentially, to defend civil rights. In many respects, though the term is anachronistic, the dissident movement was calling for *glasnost*. There is no doubt that this produced a very worrying situation for much of the Soviet leadership, for it could not be sure just how deep-rooted and widespread this new phenomenon of articulate and relatively unfearful protest was.

The movement soon spawned *samizdat* (literally, self-published, often typescript or mimeographed works, an ironic play on the official acronym *gosizdat*, the term used to describe state publishing houses). There was also *magnitizdat* (the taped version) and *tamizdat* ('over there', or smuggled out works, which often found their way back via Western radio stations that were accessible to Soviet listeners). In 1968 the dissidents started the bimonthly *Chronicle of Current Events*, a diary of information about political prisoners and human rights violations. One thing led to another. There were relatively organised groups such as the Committee on Human Rights from 1970 and the Helsinki monitoring groups from 1976 which sought to draw international attention to the dissidents. These not only achieved considerable coherence over time but their members were quite open about their involvement. The authorities went to considerable lengths to control such activity, notably in the late 1960s and early 1970s and again around 1980 (at the time of the Moscow Olympics), but were never completely successful.

The Limits of the Dissident Movement

In practice 1968 proved, in this field as in so many others elsewhere in the world, to be an untypical high point of rebellious activity. The authorities appeared to learn certain lessons, notably that show trials were counter-productive and that other traditional police state tactics could instead gradually take much of the drive out of dissident activity. The KGB, for instance, deployed measures such as physical violence and intimidation, selective arrest and imprisonment in labour camps and enforced treatment with drugs in psychiatric hospitals. More subtle sanctions included loss of job or damage to career, pressures on other family members or even, as the writer Vladimir Voinovich once described, interrogation sessions at which the victim would be offered poisoned cigarettes (Voinovich 1977).

However, arguably the most effective regime tactic was the 1971 decision to allow large numbers of Jewish dissidents to emigrate to Israel. This did nothing to diminish the widespread Jewish campaigns for emigration, but it deeply divided and demoralised the dissident movement, as arguments inevitably arose about whether it was not better to stay and fight. Many of the most vocal dissidents had been Jews or members of other national minorities such as the Ukrainians, the Crimean Tartars or the Lithuanians. The authorities meanwhile selectively allowed other dissident groups such as the Volga Germans as well as numerous individual writers, artists and campaigners the chance to emigrate to the West, and many did so during the 1970s. In short, dissidence proved to be a controllable activity.

Furthermore, Soviet dissidents were often very isolated politically within the Soviet Union. It was never difficult for the Soviet media to portray Jews seeking to emigrate to Israel as fundamentally disloyal and unpatriotic. Many dissidents themselves commented bleakly on the deeply ingrained Russian *meshchanstvo* tradition (i.e. petty bourgeois philistinism), the blank apathy of the peasantry, or the refusal of the educated career-minded professional classes to focus on anything beyond the family's weekend *dacha*. Not least, the working class under Brezhnev were politically quiescent, partly because of alcohol, partly because many workers benefited from the regime's policies insofar as they had job security, a higher standard of living than before, and some significant freedoms, such as the ability in practice to change jobs and better themselves. Significantly, about three-quarters of the working classes approved the Soviet invasion of Czechoslovakia in 1968, quite unlike the dissidents or indeed many of the younger and more educated party members (Zaslavsky 1982, p. 25). By the end of the Brezhnev era popular support for the regime may have been in decline but, as Bialer has observed, what was most striking 'was the absence of strong opposition' (Bialer 1986, p. 36).

Dissident Thought: Medvedev, Sakharov and Solzhenitsyn

Dissident political activity may have been ultimately controllable, though at a price. Dissident political thought, however, has proved more pervasive. Russian intellectual dissidence during the 1970s was often divided, but it did produce a remarkable semi-clandestine national debate, in some respects not unlike that of the nineteenth century, and in part closely foreshadowing the 'new thinking' of *perestroika*. This can be demonstrated in the contributions of three of the most articulate and influential dissidents, Medvedev, Sakharov and Solzhenitsyn.

The historian Roy Medvedev was the son of a Red Army officer purged by Stalin in 1941. Notwithstanding this, Medvedev had been a youthful and idealistic member of the party, only breaking with it in 1969. Subsequently he wrote several major *samizdat* works including a monumental attack on Stalin, *Let History Judge* (1971) and a lengthy political analysis and programme of reforms entitled *On Socialist Democracy* (1975). Medvedev was essentially a reform Marxist who asserted the need to return to true Leninist democracy. The democratic socialist possibilities inherent in the Revolution had never really been put to the test. Proper democratisation was both necessary and inevitable. It was crucial economically as well as morally and politically, for 'there is a great contradiction in our society between rapid scientific, technological and economic progress and an excessively centralised bureaucratic system, blocking further development'. However, such reform had to come from the party, from above, from within the system. It could not come from below or from the West. Ideally, an institutionalised second 'truly Marxist–Leninist' opposition party was needed to produce the spark of real democracy and the competition of fresh ideas.

Medvedev was a cautious reformer, concerned to persuade the leadership towards timely change rather than to bring down the system. This was also essentially true of Andrei Sakharov, although his analysis of the Soviet system became much more critical over time. By the 1970s Sakharov had broken with Marxism, taking an increasingly liberal and humanitarian line. As a nuclear physicist he had played a large part in the development of the H-bomb under Stalin, and had been duly rewarded with membership of the Academy of Sciences in 1953. But he came to view the nuclear weaponry which he had helped create as a danger rather than a blessing. Sakharov broke with the regime in 1961, after arguing publicly with Khrushchev. 'It was a basic break', he later wrote. 'There was no point in arguing. I was driven to a life of dissent.'

In Sakharov's principal writings, *Progress, Coexistence and Intellectual Freedom* (1969) and *My Country and the World* (1975), he argued not just that the Soviet system was over-centralised and morally corrupt but fundamentally inefficient. 'We are falling behind the West economically and technologically because of anti-democratic traditions and norms of public life which appeared during Stalin's time and have still not been completely removed.' What was needed was Westernisation in the sense that 'a democratic mode of development is the only satisfactory one for any country'. This must involve among other things 'an end to irrational and irresponsible censorship' which greatly hinders the proper flow of scientific knowledge, the 'complete exposure of Stalin', an end to élite corruption and privilege and international arms control agreements to tackle the growing menace of global insecurity, hunger and poverty.

Sakharov combined writing with an active dissident life, campaigning for the release of fellow dissidents and for human rights in general. He won the Nobel Peace Prize in 1975, but meanwhile lost his right to continue scientific research in the Soviet Union. In 1980, for criticising the Soviet invasion of Afghanistan, he was exiled to Gorki, a city on the Volga, only 250 miles from Moscow but closed to foreigners. By 1983 Sakharov had become sufficiently disenchanted with the regime to support NATO's decision to 'negotiate from strength' with the Soviet Union and position Cruise and Pershing missiles in Western Europe, although he had been a long-standing advocate of global nuclear disarmament.

The third major figure was Solzhenitsyn, who had shot to fame in 1962 as the author of the novel *One Day in the Life of Ivan Denisovich*, one of the most shocking exposés of life in a Stalin prison camp ever officially published. After a relatively brief phase at the cutting edge of Khrushchev's de-Stalinisation campaign, Solzhenitsyn fell from favour under Brezhnev. None of his major works, including two full-length critical novels about the Stalin era, *Cancer Ward* and *The First Circle*, which assisted his gaining the Nobel Prize for Literature in 1970, were published in the Soviet Union thereafter. Solzhenitsyn publicly denounced the whole panoply of state censorship, being expelled from the Writers' Union as a consequence in 1969. He then organised the publication of his writings abroad, including the seven-part *Gulag Archipelago*, an 'experiment in literary investigation'. This work was a sustained condemnation of the entire Soviet prison camp history and also an indictment of Lenin and Marxism. The regime, finally losing patience, forcibly expelled Solzhenitsyn from the Soviet Union itself with a one-way Aeroflot ticket in 1974.

Solzhenitsyn, unlike Sakharov, responded to such pressures by eventually developing a fundamentally anti-Soviet political credo. This was most succinctly set forth in a *Letter to the Soviet Leaders* written in 1973. This confirmed his position as, in effect, a liberal (i.e. not anti-semitic) Russian nationalist, with intellectual roots in the nineteenth-century Slavophil movement, an Orthodox Christian moralist. He denounced Russia's barbarity as uniquely horrible. Marxism he rejected utterly as a false God.

'This ideology bears the entire responsibility for all the blood that has been shed . . . This ideology does nothing but sap our strength and bind us.

(Solzhenitsyn 1973, p. 34)

A patriarchal Christian order needed to be reconstructed. There should be no more foreign adventurism or obsessions with industrial materialism. Soviet urban life was 'utterly unnatural', and should give way to a concentration on small-scale rural development, notably in the north and east of the country. Western democracy had 'dangerous, perhaps mortal, defects', for multi-party systems merely divided a nation. 'Are there no extra-party or strictly non-party paths of national development?' The West was spiritually and morally confused: why surrender to its cultural imperialism?

These three men, a Leninist, a liberal and a Russian nationalist, were syptomatic of a deeper ferment in Soviet intellectual life under Brezhnev. But beneath the divisions, certain common themes were apparent. Virtually all the intellectual dissenters of this era focused on questions about freedom of expression and intellectual freedom as well as on the need for legal and political rights. Many agreed on the need for moral and spiritual regeneration, not just pragmatic reformism. Sakharov as much as Solzhenitsyn saw the need for individuals to examine their consciences. None doubted that the Brezhnev era was profoundly corrupt and stagnant.

Perhaps the most telling parallel is that all three of these men, along with countless others, shifted from being true believers in the Soviet system to loyal critics and then to outright dissenters. They were driven to this position largely by the actions of the Soviet regime itself. 'Tyranny', as Dostoevsky wrote 'is a habit'; it also, as any Marxist would observe, contains within it the seeds of its own eventual destruction.

Perestroika and the Dissident Achievement

Just what did the dissidents achieve in the Brezhnev era? They certainly did not destroy the system, nor did they have any success in effecting reforms within the country, but they were able to put the leaders under considerable pressure internationally. The most prominent of them became 'untouchable' in a sense and could not be made to disappear into the *gulag* as would have happened under Stalin.

Soviet leaders wanted détente in Europe, and because of this were less ruthless with many of the better known dissidents than might otherwise have been the case, for in order to achieve any lasting détente it was necessary not to alienate Western opinion totally. As Pavel Litvinov put it in 1974 after his forced departure from the USSR, 'I want you all to understand that we have survived because the West exists'. The Soviet leaders were eventually forced onto the defensive, both diplomatically and politically. Solzhenitsyn's powerful metaphor of the *gulag* system as a scattered archipelago within the Soviet borders, and the repeated and well-publicised campaigns about human rights violations, all did enormous global damage to Soviet prestige and influence. Even West European communists talked increasingly of the 'Soviet lesson' rather than the 'Soviet model'. By the end of the Brezhnev era, the Soviet Union had fewer foreign intellectual friends than it possessed even under Stalin, a notable fact given that by no stretch of the imagination was life in the Soviet Union in the 1970s worse than it had been in the 1930s.

In the end, however, the dissidents almost certainly had a major and lasting domestic impact in helping to set the agenda for Gorbachev. *Perestroika* stemmed at least in part from the fact that reformist members of the party leadership had quietly digested a lot of dissident thinking during the Brezhnev years even if they could not put it into practice. It is a reminder that, although the Brezhnev regime may have been in large part able to control dissident activity, it was far less effective at preventing the spread of unacceptable ideas which even resulted in some outwardly loyal officials being called 'internal émigrés' at heart.

There is a considerable irony of history about all this, given the extent to which hitherto dissident ideas under Gorbachev became suddenly not just tolerated but officially encouraged and put into practice. Gorbachev remarked at the 27th Party Congress that *perestroika* was possible 'only through democracy . . . free labour and free thought in a free country' and this was plainly not meant simply as a slogan, as subsequent events have shown. By 1988 the press was describing Brezhnev era dissidents, who had been gaoled for their views, as people of 'great civic courage'. According to Amnesty International, almost all the 600 political prisoners still incarcerated in 1986 had been released by the end of 1988.

Then Sakharov himself was allowed to return to Moscow in 1986 and has publicly supported major aspects of the Gorbachev reform programme, appearing on several occasions at public meetings chaired by Gorbachev, as an honoured participant. He specifically backed several regime initiatives, not least Gorbachev's strategy for nuclear arms reductions that first bore fruit in the shape of the INF Agreement with President Reagan in December 1987. Meanwhile he continued to campaign for the release of dissidents and spoke openly of the still 'half-hearted and contradictory' nature of reform.

Medvedev's ideas, too, have now been partially accepted. The rise of informal groups since 1985, and the official sanctioning of this admittedly limited degree of political pluralism, have opened up Soviet politics more than at any time since the 1920s. Moreover, some of the informal groups have been intellectually and politically close to Medvedev himself, as the officially sanctioned 1987 Declaration of the Federation of Socialist Clubs indicated. This publicly called on all independent groups and clubs to support *perestroika*, and to strengthen democratisation, while at the same time recognising as constitutionally correct the leading role of the Communist Party. The Communist Party youth newspaper, *Komsomolskaya Pravda*, paid official tribute in 1988 to Medvedev's role in paving the way for such developments. 'His work is stunningly truthful and sincere . . . challenging us to debate and appealing to our consciences.' Some of the more liberal journals such as *Novy Mir* have even argued for the publication of Solzhenitsyn's works, praising them for their truthfulness and courage, although the party leadership itself appears to be still opposed to any such move.

Other dissidents in exile remained initially unimpressed by all this, many regarding *perestroika* as a mere façade, and Gorbachev as a flash in the pan. Bukovsky wrote in 1987 that 'Gorbachev does not want to change the system; he wants to save it, along with his own skin.' Meanwhile, the Jewish dissident Anatoli Shcharansky claimed that actually 15,000 to 20,000 were incarcerated for their beliefs.

The greater freedoms of the *glasnost* era have actually created a new wave of outspoken and active dissident groups, some of which have been harrassed by the authorities in traditional ways. Attempts by a coalition of radical groups to establish an opposition political party, the Democratic Union, for example, in 1988, were deemed unacceptable, not least because there do remain some limits to *glasnost* and *demokratizatsia*. A multi-party system is out of bounds. So, too, are the workings of the inner-party leadership, and many military and security matters. Equally, criticism of Lenin remains essentially uncharted territory.

Nevertheless, a certain irony remains. Since 1985 much of the pre-existing dissident movement has been swept into the official reformist tide, many dissenters openly supporting Gorbachev – and not surprisingly, for the range of topics open for discussion is now wider than at any time since the early days of the Revolution, and political activity accordingly less fettered. During 1987, for instance, the Soviet media openly debated an enormous range of specific matters – should there be more churches for believers? what is the true state of public health care? why do the sons of the élite often appear to avoid military service in Afghanistan? how rife is corruption even within the military and the KGB? do labour camps serve any useful rehabilitational purpose? what is the extent of and justification for élite privilege? what strikes and disasters have actually occurred? why have national economic statistics continued to be inaccurate? It also tackled a range of questions about Soviet history, as well as confronting basic issues about *perestroika* itself. Was it muddled? Why was there cynicism, misunderstanding of it or opposition to it? What costs were involved for ordinary people? Was price reform desirable? Was collective or state ownership really a better form of socialism? There was a genuine pluralism in official debate, some of it mirroring the arguments that had only been possible in *samizdat* in previous years, notably on highly charged matters such as the Stalin past, or anti-Semitism. Since 1987 this has become even more marked.

By comparison with the past, Soviet public life under *perestroika* has been a veritable Babel of debate and controversy, and Brezhnev's dissidents, in indirect ways, helped create this phenomenon.

Conclusion

Broadly speaking, our conclusions in this chapter, therefore, are threefold. First, the regime has shown some skill from time to time in adapting its official ideology to changing circumstances. Second, the official ideology and the wider political culture are deeply interwoven. Third, as the dissidents remind us, the hold of a single all-embracing belief system on modern Soviet society is far from complete and, irrespective of how efficient the regime is, may be unavoidably slackening. The gradual emergence of a civil society in recent years suggests that Soviet leaders in future may have to be content with a much more pluralist and secular belief system in which people back the regime not out of faith or fear, but because their support has been in effect rationally mobilised.

Further Reading

White and Pravda (1988) provide a recent series of studies on Soviet ideology: its content, functions and effectiveness, and how these have changed over time. Evans (1977) discusses the Brezhnev era concepts of 'developed socialism'.

The related questions of political culture and society are the subject of studies by White (1979) and Brown (1985b). Tucker (1987) and Lewin (1988) both discuss the possible development of a 'civil society'. Harding (1984) focuses on the key role of the state and its place in the Soviet system.

There is a very large literature on Soviet dissidents. Two general studies are Alexeyeva (1985) and Shatz (1980), which put the phenomenon into an historical perspective, as well as discussing the very eclectic nature of dissident thought. Such thought includes Sakharov (1969, 1975), Solzhenitsyn (1974, 1975) and R. Medvedev (1975) as well as Shragin (1978), Zinoviev (1978) and Amalrik (1970). Accounts by dissidents of their own experiences include Bukovsky (1978), Etkind (1978) and Litvinov (1969). Lakshin (1980) reveals some of the tensions between dissidents. The trial of Daniel and Sinyavsky is the subject of Labedz and Hayward (1967).

The research reports produced regularly by Radio Free Europe and Radio Liberty provide abundant further information as, in its own way, does the Soviet press, translations from which are published regularly in the Current Digest of the Soviet Press.

4

The Communist Party of the Soviet Union: The Politics of Power

The Communist Party of the Soviet Union is officially the 'core' of the political system, the 'leading and guiding force of Soviet society'. It not only possesses unrivalled power and authority, accumulated through more than seventy years of rule, but it binds these together with an official ideology that is tantamount to a national ethic. Moreover, its past achievements, particularly in transforming the Soviet Union into a modern superpower, are widely accepted within the country. The party itself may claim that its position is justified ideologically, that its 'profound knowledge of the laws of social development' enables scientifically 'correct' policies to be pursued, but for many citizens there is simply no obvious, let alone better, alternative to this single, centralised élite that can rule over such a vast and complex land. It therefore has considerable political strengths.

However, as earlier chapters have shown, the single party is by no means an ideal instrument of rule. It is far from clear that such an entrenched élite has the necessary flexibility and skill to ensure the effective running of a modern economy and society, let alone the determination and energy to carry through the transformations demanded by *perestroika*. Can it still claim to be, in the Leninist tradition, a disciplined vanguard, a galvanising force for planned change, or has it become an increasingly conservative and rusty machine, itself a major cause of the very stagnation *perestroika*

106

seeks to attack? The question is a central one, for Gorbachev is the product of the party and ultimately dependent upon it for success. The party meanwhile has thrived on the status quo and has much to lose from radical change.

In the first part of this chapter we shall consider some of the basic characteristics of the party, including its membership and structure as well as its methods of rule. In the second part we shall turn to questions of its continuing and future effectiveness, and the major changes now under way.

The Mass Party Membership

One of the most striking features of the modern party is its sheer size. In early 1917 there were fewer than 24,000 Bolsheviks. By 1953 over 6 million people belonged to this vanguard party, and by the time Brezhnev died in 1982 this had risen to more than 17.5 million, or approximately one out of every eleven adults in the country. By 1988 there were over 19 million party members. This apparently inexorable growth has taken place despite occasional weeding-out campaigns (since Stalin's time aimed largely at 'non-political' failings such as indolence, drunkenness or corruption). Such campaigns have eliminated relatively few (347,000 in 1971–4 and only 80,000 in 1981–6, one quarter of those in Moscow alone) and have done little to hinder overall growth, which has continued despite various controls.

Why has this happened? Part of the explanation is simply demographic. The party's own growth has paralleled that of the Soviet population. There is also continuing tension between the leadership's desire for exclusivity and vanguardism on the one hand, which would make the party theoretically more coherent and easier to manage and, on the other, its pressing need for a sufficiently broad base to be properly representative of Soviet society as a whole (Rigby 1968, p. 5). To some extent this balancing act has been effectively maintained. Although the party has many of the characteristics of a mass movement rather than an élite, party membership to this day is still a generally respected achievement for any citizen, a public hallmark of the fact that a particular individual possesses qualities that society values. More people apply for membership than are actually admitted.

Of course, this is in part because party membership is also widely seen as a comfortable guarantee of security and status and an access route to scarce goods, closed shops, better housing, career advancement and western travel. This has been the case since 1917 and is both frequently criticised and totally unavoidable. As the party's theoretical journal *Kommunist* put it in 1985, the party contains 'far too many cynical young careerists . . . people who should not be allowed within gunshot range of the party ranks.'

Sheer size must also adversely affect the party's political coherence. Internal divisions at any level can be found even in small political parties in the West, but the nature of the Soviet Communist Party imparts a special quality to this, particularly given the binding tradition, dating from 1921, that there can be no organised factionalism. Such a party is by definition, in the phrase of Raymond Aron 'monopolistic but not monolithic'. The problem can go deep, as one, admittedly dissident, ex-member, Efim Etkind, has put it:

> In the West you choose to join a party because you want to. Not so in the USSR. If one is a party member, what does it mean? Is he one of us or one of them? Is he a Leninist of the old guard . . . a soldier of the war against fascism . . . . a careerist . . . a weak and unprincipled victim of intimidation? Or an idealist? Or a simple-minded conformist? Or a sceptic but now condemned to carry his party card to his dying day or until the time when his heretical views come to light and he is expelled? The problem is you can't *leave* the party. To do so would be like committing civic suicide or applying to emigrate . . . [you are] a cog in a machine.
>
> (Etkind 1978, p. 7)

Just what this vast membership stands for politically is not necessarily easy to determine.

Other characteristics are rather clearer. The CPSU is not essentially a working-class party, although it does retain a lingering Leninist attachment to this tradition. At times it appears still proud that as many as 40 per cent of the Soviet industrial labour force consists of manual labourers, a fact that could increasingly be seen as an indication merely of economic backwardness. Having paid due homage to the working class as the 'leading force', the 1977 Soviet Constitution stresses how the party is the 'party of the whole people' and that all three main social groups have a legitimate role to play in building communism, as Table 4.1 implies.

Table 4.1 CPSU Composition by Social Groups (%)

	'Blue-collar'	Collective farmers	'White-collar'
1956	32.0	17.1	50.9
1966	37.8	16.2	46.0
1976	41.6	13.9	44.5
1986	45.0	11.8	43.2

Source: Miller (1987), p. 98.

Several points are worth noting about these official figures. First, they indicate social class at the time of enrollment, not current employment. Second, blue-collar includes state farm workers as well as industrial workers. Ideologically all state employees are regarded as equal. As a consequence the figures overstate the real number of 'workers at the bench' who are party members, and correspondingly understate the number of white-collar workers. Miller has calculated that in practice by 1986 probably between 20 and 25 per cent of all white-collar workers or retired white-collar workers were party members, but that only about 7 per cent of all blue-collar workers and only about 12 per cent of all collective farm workers were. On the other hand, though the figures over-represent blue-collar workers, the figures for collective farm workers are a fair reflection of the declining share that this sector has in the workforce. Party recruitment policies in recent years, meanwhile, have boosted considerably the numbers of blue-collar workers in particular growth areas of the economy such as the chemicals and electronics industries and the energy sector.

There are other distinct characteristics about party membership. It is a disproportionately male body. In 1986 some 53 per cent of the population, but less than 29 per cent of the party, were female, although this latter figure did represent a rise from only 24 per cent in 1976. It is also disproportionately Slav in composition. Slavs formed about two-thirds of the population, but almost four-fifths of the party in 1986. At the same time only 7.5 per cent of the party, but about 18 per cent of the population, were Central

Asians. The people of the Baltic states were also notably under-represented although, while in this case a lack of political commitment might play a large part, in Central Asia it is more likely to be a combination of the very high proportion of children in the population and large-scale local post-Brezhnev anti-corruption drives. One further characteristic is the relatively high level of educational attainment amongst party members. Approximately one in three have full university education or the equivalent, as opposed to less than 10 per cent of the population as a whole.

In short, the party is a heterogeneous and diverse body, like Soviet society itself, and necessarily in a state of flux. It is relatively well educated and less recognisably proletarian than in the fairly recent past. Some sort of balance between exclusivity and representativeness has been attempted although it is a matter that requires continual attention (Harasymiw 1984). In 1987, for example, Gorbachev drew particular attention to the continuing under-representation of women and the tendency for the party still to err on the side of quantity rather than quality when recruiting new members. It is not out of the question that he will seek to control more rigorously, or even cut, the size of the party.

The Party Elite: the *Apparat* and the *Nomenklatura*

Nineteen million people do not 'rule' the Soviet Union in any clearly definable sense. In theory, the party recruits the more advanced, politically conscious section of society as a disciplined vanguard. In practice, most party members, the rank and file, have little power and lead normal lives. As Hill and Frank put it, members of the vanguard are also 'parents, shoppers, workers; they, too, travel by bus and underground to and from work; they visit the theatre and cinema, they take their families to the Black Sea in August; they celebrate New Year by dancing until dawn; they have hobbies like everyone else' (Hill and Frank 1987, p. 19). What the party does expect from them is unswerving loyalty and preparedness to take on considerable and often thankless tasks. It is one thing to be part of the vanguard constructing the heroic Baikal–Amur Railway in Siberia, but quite another to cope with inadequate housing, a shortage of equipment or an unmotivated workforce in sub-zero temperatures several thousand miles from home.

Who, then, really rules the Soviet Union? There are many ways of considering this, as we shall see, but two basic categories are worth briefly examining at this point, the *apparat* and the *nomenklatura*, for they reveal something about how the party itself has traditionally been run and about how it has infiltrated all other Soviet institutions.

The *apparat* is the party machine of full or part-time salaried functionaries. These people, scattered widely right across the country but with their largest concentration in Moscow, are thought to number somewhere between 100,000 and 200,000, although estimates vary widely. They include many of the most highly trained and experienced personnel and represent, as it were, the party's inner core, not only shaping policy but overseeing its implementation. To critics these are the party 'bureaucrats', the 'apparatchiks', a caste apart even from ordinary party members, let alone other citizens. A crucial part of their power is the patronage that they dispense through control of the wider *nomenklatura* system.

The *nomenklatura* technically consists of two lists: one of posts to be filled and one of the 'great and good' to fill them. The party *apparat* at each level controls a range of *nomenklatura* appointments. Thus, at Central Committee level, the *apparat* allocates personnel to key positions in the central ministries, the KGB, the military, the media and even the Orthodox Church (Voslensky 1984, p. 75). At local level, the party *apparat* appoints head teachers, trade union officials, local enterprise managers and municipal adminis-trators. Nationally, according to Voslensky, there are about 750,000 *nomenklatura* posts and a corresponding pool of about one million names, virtually all of them party members. This patronage tradition, which infiltrates the party into all areas of public life, has been a major ingredient of the glue that has held the Soviet political system together. Many observers consider the *nomenklatura* – which includes the party *apparat* itself but is much wider – to be the real ruling élite, or even the 'ruling class', inasmuch as it is possible to define it (e.g. Nove 1975). Let us meanwhile look more closely at how the party itself is structured and how this élite rules.

Party Structure and the Leading Party Bodies

The party's basic building block is the Primary Party Organisation
or cell, derived from the pre-revolutionary underground tradition.
Nationally there are about 400,000 cells, each party member
belonging to one. Most are quite small, 40 per cent having 15 or
fewer members, and most are situated in the workplace so that
members can gather to disuss the latest party directives or
problems within the institution where they are based, meetings
often taking place during the lunch break. Beyond the cell, the
party is organised territorially, like political parties elsewhere,
paralleling government organisations at local, regional, republican
and national levels. Each level has its own hierarchy of conferences,
congresses, committees and first secretaries. If this seems complex
it must be remembered that the party is in the business not just of
keeping its own internal affairs in order but of taking ultimate
responsibility for the overall running of the country. Communication
at each level involves a range of methods, from shop-floor
propaganda to wall sheets, posters, newspapers, journals, radio
and television. Increasingly, there are specialised approaches for
particular areas. Thus a student party cell may well get a more
sophisticated treatment of, say, foreign affairs, than a rural party
cell, which may get a somewhat more regular and basic coverage
of, say, agricultural policy.

The key organisational principles behind this party structure are
the Leninist ones of Democratic Centralism, as defined in the
party rules:

(1) All leading party bodies are elected.
(2) Party committees report periodically to their appropriate conferences
    and congresses at their level as well as to higher bodies.
(3) There is strict party discipline and subordination of the minority to
    the majority.
(4) The decisions of higher bodies are binding on lower bodies.

In practice the last two rules have been very firmly adhered to
throughout almost all Soviet history. The first two, by contrast,
have normally been honoured in the breach. This led Gorbachev
in 1988 to remark that democratic centralism had long since given
way to 'bureaucratic centralism'. Hence the concerted attempt

under *perestroika* to revitalise the party, and strike a different balance between bureaucratic centralism and democratic account-ability. Although Soviet history itself is unique, this experience has parallels elsewhere. Political parties generally set some store by discipline and hierarchy and frequently have quite recognisable élites distinct from the rank and file.

We shall now consider in more detail the élite or leading party bodies and their relationship to the wider political system.

The Party Congress

The Party Congress is formally the 'supreme organ' of authority, but in practice its powers and expectations have been very limited. Since 1971 the Party Congress has met every five years, at the start of each Five-Year-Plan. Prior to that it met very irregularly. There was no Congress at all between 1939 and 1952, although it was supposed to be convened every three years. Congresses were meant to occur at four-year intervals between 1952 to 1971, but this happened only once in 1956. Modern Congresses gather together over 5,000 delegates from right across the Soviet Union, as well as fraternal foreign visitors, and have considerable ritualistic and symbolic importance in providing the leaders with an authoritative setting in which to proclaim national goals for the next five years. All this is accompanied by saturation media coverage for the ten days or so that each Congress lasts. But the individual delegates themselves are there essentially to form an audience for the leaders to address rather than to participate in active decision making. For many, the occasion is primarily a reward for local political activism and a special chance to visit the capital. The Congress delegates do elect the Central Committee of the party, which in turn elects the Politburo, but this, too, is traditionally a routine piece of political theatre.

This was not, however, the case with the extraordinary and very lively Party Conference of 1988 – the first since 1941 – called by Gorbachev to consider further reforms. Much of this was genuinely unscripted, its decisions – discussed later in this chapter – putting much public pressure on the Central Committee and the Politburo to maintain the *perestroika* process.

The Central Committee

The Central Committee is a much smaller and politically more notable body. In 1986 there were 307 full members and 170 candidates (candidates attend but do not vote; many in due course are promoted to full membership). About 40 per cent were *apparat* officials, 30 per cent were from government ministries and the rest were largely from the military, the police, the diplomatic, cultural, judicial, scientific and media élites. In addition, there were the customary token numbers of milkmaids and cosmonauts. Essentially, the Central Committee is an assembly of institutional and regional representatives, chosen in large measure ex officio – the *nomenklatura* élite, as it were.

The political power that flows from this is real though limited. The Central Committee provides the top leadership with its most obvious pool of political talent. It has on occasion proved a crucial forum for a divided Politburo. In 1957 Khrushchev successfully and uniquely appealed to the Central Committee to reverse a Politburo decision that he should resign (see Chapter 2). In 1964, when faced with a similar situation, the Central Committee appears to have backed the anti-Khrushchev majority in the Politburo. In more routine circumstances the Central Committee could well be a forum for communication and debate, formal and informal, between the *nomenklatura* élite and the Kremlin leadership. This has clearly been the case since 1985, with Central Committee meetings, if nothing else, giving the leadership a chance to gauge the wider party mood about *perestroika,* and if possible establish a broad consensus. A specific example was the debate on party rules which took place in the Central Committee in 1986. This resulted in a tightening up of discipline; since then many party members guilty of corruption have had to answer to the police courts like non-party members. At the same time, the Central Committee, after some semi-public debates, decided not to reintroduce Khrushchev's rules about limiting the length of tenure of party officials, perhaps not surprisingly, given that nearly 60 per cent of the Central Committee had been appointed under Brezhnev. It was only the 1988 Party Conference which over-turned the decision.

Thus the Central Committee is an important leadership forum, maybe increasingly so in an era of *demokratizatsia*. However, it also needs to be borne in mind that it normally meets only twice a year, usually for one day at a time, and that although the Central Committee has powers to 'direct the activities of the party' between Congresses, it is in practice the Politburo and Secretariat that do so, in the name of the Central Committee.

The Politburo and the Secretariat

The Politburo and the Secretariat have traditionally formed the apex of the political leadership. In theory, the Politburo merely 'directs the work of the Central Committee between plenary meetings' and the Secretariat merely 'directs current work', but these phrases can be translated to mean that in practice the Politburo is the top policy-making body, with the Secretariat as its administrative arm. Its nearest British equivalent is the Cabinet. The Politburo itself has no set size but in recent years has generally fluctuated at about a dozen members at any one time – all men and all full Central Committee members. In accordance with the practice started by Lenin it normally meets once a week starting at 11.00 a.m. on Thursdays; it rarely votes on issues, preferring to reach a consensus view wherever possible. It has to some extent sought to cope with the sheer volume of business by delegating to sub-committees which may include candidate as well as full members. On occasion outside specialists are brought in to address particular topics, Gorbachev having made notable use of reform minded academicians. Since 1982 *Pravda* has published a weekly report on Politburo meetings giving fuller details than before of the agenda and conclusions, though such information remains very limited. On August 13th 1987, for example, the Politburo apparently discussed and agreed to:

(a) accelerating the development of the chemicals industry and its related technologies;
(b) a proposal to publish a 10-volume work on 'The Great Patriotic War of the Soviet People';
(c) additional measures aimed at preventing AIDS in the USSR;
(d) 'certain other aspects of party and state life'.

As this laconic last phrase indicates, the inner workings of the Politburo remain largely unknown. The precise role played by particular people, the importance of candidate members, Secretariat officials or representatives of other institutions remains unclear and so, too, does the extent and nature of political debate and division.

Splits over policy have certainly occurred within the Politburo although, if nothing else, the modern traditions of collective leadership and the Leninist inheritance of anti-factionalism have often resulted in at least a façade of unanimity. However, it is known, for example, that there were serious divisions over policy and personality in the mid and late 1960s involving two ex-KGB chiefs, Alexander Shelepin and Vladimir Semichastny, who appear to have advocated much more Stalinist measures (Gelman 1984, p. 76). In the 1970s there were serious disputes about détente involving in particular the Ukrainian First Secretary, Pyotr Shelest, who was eventually dropped amidst accusations of 'economic nationalism' or excessive special pleading for the Ukraine. Shelest, it transpired, had also been a leading Politburo advocate of the invasion of Czechoslovakia in 1968. In the early 1980s there were disputes over the succession, not least in the context of how to handle élite corruption. *Perestroika* has certainly created new debates although it remains unclear whether these have led to an increasingly divided Politburo – reformers versus conservatives – or whether the differences are merely about the pace and scope of reform, with agreement on essentials. The sacking of a particularly outspoken reformer, Boris Yeltsin, from his position as a candidate Politburo member in 1987, and the downgrading of Yegor Ligachev in 1988 – widely seen as the main spokesman for the conservative party apparatus – could be explained either way.

Suffice it to say that, while the Politburo, whose functions can be compared in many respects to a British Cabinet, must be a cockpit for continuous leadership debate and tension, modern General Secretaries have almost invariably managed to preserve some overall consensus. The dismissal of Khrushchev in 1964 remains the exception that proves this rule.

The Politburo, however, is only as good as the information and expertise that it commands. Hence the Secretariat, which, as Hough has described it, acts as the 'eyes and ears' of the Politburo and thus has great political significance (Hough and Fainsod 1979, p. 430). There are normally about a dozen Secretaries, each responsible for a designated area of policy, such as economic administration, international affairs, ideology, and party cadres. Between them they are expected to appoint the party *apparat* and thus control the wider *nomenklatura*, provide policy papers for the leadership and verify the implementation of Politburo decisions. Whether they achieve all this is another matter. The Brezhnev era Secretariat was publicly criticised in 1986 for being 'lazy, out of touch and merely duplicating central government ministries'. Significantly, Gorbachev rebuilt it very rapidly in 1985–6, and went a stage further with the creation of new Central Committee Commissions in 1988 (see p. 139), in an attempt to encourage more long-range strategic social and economic thinking from it rather than sheer 'parallelism'. This will not be easily achieved, if only because the endemic and widespread traditions of 'report padding' make it very difficult to get accurate information from below. Ultimately, then, the leadership is dependent on the wider party *apparat*.

The General Secretary

The General Secretary has traditionally been recognised not by the Party Rules but by custom and convention as the leader of the Politburo. His position, like that of the British Prime Minister *vis-à-vis* the Cabinet, has thus been both constitutionally and politically an ambiguous one, for 'power' is not a finite commodity but something that depends very much on circumstances and individuals. Although the collective Politburo might have been for much of the post-Khrushchev era a 'self-stabilising oligarchy', as Rigby has characterised it (Rigby 1970), the character and style of the General Secretary has always been crucial in shaping the workings of the leadership.

Stalin, as Milovan Djilas, a member of the Yugoslav Communist leadership in the 1940s, has shown, wielded enormous influence over his Politburo. It 'resembled a patriarchal family with a crotchety head whose foibles always made his kinsfolk somewhat apprehensive' (Djilas 1963, p. 64). Politburo meetings, as Khushchev himself described them, were rarely formal and often took the shape of 'interminable, agonising dinners' late at night. Stalin did everything himself: he would 'just make a decision and issue a decree' (Khrushchev 1971, p. 267). Khrushchev's Politburo was much less cowed and sometimes prepared to reject or reverse Khrushchev's energetic handling of issues. Brezhnev, although dominant for a large part of the time, operated in a more businesslike and collegiate manner, trying to encourage collective agreement through discussion rather than imposing his own solutions (Brown 1980). Quite apart from anything else Brezhnev was, like other General Secretaries, initially the product of the collective Politburo, and his ability to recruit or dismiss members from the leadership was always significantly less than that of, say, the British Prime Minister *vis-à-vis* the Cabinet.

Gorbachev has been very much more vigorous than the latter-day Brezhnev, but neither he nor other recent Soviet leaders have always achieved what they have wanted. Indeed, under Gorbachev Politburo sessions, according to one of its 1988 members, Lev Zaikov, could last for up to ten hours at a stretch in the search for consensus on major issues. Gorbachev's sheer skill and charisma, however, have placed him in an unusually commanding position, and may enable him to resolve some of the ambiguities of leadership by also assuming the newly created post of executive President. This is discussed further at the end of the chapter.

How the Party Rules: The Theory and the Practice

This brief description of the party's structure and of its leading bodies underlines the essentially Leninist nature of it all, epitomised in the principles of democratic centralism. The party is hierarchical, it is disciplined, it does not indulge in factionalism, and 'armed with Marxism–Leninism' it is a vanguard which knows what it is doing. To this can be added one other basic tenet of party rule. The party directs but does not supplant other government and state bodies. Its function is to command the firm political and strategic high ground, but not to get stuck in the muddy low ground of 'bureaucracy' and 'administration'. The party rules but it does not, at least in theory, govern the country, in the sense that it has never dispensed with traditional institutions such as the government ministries, the police, the military, enterprise managers or the local councils and parliamentary bodies (soviets) which, constitutionally, make the laws. These it infiltrates and shapes, but does not supplant.

But how true to life is this Leninist ideal? Is Soviet politics really such a simple, hierarchical and compartmentalised matter? Even the brief descriptions above imply that the reality is more complex. So, too, does the widespread contemporary evidence about resistance to *perestroika* within the party, and Gorbachev's own criticisms of the party. After all, if the ideal were a reality, the formulation and implementation of *perestroika* would be a very much more straightforward matter than it is.

In practice, these Leninist norms are far from irrelevant. It is the party, and particularly its leadership, which decides on the 'authoritative allocation of resources' at all levels, and there is no serious challenge to this tradition. Solzhenitsyn's 1963 short story, *For the Good of the Cause*, portrayed as a routine matter the uncomplaining acceptance by local party officials of decisions taken by higher authority, in this instance the unpopular requisitioning for a research institute 'in the national interest' of a much needed new school building. In 1981 it was the party leadership, under a Politburo troubleshooter, not government ministers, that commandeered resources to reorganise the Soviet gas pipeline programme on military lines after a series of significant setbacks. The party apparatus, ultimately at Secretariat and Politburo level, co-ordinated the handling of the Chernobyl disaster in 1986, and has subsequently continued to define the national nuclear energy programme. Even powerful regional party secretaries have very little say in, for instance, foreign policy making. Hierarchical rules do apply (Frank 1985).

Moreover, the party has historically been very effective in infiltrating and directing non-party bodies while at the same time not 'supplanting' them. The soviets are a case in point. Soviets originally mushroomed during the Revolution as more or less spontaneous mass assemblies. The Bolsheviks, despite Lenin's 1917 slogan of 'all power to the soviets', soon came to mould them to their will and thus soviets from village and town level to the Supreme Soviet in Moscow traditionally ratified and explained party policy, from Lenin to Gorbachev. Nationally, out of some 2.3 million soviet deputies, rather less than half are party members, but the law-making functions of all soviets are essentially under party influence, directed by the party *apparat*. The independent political significance of the soviets has consequently been marginal.

The Council of Ministers, too, fits this pattern. In the narrow sense it is the government of the Soviet Union, constitutionally the 'highest executive and administrative body' and formally responsible, as in a parliamentary system, to the legislature, the Supreme Soviet. In practice it has very limited independent authority. All its members belong to the party and were appointed by it. They are not just rubber stamps, if only because they do influence the detail of governmental and legislative activity. They inevitably possess insight and expertise not otherwise necessarily available to the party apparatus leadership itself, and can to some extent become champions of or captives to these often very powerful vested interests. The party apparatus, however, has remained the 'leading and guiding force', if only because the Council of Ministers has until now been an unwieldy body. It has usually comprised over 100 people, ranging from leading ministers, some of whom are also members of the Politburo, and men of substantial political influence in their own right such as the ministers of finance, defence and foreign affairs, to a vast array of lesser officials. It also includes the chairmen of state committees such as the KGB, the Central Statistical Administration, the State Bank and the State Planning Committee (Gosplan). This sheer size also underlines the continuing point that the party, though it strives to 'direct', has sought not to 'supplant', having preferred until now to rule through this very fragmented and somewhat archaic ministerial structure, much of it inherited from the revolutionary era.

Thus Leninist tenets of party control and democratic centralism have always mattered. There are, however, some important qualifying factors that need to be taken into account in assessing how the party has traditionally ruled in practice over the decades.

1. Institutions are in some respects a poor guide to the distribution of power in the Soviet Union. Power has often been an arbitrary and personal matter, wielded by politically unaccountable chieftains. The decision to publish Solzhenitsyn in 1962 was taken only after his editor, Alexander Tvardovsky, petitioned Khrushchev personally, and Khrushchev had a small number of copies of *One Day in the Life of Ivan Denisovich* secretly printed and numbered and distributed to Politburo members with the instruction that they read it. Without such an intervention, Solzhenitsyn might never have been published.

Similarly, the poet Yevtushenko was only able to get a work dealing with Soviet neo-Nazis (among other things) published in 1985 after direct appeals from his editor, Vladimir Karpov, to Gorbachev. The development of institutionalised power has been limited. Thus, decrees and resolutions have variously emanated from the Supreme Soviet or from the Council of Ministers or, as is more usual, jointly from the Council of Ministers and the party Central Committee. This is constitutionally a messy arrangement, as Gorbachev implied at the 1988 Party Conference, but the Soviet Union has not normally been run by legal minds.

2. The party has not always succeeded in 'directing' other institutional bodies. Under Brezhnev, the State Planning Committee was, according to Yeltsin, a 'law unto itself' at times. The same has been true of the KGB. The party Secretariat appears to have lost significant hold over the Ministry of Foreign Affairs in the first part of the 1980s. The party's power over other institutions is not absolute and varies both with time and circumstance. Many small towns, for instance, have been dominated less by the party *apparat* than by a single enterprise under one central ministry. In such company towns economic power, and thus political influence, may well have rested with the enterprise management and the responsible ministry, rather than with local party officials. In 1981 local soviets, for instance, controlled only 40 per cent of the public housing stock in the country, much of the rest being the property of local enterprises and their ministries. Little has been done to redress this imbalance despite a target of 100 per cent for 1985 and the real difficulties it creates for the party's local *apparat*. The writer Daniel Granin discussed this specific problem in a 1980 novel, *The Picture*. His provincial party leader was far from being an all-powerful satrap:

> If he were asked what the main worry of his life was, the main business or, rather, the main desire, without a second thought he would answer: to have a housing block *to spare*. Literally, *to spare*.
>
> (Crouch and Porter 1984, p. 91)

3. The opposite point, confusingly, has also been true. The party,

particularly, according to Medvedev, at the regional level, has often not only directed but also supplanted (Z. Medvedev 1986, p. 69). Here, 'party bosses rule like dictators.' 'Supplanting (*podmena*), parallelism and petty tutelage' have been frequently criticised in practice. In an authoritarian and centralised system with no clear boundaries for party activity, they are probably impossible to avoid, for distinctions between 'politics' and 'administration' are more than usually difficult to preserve. The party may decide policy. But what is 'policy'? The strategic decision to build the Baikal–Amur Railway? Or the actual route to be taken, the timescale, the co-ordination of all the physical and human resources to make such a hero project succeed? 'Policy' is to eliminate the transport bottlenecks that annually bedevil the collection and storage of the harvest. But which body identifies the nature of the problem, gathers the evidence, proposes and implements policy solutions? All these stages are interlinked. The party has inevitably and unavoidably found that it is often dragged down into the muddy waters of day-to-day detail.

4. The party *apparat* itself has interests and is not entirely indivisible. Modern Soviet leaders, for instance, have been understandably cautious in handling the 156 *obkom* secretaries, and the 14 republican first secretaries, who are a key building block of the Central Committee, its largest single group. These men, in a sense heirs of the Tsarist provincial governors, are crucial to the leadership's success or failure, being the effective political bosses of their regions (Hough 1969). Khrushchev alienated them, particularly with his 1962 decision to split the party into separate agricultural and industrial hierarchies. Brezhnev instead left them alone, recruiting replacements from within each locality rather than imposing co-opted outsiders. Gorbachev, a typical example of this career pattern under Brezhnev, has, by contrast, moved far more men in from outside if only to tackle entrenched local corruption. Either way, the party *apparat* is not necessarily a rubber stamp of the Politburo. It successfully sabotaged attempts at economic reform after 1965, as discussed in Chapter 6. It successfully opposed food price rises planned for 1970. It has often resisted *perestroika* and *demokratizatsia*.

5. Political links across institutions are a familiar fact of life. Local political 'families', which indulged in cronyism, report padding or other unacceptable habits, were present in Lenin's time. An early Soviet leader, Anastas Mikoyan, in his memoirs published in the 1970s described such cases occurring as early as 1922. The 1941–5 war created its own special bonds of comradeship, too, that survived long afterwards. Provincial or republican party leaders have sometimes run flourishing networks of local support that cut across party and government lines, as in Central Asia or in Moscow itself in the latter years of Brezhnev. Such fiefdoms are as much a part of the Soviet political system as are earlier Leninist norms. In a sense they were partly a consequence of the Leninist rule banning factionalism on issues. Over the years this tended to emphasise the politics of personal loyalty, chieftains and clients, rather than the politics of informed political and public debate.

6. Orders from above – democratic centralism notwithstanding – simply have not in practice usually had the 'force of law' behind them in the sense that, for example, failure to fulfill the traditional economic plan leads to legal sanctions for those held responsible. At most, failure has resulted in party reprimands, non-promotion and so on. Twenty-five per cent of all state enterprises failed to meet their financial targets in 1986, but mass legal action did not follow. The party *apparat*, particularly *obkom* secretaries, have traditionally ruled as fixers and co-ordinators and their methods have not always even been technically legal. Yanov has described how the *obkom* secretary in particular 'is the only person who has the authority and power to order an all-Union dragnet, so to speak, for scarce raw materials. He alone can call . . . the Masters of other provinces and offer them a deal. He always has in reserve some raw material that is in short supply in another province, and there is always an opportunity to exchange it for what "his enterprises" need' (Yanov 1977, p. 24). Part of the strength of the *apparat* has been precisely this ability to cut corners and achieve results. The use by enterprise managers of *tolkachi* (pushers) to get scarce supplies for an industrial enterprise, often by black market bargaining, has been a commonplace and a tacitly accepted practice.

Several important conclusions follow from all this. First, since Stalin the party has increasingly ruled not through coercion but through consensus and compromise, involving both formal and informal rules of political behaviour. Second, institutional relationships, particularly those between party and state organs, vary with time and with place and can be quite complex. The resulting administrative apparatus is often very inefficient and expensive.

Third, there are conflicts in the political process, not just over people and policy, but because there are different institutional or group interests. These factors are by no means unmanageable, but they do imply constraints on the power and authority of even the Politburo leadership. Daniels has argued that, as a consequence, a better way of thinking about power is to see it not as strictly Leninist and hierarchical but as a 'circular flow', with the top preserved in office because the middle level supports them, and vice versa – at the very least an implicit bargain among the political élite (Daniels 1971, p. 20). In the fast-changing era of *perestroika*, it is not clear even that this tacit bargain is a paramount feature. What is at least as striking is the image of a reforming leadership face to face with a relatively unresponsive party machine, the bargain no longer what it was.

In short, the Soviet Communist Party is a more complex and changeable phenomenon than might at first be thought. It is not, and never has been, a static entity, and it is no more easily susceptible to analysis than political parties elsewhere.

The Effectiveness of the Party

Such complexities and changes are not necessarily a sign that the party is losing its grip. On the contrary, it would be odd if the party had not responded to changing circumstances. Is its effectiveness nevertheless in decline? Many have argued that the party is inherently incapable of responding to modern challenges with anything other than half-baked reformism, implying at best a slowly declining level of future effectiveness. Certainly, the party's ability to adapt to change since Stalin, as suggested in Chapter 2, has been mixed. Overall judgements about effectiveness, however, are difficult either to prove or disprove. In the second half of this chapter we shall therefore focus specifically on three areas of concern that have received widespread attention. The first of these is whether the party has sufficient control over powerful interest groups, notably the military. The second is how effective it is at recruiting the brightest and the best into its own leadership ranks. Finally, we consider the question of just how resistant to reform, how great an obstacle to change, the party *apparat* has proved to be, and what changes are now under way to correct this. All three are crucial tests of the party's wider political effectiveness.

1. The Party and the Military: Who Rules?

Soviet society and politics since Stalin have witnessed not just the rise of dissidence but of mainstream public opinion as a serious political factor, notably on environmental questions in the 1970s, and on an increasingly wide range of issues subsequently. This rise of a civil society, as discussed in the preceding chapter, has considerable and possibly historic significance. Its roots are to be found in the now quite long established post-Stalin pattern of institutional interest groups. Just how coherent such groups, for example, the military, the KGB, the central planners or the party *apparat*, have been is debatable. Some well documented cases of educational or legal or economic reform in the 1950s and 1960s showed that any identifiable institutional group was in practice likely to be very divided (Skilling and Griffiths 1971). However, even the existence of factions within institutional groups was still a significant development, pointing to the fact that, increasingly, the party had to rule by consensus and compromise, building coalitions of political support, not by issuing blanket decrees or by the use of coercive methods. Has the party as a result been in danger of losing or seriously weakening its leading role? Perhaps the best way to consider this is to take the case of the Soviet military.

Even twenty years ago the civil–military relationship was being described by Kolkowicz as 'essentially conflict-prone and thus . . . a perennial threat to the political stability of the Soviet state', thereby implying that the party is constantly on the political alert in fear of a coup. It is now widely considered that this is not the best way to think about the Soviet civil–military relationship or, by analogy, the party's power and authority over any of the other entrenched non-party élites. It is after all a noteworthy fact of Communist regimes globally that, by and large, they have not degenerated into military regimes, unlike so many other non-communist polities. Basic civilian party control over the military is as enduring a fact of Soviet life as it is of British or American life. It is not out of the question that the military could physically seize power in the Soviet Union in the event of a major crisis, nor would it be impossible to justify this ideologically. The precedent of military rule in Poland after 1980 – exceptional and temporary measures at a time of national emergency – already exists. But in the Soviet case this remains an unlikely scenario.

Why should this be so? Several factors are at work here. The party itself has infiltrated a very thorough network of political controllers into the military, originally derived from the Civil War experience of committed Red Commissars working alongside the military professionals. The KGB provides a separate source of intelligence for the party, too. Meanwhile, the military and the party are culturally interlinked (Odom 1973). Both are practitioners of hierarchy, order and discipline; both are heavily involved in patriotic civic training work, the party through its youth movements, the Young Pioneers and the Komsomols, the military through the tradition of national service enlistment. In terms both of status and rewards the officers have been well treated. Over 76 per cent are party members and a further 15 per cent members of the Komsomol organisation. The military as a whole still bask in the reflected glory of 1941–5, and derive prestige from the fact that Soviet superpower status is largely based on military criteria. Professional *esprit de corps* has been encouraged, not least by the granting, since Khrushchev, of relative independence to the military on career promotions.

Above all, the military sector as such has been given a major share of resources. The nineteenth-century historian Klyuchevsky described Russian life as one in which 'the state swelled up, the people grew lean'. This could be applied to the Soviet economy and its military expenditure priorities in recent decades. It is commonly estimated in the West that at least 12–14 per cent of Soviet GNP is geared to military expenditure, approximately twice the percentage figure of the United States. Moreover, the military have been able to extract qualitative as well as quantitative achievements from the Soviet command economy. Quality control systems have been applied to defence procurements in a way that the civilian sector of the economy has until now been denied.

The overall result has ensured that the party leadership has never been under any serious threat of a military coup. The 1937 Tukhachevsky 'plot' against Stalin was a crude frame-up believable only in the atmosphere of political hysteria at the time. Marshal Zhukov's dismissal by Khrushchev in 1958 for supposedly Napoleonic ambitions was based on charges that were somewhat removed from reality. There is limited evidence of any major divergence from, let alone challenge to, party policy in crises such as Czechoslovakia in 1968, Afghanistan in 1979 or Poland in 1980–2. Differences of emphasis certainly existed in all these and other cases. The military tried quite hard to stall détente in the 1970s. According to certain accounts some within the military were prepared to use nuclear weapons against the Chinese in 1969 (Shevchenko 1985, p. 165). But to the extent that there are divisions, as suggested earlier, they have tended to be within the military and within the party leadership at least as much as between them. Ultimately, the leading role of the party has survived.

The so-called Ogarkov affair of the early 1980s reinforced this point. In 1981–2 Marshal Ogarkov, the army Chief of Staff and deputy Minister of Defence, publicly took issue with the Politburo over the winnability of nuclear war. Ogarkov argued that nuclear victory remained an 'objective possibility', that the military could, if necessary, still deliver victory. The Politburo, notably Defence Minister Ustinov, authoritatively countered that 'to count on victory in the arms race and in nuclear war is madness . . . there can simply be no such thing as nuclear war'. Then, in 1983–4, Ogarkov shifted ground and began to imply that the military could no longer count on gaining the necessary technological benefit from the command economy, that the weaknesses of the civilian economy were now beginning to hamper the military effort. The international uncompetitiveness of Soviet technology was dramatically apparent, for instance in the Israeli destruction of Syrian-owned Soviet equipment in the Lebanon in 1982. A 1985 US Pentagon report showed that in twenty areas of high technology with military applications, the USSR was leading in none, tied with the US in five, and was falling yet further behind in several others.

Ogarkov's views in both cases were part of a traditional military plea for more expenditure. Nonetheless, Ogarkov intruded into a highly charged élite debate about the Brezhnev legacy in the early 1980s, indicating that even the military were not entirely opposed to economic reform. For his pains he was demoted, a reminder that the party ultimately wielded the power of veto over policy debate.

Nevertheless, the party has incurred three broader costs with the military. First, there is the sheer economic drain and the systemic distortions of the economy that the military involve. Military expenditure growth, 1977–84, was held down by the party leadership to only 2 per cent per annum in real terms – when NATO was committed to 3 per cent – but this was still growth at the expense of the non-military sector. Public discussion within the Soviet Union has under *glasnost* increasingly been prepared to treat military expenditure as an essentially wasteful activity, absorbing both human and material resources that could otherwise be more beneficially employed.

Second, this expenditure may have had at least the political benefit of keeping the military quiescent. The Brezhnev era strategy was to buy off groups as far as possible, if only, in the case of the military, as a reaction to Khrushchev's unpopular tendency both to cut expenditure and – as the military saw it – meddle in areas of military doctrine. The result was that in 1964 the military were conspicuously disinclined to continue supporting Khrushchev politically. By the 1980s, as already indicated in Chapter 2, this policy of buying off had a political cost of its own in contributing substantially to the international undermining of the credibility of détente. If détente meant a Soviet commitment to a lessening of tensions in Europe, ran the argument in Western chancelleries in the late 1970s, then the continued high levels of Soviet military expenditure and the deployment of new weapons systems simply ran counter to that professed goal.

Thirdly, it has not always been clear in recent years whether the strategic and technological niceties of the nuclear age have been fully understood by Soviet political leaders themselves. Khrushchev in his memoirs illustrated how modern compartmentalisation of knowledge can adversely affect the military:

Our fleet was [engaged in staff maneouvres in the Black Sea, witnessed by Khrushchev] sinking enemy ships right and left . . . [the commander] was terribly cocky . . . Finally, I couldn't restrain myself . . . If this were a real war and not just a map exercise, your ships would all be lying at the bottom of the sea by now . . . He looked at me with complete surprise [as Khrushchev told him he had ignored the enemy's missile-launching planes 'which would surely be involved.' 'We have such a system ourselves so surely the other side has it too?'] 'Comrade Khrushchev, I've never heard of missile-launching planes before. You're telling me something entirely new'. 'Then it's our own fault,' I told him. 'All this information must be classified.'

(Khrushchev 1977, p. 64)

This dilemma also works the other way: in a complex world, the party leadership can become overly dependent on military advice. The issue in the end is therefore not so much that 'the generals are coming' but that incrementally military and strategic priorities come to dominate the political political agenda and distort the national economy (Colton 1979, p. 286).

Gorbachev has sought to tackle this problem. Military *perestroika* has required that the military see themselves as not apart from, but a part of, the Soviet economy. In 1986 Gorbachev spoke about the need to limit the military burden: 'only that which is strictly necessary' must be acquired, implying that this had not recently been the case or was still not what the military themselves wanted. At the 1986 Party Congress the stress was on 'acceleration' of light and consumer industry. 'The top priority will be given to the development of light industry and other industries that directly meet consumer demand.' Greater productivity and innovation were required from heavy industry – and, by implication, the military sector – rather than more resources. As the largest consumers in the Soviet economy, the military are bound to have been significantly affected by *perestroika*.

Moreover, as outlined in Chapter 2, the thrust of military and foreign policy under Brezhnev has been criticised as excessively and counter-productively military in orientation, not least the stationing of SS-20s in Europe in the late 1970s. Overseas aid, which was very costly and unpopular, has also come under attack. The naval chief, Admiral Gorshkov, was retired in 1985 amidst evidence that the new leaders felt that the great expense of the Soviet navy had not led to a comparably enhanced strategic or ideological reach globally. There has been a substantial renewal of the military leadership, coupled with a lowering of its collective visibility both on major ceremonial occasions in Red Square and within the Politburo and Central Committee. The 1987 Central Committee contained only 30 members of the military, as opposed to 41 in 1981.

Just how far the military-strategic nexus will adapt to *perestroika* remains unclear. There was evidence of specific military opposition to Gorbachev's 1985–6 moratorium on nuclear weapons testing, and in general the 'new thinking', particularly with its emphasis on future European conflicts being local and containable, was seriously at odds with established Soviet military doctrine. This still expounded the view in 1988 that war would not be a chance or local incident but the decisive clash between two antagonistic social systems. What has been clear since 1985 is that a considerable effort has been made to sharpen the leading role of the party within the military, and that *perestroika* has occurred at a time of significantly lowered military prestige within the Soviet Union.

The war in Afghanistan was the main cause for that. This 'bleeding wound', as Gorbachev characterised it, gave the military real operational experience, but at the cost of undermining their prestige not just within the party élite but amongst the young. *Glasnost* has accelerated this process, together with stories of bullying and corruption in the ranks, and may well have assisted the Politburo in coming to its 1986 decision to seek a political rather than a military settlement, gradually withdrawing Soviet troops and working to install a broader-based leadership in Kabul acceptable to Washington as well as to Moscow.

Overall, the party–military relationship is a complex one but, as with other party–group relationships, it is neither unmanageable nor destabilising. Military expenditure and development are, in the end, an inescapable commitment and the political tensions they create are, in a sense, routine matters. However, as the military case illustrates more widely, the party may be constrained to some degree by the entrenched nature and by the professional and technical expertise of such non-party interests, making radical change from any direction very hard to accomplish. In the process of infiltrating other bodies, the party has itself been infiltrated in return.

In the end the most intractable problems for the party leadership may lie not with the military or any other such group, but within the party *apparat* itself, for it is the party that remains the key institution in Soviet politics, both as a force for change and as a defender of the traditional status quo. It is to this body that we now turn, looking first at questions of the party's leadership recruitment record.

II. Leadership Recruitment: The Brightest and the Best?

The ability of any political system to recruit competent leadership is a standard test of its performance, and we now consider the Soviet Communist Party in this light, focusing in particular on two sorts of questions. What kinds of leaders are recruited and why? How effective has the party been at leadership renewal? In Table 4.2 we list the top ruling élite in 1988, the two dozen or so at the very apex of political power. Full members of the ruling Politburo are listed first, a group whose status is clear enough. Since 1917 there have only ever been just over 80 full Politburo members, a self-selected élite. Second is the more ambiguous group of candidate members. These may be merely on a stepping stone to full membership, but full membership is neither an inevitable outcome nor is candidate membership a necessary prerequisite to full membership. Their precise standing is unclear. Some, resident in Moscow, may well have more day-to-day influence than those who fly in from distant republics or provinces only once a week. Third, we list any Central Committee Secretary who is not also a Politburo member or candidate, for all Secretaries are undeniably powerful figures in their own right, key directors of the party *apparat*. On any realistic assessment of the top leadership, all three groups need to be considered.

As the table well illustrates, a notable characteristic of the leadership is the degree of institutional infiltration and interlocking that exists. Curiously, the Politburo, though in principle an arm of the Party's Central Committee, is in practice a much wider gathering than that might imply, for it brings together key party state and government officials, some of whom have no specific post within the party *apparat* itself. In effect, since Stalin, the Politburo has increasingly acted as a regular forum for the key élite *apparats*. Thus, typically, it included in 1988 not just senior Secretariat figures with responsibility for ideology, defence and the economy,

Table 4.2 The Soviet Leadership, November 1988

Name	Responsibility	Secretariat duties	Date of birth	Date into Politburo	Nationality
POLITBURO MEMBERS					
GORBACHEV	President, Praesidium Supreme Soviet. General Secretary, CPSU	General	1931	1980	Russian
VOROTNIKOV	President Praesidium Supreme Soviet Russian Republic		1926	1983	Russian
ZAIKOV	First Secretary, Moscow Gorkom	Military Industrial Complex	1923	1986	Russian
LIGACHEV	Chairman, Agriculture Commission	Unspecified	1920	1985	Russian
MEDVEDEV	Chairman, Ideology Commission	Ideology	1929	1988	Russian
NIKONOV		Agriculture	1929	1987	Russian
RYZHKOV	Chairman, Council of Ministers USSR		1929	1985	Russian
SLYUNKOV	Chairman, Economic and Social Policy Commission	Economic Admin.	1929	1987	Belorussian
CHEBRIKOV	Chairman, Legal Policy Commission	Admin. Organs	1923	1985	Russian
SHEVARDNADZE	Minister for Foreign Affairs		1928	1985	Georgian
SHCHERBITSKY	First Secretary, Ukraine		1918	1971	Ukrainian
YAKOVLEV	Chairman, International Policy Commission	Foreign Policy	1923	1987	Russian
CANDIDATE MEMBERS					
BIRYUKOVA	Deputy Chairman, Council of Ministers		1929	1988	Russian
VLASOV	Chairman, Council of Ministers Russian Republic		1932	1988	Russian
LUKYANOV	Vice-President, Praesidium Supreme Soviet		1930	1988	Russian
MASLYUKOV	Gosplan Chairman		1937	1988	Russian
RAZUMOVSKY	Chairman, Commission on Party Work and Cadres	Party Cadres and Organisation	1936	1988	Russian
SOLOVEV	First Secretary, Leningrad Obkom		1925	1986	Russian
TALYZIN	Soviet representative, Comecon		1929	1985	Russian
YAZOV	Minister of Defence		1923	1987	Russian
SECRETARIAT (other than those listed above)					
BAKLANOV		Military Industrial Complex	1932	1988	Ukrainian

Apart from Gorbachev, these lists are in (Cyrillic) alphabetical order.

but also the Chairman of the Council of Ministers, the Ministers of Defence and Foreign Affairs, and the Chairman of Gosplan. This pattern became particularly firmly established in the early 1970s when the Politburo recruited the then KGB chief Andropov, the Foreign Minister Gromyko and the Minister of Defence Marshal Grechko, as well as the First Secretaries of the Ukraine and Kazakhstan, politically two of the more important republics. There are no written rules guaranteeing seats to any constituency of this kind, any more than there are rules to guarantee the status and power of the General Secretary himself, for we are dealing with unwritten conventions that can and do shift with time. Nonetheless, there has been a clear tendency since Stalin for the Politburo to develop some degree of institutional representativeness, like the wider party itself.

What sort of people comprised the top leadership in 1988? First, it was a relatively well-educated body in the sense that all had completed higher education, though traditionally this has usually meant highly specialised technical training, often in engineering subjects, rather than in law, the humanities or the social sciences. Men like Gorbachev with his law degree, or Eduard Shevardnadze who trained as a teacher, or Alexander Yakovlev who spent a year in the 1950s as an exchange student at New York's Columbia University, remain exceptions. Secondly, the leadership was male, the only exception in 1988 being Alexandra Biryukova. There has only ever been one female member of the full Politburo, Khrushchev's Minister of Culture, Yekaterina Furtseva. Third, as a general characteristic, most leaders had been involved in party work from very early on in their adult lives. Only a few (Yazov in the military and Ryzhkov in industrial management) had careers centred entirely in organisations other than the party *apparat* itself. Most worked their way up within the party very steadily, typically spending at least some time in office as an *oblast*, or republican first secretary, on the way. Finally, most were ethnic Slavs, generally Russians, the only 1988 exception being the Georgian Foreign Minister, Shevardnadze.

Does this set of very easily described norms suggest a very narrow leadership? Has leadership recruitment put the emphasis on orthodoxy and safety rather than skill and talent? The thesis that this has been the case has often been advanced, most notably by Brzezinski in 1966. He argued that the Soviet leadership was inevitably degenerating into a conformist group of unimaginative and self-selected second-raters, bureaucrats of the worst kind (Brzezinski 1969). Degeneration, like effectiveness, is a long-term and subjective matter and difficult to prove or disprove, particularly given our limited knowledge of the Soviet leadership. One indicator that has often been considered is the extent to which the Politburo has recruited technocratic specialists or all-rounders ('dual executives') with both party work and industrial or agricultural management experience, rather than mere party *apparat* bureaucrats. The empirical evidence here, though, is inconclusive for different patterns exist and in any case, even if the poorly educated party bureaucrats have now largely disappeared, the contemporary leadership may still not necessarily be adequate in more demanding times.

What we can do, however, is consider briefly why the particular people who made up the 1988 leadership did indeed reach the top. Several distinct and not particularly 'degenerative' factors certainly appear to be at work. Of those listed in Table 4.2 some had records of substantial political achievement behind them before being co-opted into the leadership. Foreign Minister Shevardnadze, for example, was a former police chief who rose to become First Secretary of Georgia from 1972–85, carrying out an energetic purge of the notoriously easy-going and corrupt Georgian political élite. In 1978 he deftly handled a series of mass demonstrations in the Georgian capital, Tbilisi, against proposals that Russian rather than Georgian should henceforth be the official language of the republic. Both Nikolai Ryzhkov and Boris Slyunkov entered the Politburo with established solid reputations, Slyunkov as First Secretary of the Belorussian Republic, Ryzhkov as the chief executive of Uralmash, an iron and steel complex, the largest industrial enterprise in the Soviet Union.

Several of the 1988 leaders had been known critics of Brezhnev and had suffered accordingly in the past. Vitali Vorotnikov had been 'exiled' to Cuba as Soviet Ambassador there, 1979–82. Yakovlev had launched a scathing public attack on Russian nationalists within the party leadership in 1971 and had been similarly banished – in this case as Ambassador to Canada.

Some of the others had been provincial party leaders who were recruited as part of Andropov's drive to put a new rectitude into politics – men who had reputations as essentially honest and sober administrators. Zaikov, promoted from Leningrad in 1986, was a case in point, as was Yegor Ligachev. Ligachev's career was an instance not just of this phenomenon, but of how men who may be dubbed obstructionist conservatives (as he was by Yeltsin, the outspokenly reformist Moscow First Secretary who was sacked as a result in 1987) are more complex than this implies. Ligachev, whose own family had suffered under Stalin, had been a rising star under Khrushchev. He was the party Secretary in the Siberian city of Novosibirsk at the time when a pioneering new university complex was created there in the 1950s and 1960s. It was soon to become a bastion of reform thinking. After a brief spell in Moscow, Ligachev was 'exiled' to Tomsk as *obkom* secretary from 1965 to 1983 where he built up a reputation as an efficient administrator who sought to tackle the growing problems of alcoholism and low worker morale well before this became politically fashionable under Andropov.

Fourthly, as Table 4.3 shows, the remarkable level of Politburo replacement between 1982 and 1988 resulted in a significantly younger top leadership. In 1981 the average age of the Politburo was 70, only three being under the age of 73. The 1981 Politburo still included the 82-year-old Latvian Arvid Pelshe who, as a delegate to the Sixth Party Congress in Petrograd in 1917, reputedly met Lenin, as well as men like Marshal Ustinov, and Foreign Minister Gromyko, whose careers had been originally 'thrust forward' by Stalin. By 1988, the average age had fallen to 62.5, only five members being older than that. More to the point, the dominant political generation in 1988 was that of men whose careers had been shaped entirely post-Stalin and to a marked degree frustrated in the latter years of Brezhnev.

Meanwhile, three cautionary points need to be considered. First, leadership recruitment remains a secretive and self-selecting matter. Whom you know clearly matters; which political 'family' or faction you belong to can count enormously. Under Brezhnev there was a marked tendency for the careers of those to flourish with whom Brezhnev had had previous career ties, notably in his native city of Dnepropetrovsk. Several of these men, the so-called Dnepropetrovsk mafia, were to be found in the Politburo itself. Under Gorbachev there are some whose careers have clearly been very closely linked to that of Gorbachev himself, such as the agriculture secretary Viktor Nikonov and Anatoli Lukyanov, also

Table 4.3 Soviet Politburo Changes, 1982–88

Politburo at Brezhnev's death	Originally elected	Deceased/ lost office	Date of birth	Politburo on 1 Nov 1988
BREZHNEV	1957	1982	1906	
KIRILENKO	1962	1982	1906	
PELSHE	1966	1983	1899	
GRISHIN	1971	1986	1914	
KUNAEV	1971	1987	1912	
SHCHERBITSKY	1971		1918	SHCHERBITSKY
ANDROPOV	1973	1984	1914	
GROMYKO	1973	1988	1909	
ROMANOV	1976	1985	1923	
USTINOV	1976	1984	1908	
CHERNENKO	1978	1985	1911	
TIKHONOV	1979	1985	1905	
GORBACHEV	1980		1931	GORBACHEV
Elected under ANDROPOV				
ALIEV	1982	1987	1923	
VOROTNIKOV	1983		1926	VOROTNIKOV
SOLOMONTSEV	1983	1988	1913	
Elected under GORBACHEV				
LIGACHEV	1985		1920	LIGACHEV
RYZHKOV	1985		1929	RYZHKOV
CHEBRIKOV	1985		1923	CHEBRIKOV
SHEVARDNADZE	1985		1928	SHEVARDNADZE
ZAIKOV	1986		1923	ZAIKOV
NIKONOV	1987		1929	NIKONOV
SLYUNKOV	1987		1929	SLYUNKOV
YAKOVLEV	1987		1923	YAKOVLEV
MEDVEDEV	1988		1929	MEDVEDEV

a student in the Moscow University Law Faculty in the early 1950s, and now a Vice-President of the Supreme Soviet and closely associated with the running of the Politburo itself.

Second, it remains as yet unanswered whether this level of élite replacement, set out in Table 4.3, is anything other than an isolated product of a specific generational crisis in the 1980s. Only two members of the Politburo recruited at any time since 1980 – Geydar Aliev, a native former First Secretary of Azerbaidzhan, and Mikhail Solomentsev, an elderly survivor from the Brezhnev era – had left office by 1988. The average age at the time of the recruitment for those elected into the post-Brezhnev Politburo was just 60, exactly the same as for those men who comprised the final Brezhnev Politburo in 1982. Gorbachev could be said to have created 'a youth opportunity programme for 55-year-olds' (Hanson 1987, p. 108). Even if the decisions taken at the Party Conference in 1988 about leadership renewals are actually implemented at every level including the Politburo (not more than two 5-year terms of office), the possibility will still exist that the system will be run by a Gorbachev gerontocracy to the end of the 1990s, in much the same way as it was in the early 1980s with the 'new thinking' somewhat in need of its own renewal. This applies at lower levels too. Over 40 out of the 72 *obkkom* secretaries in the Russian Republic were replaced between 1985 and 1987 alone, but virtually all of these were simply Brezhnev era retirements. Hardly any post-Brezhnev appointees have yet to be replaced.

Third, even 'new' leaders are extremely remote and cocooned from normal life and can be eventually very out of touch. The Brezhnev era demonstrated this only too well. As Academician Sakharov has written, the leadership 'has built its own life style, its own sharply defined position in society . . . its own language and way of thinking' and sees itself as largely irremovable (Sakharov 1975, p. 25). The Brezhnev Politburo was almost certainly unprepared for the depth and scale of global reaction to its decision to send troops to Afghanistan in 1979. More recently, the Gorbachev leadership appeared to be taken by surprise at the demonstrations and riots in Kazakhstan in 1986 following the replacement of the (corrupt but native) Kazakh First Secretary Kunaev by a Russian. Meanwhile the relative inaccessibility and unaccountability of the leadership, even in conditions of *glasnost*, has meant that the Politburo has been slow to draw satisfactory distinctions between (legitimate) élite privilege and (illegitimate) élite corruption, or to recognise that this failure in itself is politically damaging.

III. The Party's Internal Perestroika: *Can the Party Reform Itself?*

The sort of views considered above, that the secretive and closed nature of the *nomenklatura* is fundamentally unsatisfactory because it breeds irresponsible, corrupt, incompetent or degenerate leadership, have long been debated in the West, but are now being openly voiced within the Soviet Union. *Glasnost* has in part been geared to persuading the party itself that its own failings are one of the reasons for what Gorbachev has called the 'pre-crisis situation' that he inherited; that the party contains a decidedly 'inert stratum of time servers' and needs radically overhauling and democratising if it is to regain its proper vanguard role. As *Izvestia* put it in 1987, the whole *nomenklatura* system is itself an 'extremely urgent' problem. There was not just too much 'permissiveness, mutual protectionism, slackening of discipline and drunkenness', but the very 'principle of equality between communists was often violated. Many party members holding leading posts were beyond control or criticism'. The undemocratic nature of the *nomenklatura* meant that 'no strong barriers were put up in the way of dishonest, pushing, greedy people'. Or as one delegate to the 1988 Party Conference put it, 'we know more about the wealth and privilege of the British Royal Family and the Reagans than we do of our own leaders.'

Moreover the party alone, Gorbachev has argued, simply does not have the resources to run the country unaided. Non-party people have to be promoted much more readily to *nomenklatura* posts. 'Join us, you are welcome' the party theoretical journal *Kommunist* implored non-party white-collar workers in 1987. Indeed, the idea of a non-party Popular Front or Union for the promotion of *perestroika* was publicly advocated by Gorbachev advisers in 1988. For the reformers, the party's leading role was in danger of being weakened by the absence of new talent and ideas, proper criticism, and a competent level of personal morality. 'We have to win back those between the ages of 15 and 30' if *perestroika* is to succeed, argued one delegate to the 1988 Party Conference, for Komsomol membership declined from 42 to 38 million between 1985 and 1988, the number of 15-year-olds joining the youth movement dropping by as much as 25 per cent. *Demokratizatsia* was therefore not a one-off policy but a strategy aimed at achieving 'deep, really revolutionary changes in our life', not least by rebuilding the bridges between the party élite and the non-party masses.

Hence the changes proposed, though not yet fully implemented, since 1986. Party members ought to be admitted only at open meetings. The *apparat* should be regularly and competitively re-elected with secret balloting of party members, rather than appointed from above, as they were for nearly seventy years. Perhaps most strikingly of all, no-one holding elected office either in the party or the state and government apparatus should in future serve for more than two five-year terms. This might come to embrace even the Politburo itself.

At the 1988 Party Conference controversial plans for other major reforms of the political system were also adopted. These are intended to create a greater degree of public accountability for the party *apparat* and more power for the soviets. Instead of being largely impotent bodies that do little more than endorse party directives, soviets will now be expected to serve as the basic unit of local government. Party secretaries are expected to become chairmen of their local soviets, right up to republic level Supreme Soviets, and directly accountable, at least in theory, to the mass electorate not just to party members. They will now be explicitly responsible for local economic and social affairs, rather than pulling strings from behind. *Apparat* officials can therefore, in effect, be voted in or out of office. The stated aim is to weaken somewhat the iron grip of the *apparat* on local day-to-day economic and political affairs, while retaining ultimate power in the hands of the party. 'We do not abandon the role of the ruling party in the country', said Gorbachev. 'On the contrary, we want to reaffirm it.'

Thus, six powerful new Central Committee Commissions have been established at the centre, chaired by Politburo members (see Table 4.2). These are intended to make the Central Committee more publicly involved in and more responsible for key policy decisions, at the same time ensuring that the Politburo itself is better informed and less out of touch than has often been the case in the past.

Anyone reviewing the state of the Soviet Communist Party on the verge of the 1990s could point to a number of positive internal party developments in recent years such as these, as well as the promise of more to come. The reforms mentioned above, together with the tolerance and indeed limited encouragement of informal groups (*kluby*), suggest that the party might be able to meet the challenges of a more complex, more demanding era and the rise of a form of 'socialist pluralism' or civil society. The party is not going to give up its monopoly of power, but it has shown some willingness to recognise that the single party simply does not represent adequately all the interests that exist in modern society. From the point of view of the many millions of highly educated middle-class professionals in the Soviet Union, not to mention

Table 4.4   The Soviet System of Government

THE OLD SYSTEM	THE NEW SYSTEM
President of the Praesidium Nominally Head of State; presided over Supreme Court; performed largely ceremonial duties.	*President of the Supreme Soviet* Chief Executive, US-style; also General Secretary, CPSU; conducts foreign and defence policy; provides overall legislative guidance; nominates members of Council of Ministers. Elected by secret ballot of the new Congress.
Praesidium of the Supreme Soviet Its 39 members oversaw ministries and issued laws but, like the President, the Praesidium was answerable to the party.	*Praesidium of the Supreme Soviet* Its 17 Vice-Presidents, mainly from the separate republics, oversee the work of committees of the new Supreme Soviet.
Supreme Soviet Technically the highest organ of State authority, this 1,500-member legislative assembly was largely a rubber stamp for the Praesidium's decisions.	*Supreme Soviet* A smaller, two-chamber parliament with real legislative duties sitting year-round to decide specific matters; answerable to the new Congress. 422 members.
	Congress of the People's Deputies A 2,250-member forum; meets annually; decides major policy issues; elects the President and the Supreme Soviet.
Local Soviets These councils supervised departments in their area but were entirely bound by local party directives.	*Local Soviets* The councils, with enhanced authority to manage economic enterprises in their area, are presided over by the party's regional secretaries.

many of the national minority groups, society has outgrown the party. The old single-minded paternalism inherent in the Leninist model of a party-taught society, with a small party of the Marxist elect shaping society into a perfect mould, is now of limited and declining effectiveness. There is considerable awareness of all this in the party leadership, and a determination to act on it.

On the other hand, there are many less positive features about the party and *perestroika*. It is possible that the 1988 reforms, which require party secretaries to be elected as chairmen of their local soviets, will actually drag the *apparat* even more deeply into day-to-day minutiae. Meanwhile, as suggested earlier in this chapter, there are often large gaps between theory and practice in Soviet party politics. All the factors discussed earlier, which put limits on the party leadership's ability to translate policy into practice, still flourish, often to the detriment of *perestroika*. Far too many party officials, as Gorbachev has admitted, 'instead of developing innovative thinking, quite often react adversely to popular activities and initiatives, viewing them almost as a natural calamity'. Raising the political culture of party cadres, so that they are responsive to criticism and party democracy and accept these things as a necessary and not a threatening feature of public life, is not a simple matter. In the end this is not just a matter of basic competence, either. Naturally enough old habits die hard, such as planting maize in the permafrost because the central plan requires maize to be planted. What is also clear is that the *apparat*, at least in part, is actually opposed to reforms that will undermine its privileges and its power, and will therefore seek to obstruct change or penalise those who do attempt to implement reforms. Greater accountability and limited terms of office may be a step in the right direction, but will not necessarily eradicate such problems.

In short, the party leadership is aware of many self-created problems and has shown some ability in tackling them, but it has had only limited success so far in grafting *glasnost* and *demokratizatsia* onto a party machine that has traditionally ruled in other ways. The problem for the Soviet Communist Party today is that it needs such reform, but is also determined ultimately to preserve, even rejuvenate, the essentially different tradition of the party's authoritative 'leading role' in society. How far it can do both is still unclear. The process of trying to democratise a one-party oligarchy without losing control politically, socially or economically is at best a tightrope act of great difficulty.

Further Reading

Hill and Frank (1987) is a comprehensive introductory study of the CPSU. Rigby (1968) discusses party membership questions in

5

Modern Society: Tensions and Inequalities

In the days of Lenin, Soviet society was still overwhelmingly rural and illiterate, its chief preoccupations often the elemental ones of fire, frost, drought and vodka. Modern Soviet society by contrast, is increasingly complex, urbanised and educated. Two-thirds of the population now live in towns or cities, many in very large conurbations indeed. By 1986 there were 22 cities with one million or more inhabitants. Literacy is almost universal, with many millions having received higher or specialist secondary education. This vast upheaval has been a consequence of the regime's core commitment to industrialisation and has, by and large, been accepted, if only because of the widespread belief that a new and socially more egalitarian society was being developed.

How successful has the Soviet regime been in creating such a society? How serious are the tensions, the inequalities and differences that undoubtedly do exist, as they do in any country? In this chapter we shall consider these questions and their political consequences, with particular reference to four areas widely considered to be particularly significant: rural–urban divisions, class and income differentials, tensions between the party and the intelligentsia, and finally the nationalities question. We shall also consider whether the combined impact of *perestroika* and *glasnost* is in practice likely to widen or narrow such divisions. What are the social consequences of political and economic reform?

The Official View

Officially, Soviet society under socialism has traditionally been characterised as one with a high level of social unity, any existing tensions being essentially 'non-antagonistic', that is to say, temporary and relatively superficial rather than, as under capitalism, systemically ingrained. Thus there are no antagonistic classes, but instead three main social or occupational groups: manual workers, non-manual workers, and peasants. In 1983, 61.2 per cent of the population were classified as manual workers, although this included several million agricultural workers on state farms. The peasantry, 12.9 per cent, officially consisted only of those working on collective farms who were technically not waged employees of a state enterprise and therefore in Marxist ideological terms traditionally placed in a different class. In practice, if we ignore this distinction and include all agricultural workers, about one quarter of the labour force is employed on the land. This is considerably more than in many Western economies, but far fewer than in even the quite recent Soviet past: in 1959 the comparable figure was about one-third.

In 1983 non-manual workers comprised 25.9 per cent of the population. This is a very mixed group indeed, ranging from junior office workers to Politburo members, from the broad ranks of the modern specialist and technical intelligentsia with higher education, such as engineers, teachers or doctors, to the much narrower stratum of leading creative writers, artists and scientists. In this sense, the non-manual group includes not just the *nomenklatura* élite and the broad 'middle classes', but also the intellectual élite, often associated in Russian history with critical opposition to the regime. Both official and unofficial studies sometimes reflect this diversity, defining the élite and the specialist or creative intelligentsia as something apart from 'routine' non-manual workers.

This heterogeneity is increasingly a feature of the other two official social groups as well, a fact recognised in many modern Soviet sociological studies. Large numbers of the manual working class are highly skilled, and many peasants are far removed from the images that this term conjures up, often being skilled workers whose culture and aspirations are, at least in part, geared to the

mainstream of modern Soviet life. Indeed, Soviet society has been
described by Lane as 'a continuum of social groups' rather than
distinct classes (Lane 1985b, p. 173).

In reality, too, it should be stressed that, although in this
chapter we focus on division and antagonism, there are significant
factors working in favour of social unity. Class antagonism is
arguably not as sharply defined or deeply rooted as in the United
Kingdom, if only because of the enormous social upheavals of
modern times, and the still quite considerable level of social
mobility. The centrally planned non-market economy has held
regional disparities down to a lower level than almost certainly
would have been the case otherwise. Moreover, as argued in
Chapter 3, ideology and political culture both provide additional
social glue.

Nonetheless, there are real cleavages in Soviet society, and their
existence became increasingly acknowledged during the 1980s.
Gorbachev, at the 1986 27th Party Congress and in later speeches
and documents, authoritatively challenged the traditional 'non-
antagonistic' view. On the contrary, he argued, on many social
questions there was, in effect, a 'crisis': different social groups had
clearly opposing interests, and it was unrealistic to assume that
change could be accomplished without conflict. In the Soviet
context such views would have been deemed revolutionary a few
years before, but they demonstrate that in the social, as well as in
the economic and political spheres, *perestroika* has involved some
very fundamental rethinking of inherited dogmas. Just how
effectively social tensions and inequalities are handled is thus of
considerable and growing importance.

Town versus Country

The divisions between town and country operate at many levels
and, although they have declined in recent decades, are still much
more marked than in most Western societies. The official
commitment to ending 'the gap between town and country' still
has much potency, even if it is manifested by way of encouraging
peasants to live in multi-storied apartment buildings in 'rural
cities'. The sheer size of the nation and the legacy of the past both
contribute to the continuing physical and mental isolation of much

of Soviet rural life. Even in 1982 one quarter of all farms in the Russian Republic were off any normal road system. In 1975 only 8 per cent of rural families had a car. Despite a significant growth in mass car production in the 1970s, even by the end of the century ownership levels will still be about fifty years behind the West (Crouch 1985, p. 171). Of course, there are great variations nationally and the picture is by no means all negative. Rural life in Estonia is very much more advanced than in Tadzhikistan. Statistically, though, in economic, educational and cultural terms, rural life everywhere is still very disadvantaged in comparison with urban life. In recent years only half as much has been spent per head on rural shops, schools and health care provision as on urban equivalents. Thus a human exodus continues as people are drawn to the cities. The rural population fell by a total of 6.9 million in the 1970s although the rate of rural–urban migration is now less than before. Many settlements are left to the old, the women and the unskilled. In Tula province in central Russia in 1986, for example, half the 'dairymaids' were of retirement age or close to it, one third of the rural population having left the region since 1970.

All this has a knock-on effect for urban life, not least in the uncontrollable growth of towns and cities, as people continue to leave the land. This has put enormous pressure on already overstretched urban housing and services, with a consequent effect on the quality of life for almost all. The phenomenon of the *limitchiki* illustrates the point. *Limitchiki* are those who have only temporary permits to live and work in a city and often stay on illegally. There may well be one million in Moscow alone, creating considerable tensions. They have been officially accused of contributing excessively to the rising levels of crime and violence, all of which does little to alleviate the traditional urban distrust of the peasantry, noticeable in any urban food market. City dwellers frequently blame the peasantry for the scarcity and price of their food supply.

The writer Valentin Rasputin has illustrated many of these social tensions very effectively, and won a considerable popular and critical following in the process. In his 1967 short story, *Money for Maria*, Kuzma the hero, a Siberian peasant, travels by rail to a far distant city to seek his brother, who left the village long ago. He can only get a first-class ticket, and runs into much social embarrassment as a result. The middle-aged carriage attendant,

> the worse for many years of travelling, was standing at his shoulder. She took his ticket and turned it in her fingers, glancing from the ticket to him and back again several times as if she thought he must have stolen or forged it, and as if she regretted that railway tickets did not carry the passenger's photograph, for nothing could be proved without a photograph. She looked down at his boots and Kuzma looked down at them too. Against the bright glass-clean carpet his mud-stained, outsize, imitation-leather boots looked like tractor treads in a flower garden. He felt ashamed and murmured apologetically: 'I couldn't get a second or third class ticket'. 'And ain't you glad', she said viciously.
>
> (Crouch and Porter 1984, p. 133)

In reality, the town and country split is complex. There is also a distinct mixture of both anger and nostalgia at the way in which the authorities have treated the agricultural economy and rural culture in recent decades, and this is voiced by many. Rasputin's 1985 short story, *The Fire*, was a remarkably bleak account of apathy, drunkenness and isolation in a remote logging camp. Writers such as Victor Astafyev, Vasili Belov, Yuri Bondarev and others have inveighed passionately against matters such as the Brezhnev era policy of allowing tens of thousands of village settlements in the Russian Republic to die a slow, planned death in order to encourage a concentration of investment in ever larger farm units. Older traditions of pride and self-reliance, of stoicism and decency crucial to a healthy rural economy, were being neglected, they argued.

The town versus country split, even if it is psychologically, culturally and economically very real, is to some extent overlaid by regional variations. These are considerable, and appear to have changed little over time (Dellenbrant 1986). The major metropolitan cities, such as Moscow, Leningrad, and Kiev have traditionally enjoyed a disproportionate share of national resources and on many criteria the highest standards of living. They have been followed, broadly speaking, by the periphery areas such as the Baltic states of Latvia, Lithuania and Estonia, and then the Caucasian republics of Georgia and Armenia. Education and health care in these regions are higher than in central European Russia, the Ukraine or Belorussia. Car ownership rates are greater in Georgia and Estonia than anywhere other than Moscow itself; Georgians have four times the national

average in personal savings; the provision and quality of housing in
the Baltic states is markedly better than elsewhere. The Baltic
states are generally better administered and have a well-developed
industrial base and thriving small-scale agriculture. The region
also has forms of access to the outside world not readily available
elsewhere. For example in Tallinn, the Estonian capital, only a
short hydrofoil trip across the Baltic Sea from Finland, local
people can watch (and understand) Finnish television. There is a
local tradition of international commerce, via the Baltic ports,
providing a range of consumer goods inaccessible even in Moscow.
Net migration rates into the area are relatively higher than into
any other region of the country.

Meanwhile, there are regions of great relative deprivation in
provincial Russia, the Ukraine and Belorussia. The great over-
centralisation of Soviet life, coupled with deliberate efforts to
maintain traditionally higher living standards in many of the more
advanced non-Russian republics, has meant that even cities such
as Gorki, just 250 miles from Moscow, where Sakharov was
banished in 1980, far away from the Western media, are genuine
places of exile for dissidents. Chekhov regarded virtually all
nineteenth-century Russian provincial towns as boring and backward. He might well have felt the same today, particularly about
the older industrial towns of central Russia. Here in some provinces
even the urban population is in decline as people leave, not least to
join Moscow's *limitchiki*. Cities such as Vladimir or Kalinin or
Smolensk, industrialised fifty or a hundred years ago, have higher
crime rates than Moscow, pockets of unemployment and very
limited budgets. Vologda, just 500 miles north of Moscow, had a
housing waiting list that was technically 200 years long in 1986.

Although great strides have been made since the Revolution,
Soviet Central Asia remains less industrialised and poorer than the
rest of the country. In 1979 only 41 per cent of the region's
population was urban, compared to 62 per cent for the USSR as a
whole. It possesses a lower standard of living and inferior access to
various welfare programmes. Equally significant, such disparities,
and the awareness of them, appear to be on the increase. Living
standards in Central Asia grew by less than 5 per cent from
1980–85, compared with over 12 per cent for the remainder of
the USSR. This is almost certainly a factor conducive to the
development of dissident nationalism in the region (McAuley

1988). Indeed, all these urban–rural and regional variations to some extent overlap with ethnic divisions, which we shall turn to later in this chapter.

The Skilled versus the Unskilled

If town and country divisions are to some extent greater than in Western societies, wages differentials are actually rather less. This is despite the fact that Soviet society is meritocratic, particular or scarce skills being rewarded with additional income as they are elsewhere. Stalin denounced wage levelling in 1930 as 'naive . . . we cannot tolerate a situation where a rolling mill operator in a steel plant earns no more than a janitor'. To encourage the development of a skilled industrial workforce, large wage differentials have subsequently been deemed essential. The variations, though less than in many capitalist economies, are still large. In 1982 the average Soviet wage was 177.3 roubles a month. Many skilled professionals were earning three times that, the military élite ten times, and the top political leadership undisclosed sums. Skilled male manual workers were relatively well paid: whereas miners were earning an average of 300 roubles, librarians were receiving only 110 roubles a month. Women earned less than men: only 60 to 70 per cent of the average male pay rate, being less skilled, and clustered in industries or professions that have traditionally been low paid, such as education or the health service. Moreover women, in a male-dominated society, continue to undertake the greater burden of domestic chores, too, a situation of which men appear to approve. On average, women spend up to 30 hours a week on housework, compared to only 12 hours for men.

At the very bottom end of the social scale there is real poverty. It has been argued that 40 per cent of urban workers are below an 'acceptable' level of income, including Stalin's janitors, as well as cleaners, drivers, storemen and pensioners, many of whom were on the minimum monthly pension of 45 roubles, although it must be stressed that welfare safety nets have been improved (Matthews, 1986). Collective farm workers for instance have since 1967 been guaranteed a minimum basic wage, which means that they are not as dependent on the vagaries of the weather as before, and less rooted to a subsistence economy. Overall, wage differentials are thus not only somewhat less than in capitalist economies, but have narrowed in recent years.

This narrowing or levelling has been most marked between managerial and technical staff on the one hand and skilled manual workers on the other. Whereas in 1940 the former earned on average twice the wages of the latter, by 1982 the advantage had shrunk to little more than 10 per cent. Or to put it another way, 'wage drift' under Brezhnev resulted in manual workers' incomes generally rising faster than productivity. As a consequence, the argument has increasingly been heard in recent years that there has again been 'too much levelling of wages': skilled managerial and technical cadres should be paid appropriately if they are to shoulder responsibilities. This has clearly not always happened. In a 1984 survey, an extraordinary 72 per cent of middle-level farm managers replied that they wanted to be demoted because they didn't consider 'the value placed on the job was in keeping with its actual complexity'. Greater wage differentials are needed if skill and responsibility are to be adequately rewarded, argue the reformers.

Wages and statistics, however, do not tell the whole story. Wages can be as much as doubled in Siberia and the Far North for comparable jobs, but the cost of living is much greater, the climate harsh and the distances back to family and friends enormous. In practice, net migration to these regions, particularly to Western Siberia, has only come about within the past decade, and at the cost of very high rates of labour turnover (Helgeson 1982, p. 131).

There is another and more serious point behind the bare statistics. It is not just money, but *blat* (connections) that matters in Soviet society, scarce goods often being allocated not by money but by whom you know. The élite, of course, has access to hand-tooled ZIL limousines, servants, closed shops, dachas, foreign travel, private coaching and privileged entry to prestige educational institutes for its offspring (Matthews 1978). But many quite ordinary people are also caught up in this inevitable pattern: if supply and demand are badly out of line, then various more or less black markets arise, housing being a classic case.

Soviet housing allocation has frequently been corrupt – not just in the spectacular ways of Kazakhstan in the 1980s, where as much as 80 per cent of the housing was reportedly allocated corruptly, but more commonly in the quite low-level manner that often applies in a 'society of connections'. A good flat is one of the scarcest commodities, and to get one quickly it is necessary to be well connected. 'Too often the decisive factor is not the waiting list, but a sudden telephone call . . . (after which) they give the flats to football players and the whole queue is pushed back', *Pravda* explained in 1973. A middle-aged lady in Astrakhan on the Volga was rumoured to have a contact with an important member of the City's executive committee. She asked 800 to 2,500 roubles for a flat. In four years some forty desperate flat-seekers, including professional people and party members, paid her a total of 50,000 roubles in bribes, before it was discovered that she had no contacts at all (Morton 1980, p. 251). Such corruption is by no means universal. Nonetheless, to put it no higher, much social life is a matter of unofficial interconnecting networks of friends and acquaintances providing mutual favours.

The existence of this informal economy poses two political problems. First, to the extent that it is associated with privilege and power, it is widely seen as ideologically and culturally illegitimate. The official value system puts a premium on inconspicuous consumption, as it were, rather than on the flaunting of wealth and material gains. Brezhnev was very proud of his private fleet of cars and his opulent dachas, but this monopoly of perquisites could never be easily paraded on, say, Soviet television. Secondly, even at the everyday level, when it is not necessarily a matter of privilege, let alone corruption, it still creates patterns that are fundamentally corrupting to individuals and highly damaging to social cohesion. Such disparities raise afresh basic questions about injustice and inequality that the Revolution was to have solved, as Gorbachev has argued on numerous occasions.

Perestroika and the Problems of Economic Inequality

In a sense such problems are manageable. The inequalities which we have outlined are probably inevitable in modern society, given the continued existence of the family and of the division of labour, which is apparently inseparable from an industrialised economy. However, there is evidence that such divisions are more entrenched than they were a generation or two ago. Soviet social mobility, though still relatively high, has declined as economic growth rates have levelled out. It is less easy to progress upwards from a peasant background than it was fifty years ago, and more likely than it was then that military officers will be the sons of military officers. In the past, if only because social mobility was so relatively easy, many benefited from hierarchy and there was still a widespread belief in equality of opportunity through the education system (Yanowitch 1977, p. 91). But by the 1980s all of this was less obvious, as the gap between rising expectations and a slowly changing reality widened. Hence the disillusionment encapsulated in the Brezhnev era saying, 'they pretend to pay us, and we pretend to work'.

One of the most effective proponents of economic *perestroika* has been Academician Tatiana Zaslavskaya, a leading Soviet sociologist. Her views and those of other reform academics have done much to shape the party leadership's thinking. Zaslavskaya argued in the party's theoretical journal *Kommunist* in 1985 that the Soviet Union had to develop a high-wage, high-output economy if it was to compete internationally (and incidentally cope with a real problem of labour shortage in many parts of European Russia). To reinvigorate the economy, better human incentives were needed. The most effective incentive was no longer – if it ever had been – a Stakhanovite storming campaign or a Hero of Socialist Labour medal, but quite simply money and an adequate supply of goods and services for that money to be spent on which would put an end to the attractions and corruptions of *blat*. 'Socialist justice consists first in encouraging and supporting those groups that make the greatest contribution to social development, and second in exercising social oversight over, and economically regulating, the status of those groups that put narrow occupational, departmental or localistic concerns above social interests and do harm to social development.'

The 'gap between price and value', therefore, needed to be eradicated, meaning in practice that prices had to rise. The traditional blanket subsidies on food or housing were not necessarily socialist. 'Socialist justice is not just providing equal opportunities for all' (and there was still some way to go here); it is not just a matter of providing freedom of career choice, or an anti-poverty net; it is also about 'making those who can pay more'. Meat prices, for instance, had been fixed since 1962, after the

Novocherkassk food riots, so that by 1987, though meat was still priced at 1 rouble 80 kopeks a kilo, the state was providing a subsidy of about 3 roubles per kilo, involving in reality an enormous though hidden redistribution of wealth in the wrong direction (Aganbegyan 1988, p. 178). Similarly with housing, some selective redistribution was needed. Rents had been fixed since 1928. Was it socially just to pay equally for unequal benefits? To pay 3 per cent of a monthly wage for a flat on Gorki Prospect in central Moscow, and exactly the same for a flat in a muddy sidestreet of Vologda or Irkutsk?

Wages, too, needed to be more unequal in order to benefit the skilled. In 1987 Gorbachev pushed this message home, arguing that 'there should be no limits on . . . legitimate wage levels'. The intention has been not just to create a more productive high-wage work force but, as it were, to outflank the black market with a high-output economy. This was crucial, because, as Zaslavskaya put it, the 'human factor' (motivation) was an essential part of *perestroika*, and one aspect of this has to be 'that everyone's rouble should have equal buying power'. At present this was not so, argued Zaslavskaya, because 'different social groups' as a consequence of privilege, corruption and so on, had 'unequal access [to scarce goods]'.

What consequences for society and politics does such a reform strategy portend? First, *glasnost* exacerbated tensions by publicising to an unprecedented degree the nature and extent of inequalities and differences. Second, economic reform could well widen rather than narrow regional differences. It is likely to widen differentials, too, particularly if higher prices are accompanied by lower wages as a result of cuts in bonus payments stemming from tougher quality control checks. (Bonuses are estimated to have accounted for between 15 per cent and 40 per cent of average manual wages in recent years, but since 1986 many workers have lost most or all of such payments.)

Politically, therefore, the leadership needs to persuade society that such inequalities – even widening ones – are either temporary or justified. This may not be easy. How are distinctions to be made between acceptable and unacceptable inequalities? Are élite perquisites a justifiable reward for great responsibility? As Gorbachev put it in 1986, 'long-established ideas' are difficult to shift, and 'unfortunately there is a widespread view that any change in the economic mechanism is practically a retreat from the principles of socialism'. But, unless existing and possibly widening inequalities can be shown to be justified, the attempt at *perestroika* will have failed in a primary task. Recent debates attempting to redefine inequality and justify it ideologically as well as pragmatically show that the leadership is aware of this, but it will not be easy to persuade either the party faithful or the non-party masses that some of the most sacred characteristics of Soviet life, promulgated for decades as the epitome of socialism (cheap housing and public transport, 'free' health education and welfare) are 'unsocialist' after all.

The Technical Elites versus the Party *Apparat*

Regional and class inequalities are by no means confined to the Soviet Union. By contrast, we now turn to a problem that does have a distinctively Soviet air to it, but which has changed very markedly over time, namely that between the party apparatus and the professional and technical élites. This is a division that still carries considerable political resonance but is now in most respects far removed from the destructiveness of earlier decades when the clash between Bolsheviks and 'bourgeois specialists' was a major fact of life.

Ideologically, the latter were not to be trusted and yet, at least in the early days, their skills were needed simply because the Revolution had not yet trained its own cadres who would be both 'red' and specialist. Many bourgeois specialists, as well as creative writers and artists, did in practice throw in their lot with the Bolshevik Revolution, but the party had at best a wary tolerance of such types and as time passed this gradually crumbled. The Stalin revolution encouraged this trend with show trials from 1928 onwards of apparently treacherous bourgeois specialists; and with the rapid rise after that date of a new technical intelligentsia, young men from working-class or peasant backgrounds 'thrust forward' through the new party schools and trained to take command of the new Soviet state.

Such specialists, part of an arrogant but insecure new ruling orthodoxy, were imbued with the revolutionary belief that there were, so to speak, no heights the Bolsheviks could not storm.

The old intelligentsia, paradoxically, had often been the most Westernising stratum in Tsarist and early revolutionary society. Many of the legal norms, educational reforms and technological advances that had been developed were largely their doing. Thus, as the dissident writer Shragin has commented, 'the Bolshevik revolution was not a break with the past but a reaction of the old Russia against the incursion of genuine Europeanisation' (Shragin 1978, p. 153). By the 1930s, as the poet Mandelstam was to discover when forced to beg for translating work, the standard response from the new Stalinist cadres to the old intelligentsia was *'ne treba'* (we do not need it) (Mandelstam 1975, p. 309).

And indeed they did not. A striking feature of the Stalin era was that distinctions between what might be termed technical and political authority were often disregarded. In the rush to build a new world, the party came to lay down the ideological law on all matters, no field of human activity being excluded. As late as 1948, for example, the music of Prokofiev and Shostakovitch was denounced as 'formalist' and 'anti-democratic'. Stalin himself was to spend time writing authoritative ideological articles on philosophy or mathematics, psychoanalysis or linguistics.

The most inglorious example of this pattern can be seen in the Lysenko affair. For a generation, Trofim Lysenko symbolised the utopian belief that the Revolution could take short cuts, that all problems could be solved, and that bourgeois specialists with their cautious traditions were indeed not needed. Lysenko had a long career under Stalin and was even described by Khrushchev as 'the ideal Soviet scientist', but in reality he was a semi-literate peasant who had initially come to Stalin's attention as a 'barefoot scientist', a simple *muzhik* with homespun and optimistic solutions to complex agricultural questions. This was an age when many held uncomplicated views about the class nature of knowledge, and Lysenko's curious mixture of ingenious and crackpot ideas proved highly infectious. He came to preside over a large share of Soviet science culminating in a major routing of the scientific élite in the Academy of Sciences in 1948. The Lysenkoites hounded to their deaths many honest and gifted people, such as the geneticist Nikolai Vavilov, and did untold damage to Soviet science, particularly agro-biology and genetics. Lysenko denounced genetics as a 'bourgeois science'. Nothing was bred in the bone, as it were. Environment and self-improvement were all. A lap dog in an appropriately wild environment would eventually sire a wolf, wheat could turn into rye, and – by extension – ordinary man into New Soviet Man.

Lysenko and his followers were only routed politically after the overthrow of Khrushchev in 1964, and as a result of a slow-burning revolt within the Soviet scientific and academic élite (Z. Medvedev, 1969). Lysenkoism has officially been damned since that time, his victims such as Vavilov being gradually rehabilitated, if only posthumously. This is not least because it illustrated better than anything else the dangers inherent in not distinguishing between political power and technical or professional authority. The damage done to Soviet science was incalculable and lasting, and right through the Brezhnev and post-Brezhnev years Soviet writers and journalists have continued to hammer home the point that a leading position in world science in the 1920s and 1930s was irrationally thrown away.

On the surface some lessons have therefore been well learnt. As Andropov put it in 1982 in a notable admission for a Soviet leader, 'we do not have all the answers'. Moreover, of course, modern Soviet professional and technical élites have long since been both 'red' and specialist. The intelligentsia today is essentially the creation of the modern Soviet educational system and is, in a sense, the major supporter and client of the regime (Churchward, 1973). Furthermore, Lysenkoism itself is now light years away psychologically: the very idea that specialists are not needed, or that Einstein's theory of relativity could be dismissed as 'bourgeois' is unthinkable. The old division between technical and political élites still exists, as mentioned in Chapter 4, but it has narrowed significantly. This in itself is one of the more notable examples of political development since Stalin.

Let us now take this a little further by taking as a case study perhaps the most dramatic and long-lasting of all these divides, that between the creative literary intelligentsia and the state.

The Writers and the State: A Case Study

Writers have been especially significant in Russian and Soviet history. The sheer power of the written word and of ideas in a traditionally closed society has made writers social tribunes, of a kind that has rarely existed elsewhere. Nineteenth-century Russian history was peculiarly dominated by the critical and literary intelligentsia rather than by the Tsar or his ministers. Soviet leaders retained some awe about this power. As Mandelstam put it in the 1930s, 'here they kill poets for their ideas'. Modern leaders, while not doing that, are still deeply involved in what is written and published by the nation's literary élite. Gorbachev, speaking to the Writers' Union Congress in 1986, characteristically said, 'you cannot imagine how much we need the support of a group such as the writers' if *perestroika* is to be made irreversible.

There is a paradox here. The regime needs writers to express ideas and debate selected questions, for by definition they are often better able to articulate and debate contemporary questions than political leaders. Many writers accept this highly instrumental role, for the tradition of social and political commitment is a deep one. The idea that intellectuals should shoulder some responsibility for creating a better society was crystallised in the debates between Nikolai Gogol and Vissarion Belinskii as long ago as the 1850s – debates about art for art's sake, with Belinskii declaring that 'a pair of boots for a peasant is worth all the poetry of Pushkin'.

Yet despite this tradition, the authorities have also feared writers, for they have feared unfettered debate. Literature may be a vehicle for positively inculcating regime values and attitudes, but it is also a potentially explosive phenomenon that needs to be controlled and censored, not least in the century of mass literacy. (Illiteracy itself was the most effective censor in Tsarist times.) Hence the very tight controls that have usually been imposed on Soviet publishing. From 1934 until 1987 writers were hardly ever allowed to publish their works unless they had the approval of the Writers' Union. Censorship covered several hundred categories of forbidden topic, ranging from domestic floods, earthquakes or epidemics, plane or rail disasters to the more usual areas of military and state security; from evidence of any improvements in living standards under capitalism to the very existence of censorship itself (Dewhirst and Farrell 1973, p. 56). At best, therefore, this has been a tense relationship, the writers both a useful adjunct to the state and a potentially oppositionist group. But what is perhaps most striking is how this relationship has changed with time.

Stalin and the Rise of Socialist Realism

With the Revolution literary life blossomed anew, but by 1934 Stalin had created in the Writers' Union a single bureaucracy of control which systematically sought to promote a specific genre of literature known as Socialist Realism. This meant, according to the old revolutionary writer Maxim Gorki, the figurehead of the new Writers' Union, that Soviet literature had to be geared to upholding socialist values, and had to be realistic (i.e. not grotesque or fantastic: easily comprehensible). Stalin, in an immortal phrase, saw writers as the 'engineers of the human soul', their very clear public function being to inspire and uplift the masses. Seventy-five per cent of all pre-1934 Soviet literature, Stalin said quite categorically, had been 'useless'.

The results, predictably, were optimistic novels about constructing the brave new world of industry, modelled on early prototypes such as Fyodor Gladkov's *Cement* (1925). The heroes were largely two-dimensional figures, such as Pavel Korchagin in Nikolai Ostrovsky's *How the Steel was Tempered*, who rejected his first love because she was bourgeois, and his second love because marriage, he argued, should wait until the world revolution had been achieved. A common theme was what has been widely and irreverently dubbed 'boy meets tractor'.

This directed writing was not necessarily without literary merit. Valentin Katayev's *Time Forward!* was a vivid and clever attempt to portray the building of a giant steel complex at Magnitogorsk in the Urals. The theme was the speeding up of time in a country where the historical development of a century must be completed in ten years, and Katayev devised techniques which conveyed a vivid impression of time in movement: objects were always in motion and landscapes were usually seen through the windows of moving trains. Equally, not all socialist realist literature conformed to the ideological canons. Mikhail Sholokhov's epic work on the Don Cossacks, *Quiet Flows the Don* (which effectively won him the Nobel Prize for Literature years later in 1965) was essentially a eulogy to the Cossack way of life which was being destroyed by the forces of revolution. But it was universally popular, not least with Stalin. So too, was Mikhail Bulgakov's play *The Days of the Turbins*, impeccably bourgeois and Ukrainian in its ideology, but with sufficient blood and thunder to appeal to Stalin. Moreover, as the Stalin era progressed, much of its literary output was written to appeal to an increasingly unrevolutionary élite. Acquiring pink lampshades became a more common activity than striving to retain revolutionary asceticism (Dunham 1976).

In short, this pulp fiction may or may not have been socialist, but it certainly filled a need at a time of burgeoning literacy. As late as 1926, at least 50 per cent of the population were illiterate, but by 1939 only 10 per cent were – a remarkable achievement by any standards (Pethybridge 1974, p. 183). The corresponding cost was also very great. The old critical intelligentsia was literally destroyed ('we do not need it') and a new society created that, although it could read, operated within a very rigid and hierarchical framework of thought. The 'thrust forward' generation of these times meanwhile ruled Soviet politics and public life until the 1980s.

The Post-Stalin Era and the Decline of Socialist Realism

Khrushchev calculatingly used writers such as Solzhenitsyn as part of his de-Stalinisation campaign. But, more generally after 1953, a thaw set in which resulted in a wider range of works being published, some quite critical of Soviet reality. Vladimir Dudintsev's novel, *Not by Bread Alone*, caused a considerable stir in 1956 by criticising bureaucrats and suggesting that the planned economy showed insufficient tolerance towards new inventions. Where did unplanned genius and serendipity fit into the Five-Year-Plan? From time to time, though, the thaw froze over again. Boris Pasternak's novel, *Dr Zhivago*, was roundly attacked, Pasternak himself being dismissed as a 'pig' and a 'weed' and bullied into renouncing the Nobel Prize for Literature which he was awarded in 1958.

Under Brezhnev the freeze appeared to go deeper. Many of the more talented writers and artists, scientists and scholars left the Soviet Union in what was often described as the Third Wave of emigration since 1917 (the others having been in 1917–21 and 1945). Writers of real talent who left included Vasili Aksyonov and Vladimir Voinovich. Voinovich had written a highly subversive comic epic during the 1960s and 1970s entitled *The Life and Adventures of Private Ivan Chonkin*, which succeeded not only in ridiculing the Soviet war effort but in suggesting that life itself was a comedy with no inner meaning. The eponymous hero was a good-natured peasant conscript whose best efforts only succeeded in unintentionally making fools of the party, the secret police, of Hitler and of Stalin himself. Aksyonov, typically, had made his mark under Khrushchev, only to become increasingly frustrated and disillusioned in later years, backing the unofficial publication of a samizdat anthology, *Metropol*, in 1979. Solzhenitsyn, meanwhile, was denounced on behalf of the regime by Sholokhov as a 'colorado beetle', anathematised and physically expelled in 1974.

Despite such frustration and waste the regime's licensed literary élite was by no means just a sycophantic chorus. On the contrary, slowly and sometimes painfully an articulate literary intelligentsia continued its post-Stalin re-emergence (Hosking 1980). Some individuals, despite all the pressures, achieved both popular and critical success and did so moreover with works that were far removed in philosophy from the obligatory optimism of Socialist Realism.

Thus, the highly influential 'village prose' writers of the 1960s and 1970s helped crystallise a national mood of doubt about the nature of Progress, and did much to encourage the rebirth of a powerful sense of Russian nationalism. Vasili Shukshin, for example, starred in a hugely popular film based on one of his stories, *The Red Snowberry Tree* (1973). This was a eulogy to the lost rural past and its supposed moral purity and, remarkably, was lavishly praised by two of the most diverse figures imaginable at the time – the exiled Solzhenitsyn and Brezhnev himself. Others, such as Rasputin, focused attention on the environmental costs of modern life. His heroes had seen the future and did not like it very much.

Urban writers such as Yuri Trifonov concentrated on the unavoidable corruptions and queues of Soviet life. The real heroes, he argued, were not the constructors of cement factories or steel mills, or valiant wartime soldiers, but ordinary people coping with the routine of everyday life (for which phenomenon, appropriately, there is a single, terse Russian word, *byt*). Moreover, like many modern Soviet writers, he proposed no solutions and offered no didactic moral. 'The writer' he said, quoting Chekhov, 'is the pain, not the doctor'.

Then there were the 'fraternal writers' from the non-Russian republics, such as the Kirghiz Chingiz Aitmatov, whose stories could be deeply tragic. In *The White Steamship* (1970) the hero was a seven-year-old who appeared to commit suicide at the end of the story, when his emotional world was destroyed after he discovered that his beloved grandfather had drunkenly slaughtered a white deer, sacred to the Kirghiz folk tradition. Aitmatov consistently explored the theme of folk memory and tradition, not least in the context of the Russification of Central Asian culture since 1917. In an influential novel published in 1980, *The Day Lasts More than a Hundred Years*, Aitmatov produced a powerful metaphor of imperialism with his account of how prisoners of the Mongols were turned into *mankurts*, memoryless slaves, by having their shaven heads wrapped in wet camel's skin. As it dried, the skin shrank, encasing the skulls and destroying forever the memory. Aitmatov's writing could be seen as a comment on the traditional Russian tendency to patronise the Central Asians as if they had had no pre-1917 existence. On the contrary: as Aitmatov's seven-year-old argues in *The White Steamship*, the Islamic peoples had a very well-developed sense of their own past. It was individual Russians who did not know the obligatory seven generations of their family trees and, he tells a visiting Russian soldier: 'Grandfather said that, if people don't remember their fathers, they'll turn bad.' 'Don't you listen to him', says the Russian. 'We're marching to Communism, we're flying in space – and what's he teaching you . . .? He's an ignorant one, backward.'

Despite the regime's best attempts, and without reading too much into such works, Soviet writers did achieve a relatively effective place as licensed critics and debaters under Brezhnev. The consistency and range of debate was far wider than at any previous time, and often quite critical of Soviet reality, sometimes exposing very painful nerves. Trifonov, in a major novel *The Old Man* (1978) for example, managed to say some bitter things about Bolshevik morality in the Civil War. Rasputin's short story *Live and Remember* (1974) dealt sympathetically with, of all things, a deserter from the Great Patriotic War of 1941–5. He returns to his home village and makes his wife pregnant. She, not wanting to betray her husband, admits to an illicit affair. Finally she commits suicide, driven to despair in the knowledge of the disgrace to which the birth of an apparently illegitimate child would expose her. Apart from anything else, here was the village community as an informing, gossipy, closed tyranny.

Other writers, such as Alexander Kron in his novel *Insomnia* (1977), managed to convey very effectively the personal betrayals and compromises that dominated academic life at the time of Lysenko in the late 1940s, which still dogged the elderly in their scientific careers even in the 1970s. On the surface the past has been buried, but in private there are some very tortured consciences, the prevailing insomnia not being confined to ex-Lysenkoite witch-hunters either: one of Kron's points is that most of those who held public positions and survived those years are compromised figures, even those who subsequently de-Stalinised with some enthusiasm.

Gorbachev and the Writers

Gorbachev's *glasnost* policy, as suggested in Chapter 2, was thus an evolutionary rather than a revolutionary development, but it did nonetheless have a dramatic impact on the literary world. In 1986 the Writers' Union replaced its old leaders, voting in writers and reformists to its board of management. With the party's consent, it agreed to scrap the organ of censorship, *glavlit*, that had so emasculated Soviet letters since the days of Lenin. Just as important, *glasnost* encouraged a real change in attitudes, with editors now much more prepared to take responsibility for what they published. The state publishing monopoly has gone too. Many writers since 1986 have set up, or been encouraged to set up, publishing co-operatives of their own with the full backing of the Writers' Union. Again, the motivation is at least in part pragmatic: the Soviet Union has very few young writers. In 1982 only 3 per cent of the members of the Writers' Union were under the age of 40; in 1987 the Moscow branch had no one under the age of 30. Loosening the rules of publication was seen as the quickest way to reinvigorate Soviet letters.

The policy of *glasnost*, too, has had a dramatic impact not just on the range of subject matter open to discussion, as outlined in

Chapter 3, but on the audience that it encompasses. Debates under Brezhnev were largely within or between the élites. To take a literary example: although Bulgakov and Mandelstam were rehabilitated in the 1970s, their works were republished in very limited editions. Bulgakov's masterpiece, *The Master and Margarita*, completed in 1940, was published for the first time in the Soviet Union in 1973, but, of the print run of only 30,000, all but 4,000 copies were exported. In contrast, the policy of *glasnost* since 1985 has involved newspapers and journals, film and television, thus reaching tens of millions of people day after day. The longer-term impact is thus incalculable, as journals start to compete for readers in the knowledge that paper and print supplies are no longer allocated solely by bureaucratic whim and that literacy and journalistic success is now not dependent on merely regurgitating the party line. The circulation of the literary monthly *Novy Mir* increased from 400,000 to one million between 1985 and 1988, for example.

As for the writers under Gorbachev, two strands have become apparent. First, writers from the past, whose works have been banned for decades are now being published, the stored-up cultural legacy of several generations. Pasternak's *Dr Zhivago* appeared in the mass circulation monthly *Novy Mir* in 1988, for example. Anna Akhmatova's poetic lament, *Requiem*, to the memory of her husband and son and all of Stalin's victims, was similarly published in *Oktyabr*, at one time under Brezhnev *Novy Mir's* chief opponent, in 1987. The wartime epic of Vasili Grossman, *Life and Fate*, the deeply anti-Stalinist works of Andrei Platonov, the poetry of Nikolai Gumilyev and even the still living dissident poet Joseph Brodsky, who emigrated in 1972 and won the Nobel Prize for Literature in 1987, are other notable examples. Meanwhile, the youth magazine *Yunost* planned to serialise Voinovich's *The Life and Adventures of Private Ivan Chokin* in 1989.

Secondly, much new or recently published work has opened up fresh areas for political debate. The elderly Anatoli Rybakov published a major autobiographical novel in 1987, *Children of the Arbat*, which dealt with the purge years, the murder of Kirov at Stalin's behest in 1934, and the exile to Siberia of the 22-year-old hero on unsubstantiated charges of political subversion. Rybakov depicted a harsh and brutal peasant life in Siberia, contrasting it with the pampered lives of the children of the élite (the Arbat being Moscow's equivalent of London's Hampstead or Washington's Georgetown). He also portrayed Stalin more unsympathetically than any previously published Soviet novel had done. From his Georgian seminary days onwards, Stalin is seen as a cynical, suspicious and cruel manipulator for whom socialism is a nonsense, and the peasants merely a lesser breed of sub-humans.

Other writers, too, have had their say. Vasily Bykov wrote about the disastrous impact of collectivisation in paving the way for the low morale of 1941. The peasants by then were so disaffected that they turned to the Germans as liberators. Sergei Zalygin wrote about the New Economic Policy of the 1920s as a period to learn from, rather than as a desperate prologue to a necessary Stalinist collectivisation, which had been the traditional and ideologically correct approach in the past. Aitmatov, in *The Executioner's Block*, dealt with the contemporary drugs problem, notably Central Asian hashish, as the real opium of the people, quoting among other things large chunks of the New Testament, no mean breakthrough in a land where the Bible has been virtually unobtainable for decades.

These are cases of writers at the cutting edge of *glasnost*, as it were. Even so, it is important to stress that functionally, just as under Stalin or Brezhnev, such work is in a tradition of public affairs writing designed to encourage support for the policies of the regime. It may follow from this and from the Brezhnev era that Soviet literature is at best now rather limited both as a literary and as a cultural phenomenon. Few would claim Aitmatov, Zalygin or Rybakov as writers of the very first rank, and many members of the Writers' Union have in practice used *glasnost* to do nothing more than settle old literary quarrels. Meanwhile, film makers have had at least as considerable an impact since 1985. Films such as Abuladze's *Repentance*, a complex and powerfully surreal attack on Stalin and Beria, have been important cultural events in their own right.

Nevertheless, the relationship between the writers and the state has changed markedly since Brezhnev as well as since Stalin. The writers have greater latitude than before, both in what they say and do and in how they regulate themselves. Many of the more significant have become once again, as in the nineteenth century, tribunes of a nascent civil society, almost a national aristocracy

that shapes opinion and influences public policy: people who are
needed but are also not quite controlled by the regime. Indeed,
their significance not just for what they write but for the campaigns
and issues that they address as public citizens has increased
markedly since Brezhnev, particularly on environmental issues.
The 'destruction' of the Russian countryside, the continuing
pollution of lakes and rivers and the Chernobyl disaster have all
been passionately debated. The war novelist Yuri Bondarev, put it
thus at the Writers' Union Congress in 1986:

> If we do not stop the destruction of the monuments of our architecture,
> if we do not stop the rape of our earth and rivers, if there is not a moral
> explosion in our science and criticism, then one fine morning . . . will
> be the last, and . . . we with our inexhaustible optimism will wake up
> and understand that the national culture of vast Russia has been wiped
> out, gone for good, has been done away with, destroyed for ever.

Note here the distinctly Russian nationalist tone of his remarks.
Bondarev went on to remark that 'our culture' is more than
'merely a Russian form of Pepsi-Cola'. The tensions between the
Soviet intelligentsia and the party apparatus may have decreased
over time, as the case of the writers suggests, and as the experience
of others such as the military, legal and scientific élites confirms.
The party is clearly much more inclined than in the past to work
with the intelligentsia, accepting that there are spheres of
competence beyond its grasp. But the tensions between the
nationalities in the Soviet Union have, if anything, become deeper
than before. It is to this problem, arguably the most intractable
and complex of all the domestic political tensions facing the Soviet
leadership, that we now turn.

The Soviet Nationalities Question

In December 1986 nationalist political disturbances in the city of
Alma Ata, the capital of the Central Asian republic of Kazakhstan
and on the old silk road from China, claimed the lives of up to fifty
people. In August 1987 unofficial mass rallies took place in the
Baltic States protesting at the forcible incorporation of Estonia,
Latvia and Lithuania into the Soviet Union under the 1939 Nazi–
Soviet pact, and demanding independence. At the same time

several hundred Tartars demonstrated outside the Kremlin demanding to be allowed to return to their traditional homelands in the Crimea from which they had been forcibly removed by Stalin. In 1988 mass disturbances in Armenia caused chaos as the largest unofficial political movement since 1917 protested at the treatment of Armenians in the mountainous enclave of Nagorno-Karabakh in the adjoining Muslim republic of Azerbaidzhan.

Arguably, these and other incidents were isolated affairs, but they are symptomatic of the fact that, as Gorbachev has said, the nationalities question is 'the most complex area of social relations' within the Soviet Union. This awareness is not new. Lenin called the Tsarist Empire 'the prison house of nations'. The British MP Henry Norman wrote in 1902 of how 'thoughtful Russians' were aware that the Empire was 'showing signs of going to pieces' (Norman 1902, p. 450). The dissident mathematician Igor Shafarevich wrote in 1974 that 'of all the urgent problems that have accumulated in our life, the most painful seems to be that concerning relations between the various nationalities of the USSR. No other question arouses such explosions of resentment, malice and pain' (Shafarevich 1974, p. 88).

Any such tensions in a sense are understandable, for the Soviet Union is the largest multinational state in the world and its national and ethnic complexities are by any standards extraordinary. There are over one hundred ethnic, tribal or linguistic groups recognised officially of which 22 have populations of one million or more, as set out in Table 5.1. Although Russians are dominant with, in 1979, 137.4 million people, they comprised at that time only 52.4 per cent of the population. Other Slavs, Ukrainians and Belorussians accounted for a further 51.8 million people, so that Slavs as a whole comprised 72.2 per cent of the population. Beyond this, however, there was and is a bewildering variety, ranging from the principal groups many of which have their own union republics to very small clans which are recognised by at best autonomous republics or regions within the larger republics. Table 5.1 gives some indication of this, with the fifteen major ethnic groups – each with their own Union Republic – listed first, followed by the most populous of the others. Some of these have their own territories, notably Autonomous Republics within the Russian Republic itself, but others are of geographically much more scattered type.

Table 5.1 *Ethnic Composition of the Soviet Union*

	Number (thousands)		% of total population	
	1959	*1979*	*1959*	*1979*
Total Population	208,827	262,085	100	100
Slavs				
Russians	114,114	137,397	54.6	52.4
Ukrainians	37,253	42,347	17.8	16.2
Belorussians	7,913	9,463	3.8	3.6
Western Nationality Groups				
Latvians	1,400	1,439	0.7	0.5
Lithuanians	2,326	2,851	1.1	1.1
Estonians	989	1,020	0.5	0.4
Moldavians	2,214	2,968	1.1	1.1
The Caucasian Peoples				
Georgians	2,692	3,571	1.3	1.4
Armenians	2,787	4,151	1.3	1.6
Azerbaidzhanis	2,940	5,477	1.4	2.1
The Central Asians				
Uzbeks	6,015	12,456	2.9	4.8
Kazakhs	3,622	6,556	1.7	2.5
Tadzhiks	1,397	2,898	0.7	1.1
Turkmenians	1,002	2,028	0.5	0.8
Kirghiz	969	1,906	0.5	0.7
Other Territorial Groups				
Tartars	4,968	6,317	2.4	2.4
Chuvash	1,470	1,751	0.7	0.7
Bashkirs	989	1,371	0.5	0.5
Mordvinians	1,285	1,192	0.6	0.5
Non-Territorial Groups				
Germans	1,620	1,936	0.7	0.7
Jews	2,268	1,811	1.1	0.7
Poles	1,380	1,151	0.7	0.4

The official view traditionally was that nationalism did not amount to a problem. It was a product of feudal or capitalist exploitation. Nation states would wither away after the worldwide socialist revolution, people merging into one internationalist brotherhood for, as Marx put it, 'the working man has no country'.

'A new historical community, the Soviet people', would arise, said the 1961 Party Programme.

But, for three main reasons, it was never that simple. First, the Soviet Union was from the outset an historic compromise between the Bolsheviks in Moscow and a series of often deeply anti-Muscovite but also anti-Tsarist national élites in the wider Empire. To hold it all together, compromises had to be made, with central party control on the one hand, but a framework of federal institutions and a theory to go with it on the other. These compromises were acceptable to the centralising Bolsheviks, for in the end they were determined to preserve the territorial sanctity of the Empire, if only to maintain the economic self-sufficiency that the Russian state had traditionally enjoyed. Nonetheless the result was an odd one, with constitutional provisions allowing the secession of individual republics and separate United Nations membership for the Ukraine and Belorussia, but very little evidence that this was anything more than window dressing.

The second complication was to do with merging: into what did the peoples of the Empire assimilate? Officially the answer was a collective new Soviet patriotism. This at least had (and still has) the merit that it promoted anti-racism as official policy and encouraged the vision of different peoples co-existing harmoni-ously within one nation state, an impeccable set of ideals. But in practice it has often seemed to non-Russians to lead to nothing more than Russification or, as Lenin termed it, 'dominant-nation chauvinism'. Certainly, a sort of unconsciously patronising or 'elder brother' attitude has often existed, summed up for example in the remark of the Bolshevik Mikhail Kalinin in 1923 that it was their task to get the non-Russians up to the point where they were 'capable of sharing the ideals of the Leningrad workman' (Bennigsen and Lemercier-Quelquejay 1967, p. 125).

Third, although it was for decades an axiomatic belief of Soviet leaders that modernisation and development would create a harmonious national melting pot, the opposite seems to be the case in practice. Modernisation appears to have increasingly stimulated rather than eradicated ethnic conflict, a situation that finds close parallels elsewhere in the world. The tendency to underestimate this on the part of the Soviet leadership has almost certainly helped make matters worse over the years. The force and tenacity of nationalism is one of the central phenomena of the twentieth century, and comments such as those of Andropov in 1982 that the nationalities question in the USSR 'has been settled successfully, finally and irreversibly' were at best self-deluding. At the Central Committee Plenum in January 1987 Gorbachev admitted as much, arguing that the 'sphere of nationality relations' was 'very complex'. The past habit of producing 'upbeat treatises reminiscent at times of complimentary toasts', rather than serious analysis of the real issues, had actually resulted in the 'negative consequences with which we are now faced'.

Anatomy of a Problem

What, precisely, are these negative consequences and how serious are they? Several specific features can be identified. First, there has been a marked increase in ethnic consciousness throughout the Soviet Union within the past twenty years. As Bialer has put it, ethnic polarisation 'is increasing faster than . . . identification with, and consciousness of, a new Soviet nationhood' (Bialer 1980a, p. 208). This applies to Russians themselves as much as to non-Russians and is visible in, for example, the mushrooming passion for local ethnographic and conservation societies. Language survival shows this very clearly, too. Non-Russian languages have in some respects strengthened their hold, particularly among the young. Even though many speak Russian as a second language, at the time of the 1979 census 47.2 million spoke no Russian at all. Attempts at linguistic Russification increasingly seem to rebound. Thus, since the mid-1970s, there has been a concerted policy to encourage linguistic Russification in the Ukraine and Belorussia to draw the Slav peoples at least closer together. Schools in these republics have increasingly had to teach through the medium of Russian rather than the local language. However, this appears to have produced a growing anti-Russian backlash, with insistent popular demands under *glasnost* that the Belorussian and Ukrainian languages be positively promoted. In Belorussia, for instance, there are more schools where English or Spanish is the language of instruction than Belorussian. Although some small ethnic groups, for instance in Siberia, have been assimilated, generally speaking this has not occurred. In 1979 only 15 per cent of all Soviet families were of mixed ethnic stock.

Meanwhile, physical movement of peoples, a common enough occurrence under Stalin and Khrushchev, has been effectively dropped since the 1950s because of the unacceptable tensions that it creates, as for example with the post-war settlement of Russians in the Baltic States in the 1940s and 1950s and in Kazakhstan at the time of Khrushchev's Virgin Lands scheme and later. A growing sense of ethnic consciousness applies not least to Soviet Muslims who are in any case united by bonds of religion and culture, history and tradition that the European Russians have always found difficult to loosen (Carrere D'Encausse 1979).

A second aspect of the nationalities problem is that the non-Russian élites have become more assertive, their political expectations higher. This is partly a consequence of education and development, partly because the party has, since Stalin, broadly adopted a policy of trusting local élites to govern their regions, albeit with Russian party and security officials and military commanders quartered there too. Under Brezhnev this flourished at least in part as an extension of his policy of 'stability of cadres, trust in cadres' which applied to the entire Soviet Union. The effect, however, was that local élites to some extent protected themselves and their peoples from Moscow and grew accustomed to this state of affairs, as the cases of Shelest in the Ukraine, Mzhavanadze in Georgia and Kunaev in Kazakhstan showed notably during the Brezhnev era. On removal from office all were publicly criticised for excessively corrupt or nationalist ways of operating or, in other words, having gained too much political latitude. A significant long-term achievement of such élites may well prove to have been in persuading Moscow that Soviet television should use local languages where appropriate, rather than provide a blanket coverage in Russian. Similarly, the abortive debate about the Autonomous Republics (which are administrative sub-divisions of the Union Republics allowing smaller national groups to conduct business in their local languages), which some in Moscow wanted to scrap in the 1970s as part of a streamlined new constitutional structure, suggested that local élites had achieved some significant bargaining powers.

Third, demographic changes are adding a highly charged further dimension. Table 5.2 indicates the figures. By the year 2000, Russians may well comprise no more than 48 per cent of the population; and a relatively ageing one at that. One in every two

Table 5.2 Ethnic Composition of USSR, 1950–2000

Nationality	1950	1960	1970	1980	1990	2000
Russian	56.8	56.1	53.8	52.0	50.1	48.0
Ukrainian	20.5	20.0	19.5	18.9	18.0	17.3
Belorussian	4.3	3.8	3.7	3.6	3.6	3.6
Total Slavic	*81.6*	*79.9*	*77.0*	*74.5*	*71.7*	*68.9*
Moldavian	1.3	1.4	1.5	1.5	1.5	1.5
Baltic	3.1	2.9	2.9	2.7	2.7	2.5
Transcaucasian	4.3	4.6	5.0	5.4	5.9	6.2
Central Asian	9.6	11.3	13.6	15.7	18.2	20.7
Total Non-Slavic	*18.3*	*20.2*	*23.0*	*25.3*	*28.3*	*30.9*

Note: Figures may not add up to 100% due to rounding.
Source: Feshbach (1983), p. 81; Feshbach (1982), pp. 317–18.

children born by the year 2000 will probably be of Muslim origin. There are considerable resource problems associated with this relative population explosion in the south which are considered in the next chapter. There are also military and international implications. 80 per cent of army officers are Russians and most of the others are Ukrainians or Belorussians. By 2000 about one third of all military conscripts will be Muslims, compared with one sixth in 1970. Many of these will have at best very poor Russian and, moreover, there is evidence that barracks life tends to heighten ethnic tension rather than act as an integrative experience (Wimbush 1985, p. 238). Acceptance of the existing disparities, whereby the prestige and hi-tech services such as the strategic rocket forces, the air force and the navy are overwhelmingly Slav, and Muslims are largely restricted to unskilled conscript labour, might be less easy in future years. Meanwhile, Central Asian troops fraternised widely with Afghans after the Soviet military occupied Afghanistan in 1979–80, and, in a slightly different context, the existence of over one million ethnic Poles on the Soviet side of the Polish border might well have dissuaded Soviet leaders from more dramatic intervention in the Polish Solidarity crisis in 1981–82.

A fourth aspect of the problem is that national and ethnic consciousness is inextricably intertwined with religion. Rule by avowedly atheist Europeans can only encourage Muslim attachment to the traditional local culture. It is thought that up to 80 per cent of Muslims retain some sort of ties to Islam. Popular Islam in its broadest social and cultural sense is a far from diminishing force. Indeed, the Soviet press has since 1983 talked about the 'growth' of religion in Central Asia. The impact of religion elsewhere, too, is very marked. Between 30 and 50 million Russians are commonly estimated to be Orthodox believers, and the influence of the church on Russian society has, if anything, grown in recent years. There are now over 6,000 priests, a far cry from the 51,000 of 1917, but rather more than there were under Stalin. The Orthodox millenium was celebrated on a grand and open scale in 1988, amidst the emergence of a new concordat between church and state, with Gorbachev calling for a 'fruitful dialogue'. There was also public self-criticism from the party of its behaviour towards religion in the past. In addition there are about five million Catholics, mostly in the Ukraine and Lithuania, about two million Jews, mainly in the Ukraine and Moscow, and there are small Buddhist communities in the Far East. In some cases, notably in Lithuania where Catholics dominate as in Poland, the church provides an alternative focus for nationalist sentiment. Religion and nationalism, in short, are distinct but closely intertwined in the Soviet Union, and apparently unsusceptible to regime pressures against them.

The key point underlining all of this evidence is that nationality cleavages, particularly between Slav and non-Slav groups, are serious and widening.

Mitigating Factors

How, then, have the Soviet authorities in the past managed to keep the nationalities question from turning into a destabilising crisis? The answers have to be sought in the evidence that, quite apart from the powers of the modern state to coerce or isolate recalcitrant peoples, there are several important mitigating factors to take into account.

First, 'nationalism' is not always the issue. The desire to be different does not always translate into demands for political independence. There is much debate amongst Western specialists on Soviet Central Asia about whether the true impact of Islam really spreads very far beyond cultural differentiation (Rywkin 1982). Abortions for instance are very easy to obtain in the Soviet Union except in central Asia, where there is considerable opposition; but this does not necessarily translate into political militancy.

Second, Russification is not an entirely negative process. The Soviet élite, as Nove has described it, is in important respects a 'non-hereditary caste system', and the Russian language once learnt is an important skill and thus much sought after. Barriers to advancement are arguably not as great for national minorities as they were for Indians or Africans under the British Empire (Nove 1975). The numbers of non-Russians speaking Russian as a second language have in fact risen markedly in recent years, from under 50 per cent in 1970 to over 60 per cent by 1979. In at least this sense a case can be made out, as Lane has done, for a 'growing homogeneity' between the various national and ethnic groups (Lane 1985b, p. 225).

Third, native élites have benefited considerably from Russian rule, having since Stalin been able to govern their own regions to a varying but almost always significant degree. This tradition has been particularly deep-rooted in the Ukraine and the Caucasus, but under Brezhnev it grew elsewhere, too, not least in the Baltic States and Central Asia. By 1976, 76 per cent of all non-Russian republican party and government leaders were indigenous cadres (Bialer 1980a, p. 214). The real victims have often been the non-titular minorities (i.e. those without a Union Republic to their name) such as the Abkhaz people in Georgia, who petitioned unsuccessfully to be allowed to secede from Georgia in 1977, or the Christian minorities in Muslim Azerbaidzhan, the subject of great disturbances in neighbouring Armenia in 1988 referred to earlier.

Fourth, some regions such as Central Asia have benefited economically from incorporation into a modern industrial state. The Muslim territories may be poor in comparison with other regions of the USSR, but compared with Muslim countries to the south, such as Iran or Afghanistan, their standard of living is far higher. Because they are part of an essentially European state, they are equipped with an educational and health care system for instance that is far more extensive than would otherwise have been the case (McAuley 1984, p. 110).

Fifth, the sheer complexity of the nationalities question has enabled the central leadership to divide and rule in time-honoured ways. Even with *glasnost*, the sheer size of the country renders people relatively ignorant of life elsewhere. Access to the local press outside a particular region is still difficult and most national and ethnic minorities are geographically very firmly rooted. Different groups can on occasion therefore be treated in different ways. Germans and Jews have been able to emigrate, albeit in controlled numbers since the early 1970s. Armenians have traditionally been allowed greater latitude towards their Orthodox church than Russians or Ukrainians, if only to nip in the bud any tendency to make common cause with Armenians in adjoining Turkey.

Sixth, there are significant tensions, as Shafarevich put it, 'between the nationalities' and not just simply between Russians and non-Russians. There are deep seated local rivalries in the Caucasus between Georgians, Armenians, Azerbaidzhanis and the many other ethnic and linguistic groups. The original justification for Russian annexation of the hitherto independent Christian kingdoms of Georgia and Armenia at the beginning of the nineteenth century was fear of the neighbouring Islamic Persian and Turkish empires. Muslims in Central Asia, meanwhile, are, as one writer has put it, 'composed of distinct and to some extent competing ethnic groups . . . the world of Islam divides as much as it unites . . . they are as likely to fight each other as outsiders (Halliday 1986, p. 25). Ukrainian complaints that their economy helped subsidise other less developed parts of the Soviet Union, discussed in the local press officially under Shelest in the early 1970s, only served to antagonise the Central Asian élites. Lithuanians showed relatively little common cause with their fellow catholic Poles in the Solidarity upheavals of 1980–82. In the 1970s Moscow's intellectual dissidents rarely saw eye to eye with Ukrainian nationalists. The deportation of the Crimean Tartars eastwards in the war was triggered off by local anti-Muslim feelings and relayed to Stalin by a Ukrainian party *apparat* only too keen to brand all the Tartars as collaborationists (Nekrich 1978, p. 33). Cross-cutting divisions of this kind have been a significant regime asset.

Finally, but perhaps ambiguously, there has been the rising phenomenon of ethnic Russian nationalism. The Soviet leadership was able to harness this relatively effectively, at least in the Brezhnev era (Yanov 1978). Much praise was lavished at Party Congresses on the 'great Russian people'. Figures from the past, even such ideologically dubious writers as Fyodor Dostoevsky, were celebrated as essentially Russian national heroes. Russians in the Central Committee rose between 1966 and 1981 from 57 per cent to 68 per cent. The destruction of ancient Orthodox churches under Stalin and Khrushchev has given way to plans for building completely new churches under Gorbachev. Whether, in the longer run, the balance between Russian nationalism and Soviet patriotism can be maintained, however, is unclear. Russian nationalism is in part a response to demographic trends, but if it means a return to Slavophile ideas, it seems more likely to divide than to unite, and thus accelerate ethnic polarisation. Both the relatively liberal Russian nationalism of writers such as Solzhenitsyn or Rasputin, often focusing on environmental issues, and the crudely anti-semitic and xenophobic views of the nationalist *Pamyat* movement which have flourished openly since 1986, are likely to widen the cleavages still further. (*Pamyat* started as a conservationist body in the 1960s, but by the 1980s was openly anti-semitic, laying the blame for just about everything on a Jewish conspiracy. 'Nothing can be changed in our country without a renunciation of Marxism as a profoundly Zionist doctrine.' Its followers sport a kind of uniform of black sweatshirts with a golden bell on the front, and claimed 100,000 members in Moscow alone by 1988.)

Gorbachev, *Glasnost* and the Nationalities

Plainly, therefore, even taking these mitigating factors into account, the nationalities question is at best a highly complex one which the leadership cannot ignore. Gorbachev applied the strategies of *glasnost* when he spoke in 1987 of the need to discuss such 'negative phenomena' as the Alma Ata riots openly, and to 'resolutely combat nationalism'. The subsequent discussion was limited, *glasnost* notwithstanding. The full casualty figures, the motivation and the organisation behind the riots, received only limited treatment in public. Perhaps this is understandable for even the discussions which have taken place on the nationalities question have independently added to the existing tensions, rather than solving anything, allowing hitherto submerged irritants to surface openly. Demonstrations in the Baltic States in 1987, basically calling for the publication of the secret protocols of the 1939 Nazi–Soviet pact which had allowed for the dismemberment of Poland and the Baltic States, had turned into organised Popular Front movements by 1988. These demanded full sovereignty over economic and political affairs. As a result, the long-term relationship of the Baltic States to the Soviet Union remains unclear. Meanwhile, as we shall see further in Chapter 6, the growing debate about resource imbalances in Central Asia under *glasnost* has proved a considerable irritant between the Russian and the Central Asian élites.

In other respects, too, Gorbachev's reforms have not had happy consequences for nationality relations. Anti-corruption drives after 1985 hit non-Russians disproportionately hard, the élites of Central Asia and the Caucasus in particular being substantially purged. In Tadzhikistan the work of Sharif Rashidov, First Secretary for almost a quarter of a century until his death in 1983, was verbally demolished amidst accusations of 'mismanagement, falsification [of the cotton crop figures], corruption, embezzlement, nepotism and bribery'. The impact of this on the Uzbek élite was considerable. In 1986 over two-thirds of the local party were native Uzbeks, but only a minority of the political leadership was. In Kazakhstan, the dismissal and denunciation of Kunaev, First Secretary for over 30 years until his replacement in 1986 by a Russian, Gennadi Kolbin, not only reversed the established trend of thirty years' duration which allowed native cadres to provide the local leadership, but triggered the Alma Ata riots. Subsequent revelations that the Kunaev 'clan' corruptly controlled up to one third of the food supplies may have pleased the (mainly urban) Russians who comprise a uniquely high proportion of the republic's population (native Kazakhs comprised only 36 per cent in 1979), but were unlikely to foster inter-ethnic harmony. Kolbin subsequently suggested that Russians in Kazakhstan ought to learn the local language – a novel proposition – but Gorbachev also spoke of the need to defend the Russian populations in non-Russian republics against local discrimination, and the contemporary Soviet anti-drugs and anti-alcohol campaigns hit hardest at the local traditions and economics of the Caucasus and

Central Asia. Moreover, Gorbachev has grasped the birth-rate nettle, which Brezhnev would not. Family planning campaigns have been introduced since 1986 in the Muslim republics in a deliberate and novel attempt to limit population growth, the first target being Tadzhikistan, where the 1984–6 birthrate was 40.9 per thousand as opposed to 19.7 per thousand for the USSR as a whole, and 16.9 per thousand for the Russian Republic.

Conclusion

In short, consciously or otherwise, the effect of recent regime initiatives may well have been to exacerbate inter-ethnic rivalries. The nationalities question has entered a new and more troubled phase, not least fuelled by the reform policy of *glasnost* (and the release from labour camps since 1986 of many dissident nationalists). In the past the sheer complexities of the issue, coupled with a mixture of sanctions, have held this vast and diverse country together. Even today the problem is still best seen not as one likely to destabilise the Soviet system itself. But it has become an increasingly crucial test of the regime's ability. Moreover, the nationalist challenge cannot be seen in isolation. It is intertwined with religion and it does exacerbate other problems facing the leadership, not least the state of the economy and demographic trends, as we shall consider more fully in the next chapter. Economic *perestroika*, for example, could well encourage greater regional inequalities which in some respects could parallel deepening ethnic divisions. Relatively prosperous and well-run republics such as Estonia are likely to benefit disproportionately from *perestroika*.

Looking back at the other cleavages that we have considered in this chapter, in particular of class and income, of town and country, similar conclusions could be drawn. *Perestroika* and *glasnost* have almost certainly heightened expectations while not necessarily providing adequate justification for continuing or widening inequalities. But in the absence of a catalyst such as economic slump or war, these tensions, although their importance may well increase, are still a long way from being politically destabilising. Social, economic and cultural tensions of this kind have only become mutually reinforcing and politically divisive in other countries if they are interlinked: if, for instance, low income were associated with ethnicity, or religion solely with rural life. The Soviet regime has in the past gone to considerable lengths to avoid any such interlinking and no doubt will continue to do so in the future.

Further Reading

Kerblay (1983) is a comprehensive study of modern Soviet society, and ranges very widely. Among other things it discusses the urban–rural divide, social mobility, population trends, and cultural and other values. Ryan and Prentice (1987) is a source book on changing social trends since Stalin. Lane (1982, 1985b) and Yanowitch (1977, 1986) consider questions of class, status, power and inequality. Dellenbrant (1986) looks at regional inequalities and variations. Matthews (1978, 1986) considers first privilege and then poverty in Soviet society, and their associated life-styles. Browning (1987) and Buckley (1986) are recent additions to the literature on women and Soviet politics.

There are several studies of the intelligentsia, including Churchward (1973), Hill (1980), Malcolm (1984) and Fortescue (1986).

The relationship between literature and politics is examined by Dunham (1976), Hosking (1980) and Marsh (1986). Many modern Soviet writers' works are available in translation, including Rasputin, Aitmatov, Grossman, Voinovich, Trifonov and Shukshin, mentioned in this chapter. Crouch and Porter (1984) contains a selection of such authors.

There is a large literature on the nationalities. Azrael (1978) is a general source book; Dunlop (1985) and Yanov (1978) focus on Russian nationalism; Wimbush (1985), Rywkin (1982) and Lubin (1984) on the Central Asians, and Carrere D'Encausse (1979) on the overall threat to Soviet stability that the nationalities question, in her view, poses.

The research reports produced regularly by Radio Free Europe and Radio Liberty, and the Soviet press itself, are valuable sources, as mentioned at the end of Chapter 4.

6

The Economic and Environmental Record

How effective is the Soviet political system? What are its strengths and weaknesses? By what criteria should we even begin to measure any such capacity? Is the Soviet system for example effective because it has protected its people, albeit at great cost, from external military aggression or from the rigours of capitalism? Can the harsh treatment of dissidents in some way be set against policies of full employment? Such questions do not necessarily yield very productive answers.

Nevertheless, as part of the process of studying any political system, we inevitably and quite understandably tend to form judgements about system strengths and weaknesses. In this chapter we seek to offer some guidelines, focusing on two specific areas of enquiry in the belief that at least some useful, though limited, assessments about regime capacity and effectiveness can be made.

First, we consider the effectiveness of the Soviet economy and the extent to which its relative achievements and failures are a product of the political system. This is a matter of the utmost importance, which has received considerable attention both East and West and has been the basic springboard for the entire *perestroika* process. Second, we look at some of the environmental problems of this vast country, for these are not only matters of considerable political controversy in their own right, but also help to illustrate some of the strengths and weaknesses of the Soviet Union's political and administrative traditions. How competent at devising and then actually implementing environmental policy is the bureaucratic apparatus? What wider conclusions can be drawn from such case studies?

Soviet Economic Performance

A key measure of the effectiveness of any political system is its ability to handle the economy. Nowhere is this more true than in the Soviet case, where economic and political power are unusually closely intertwined and economic growth has always been seen as a particularly significant goal. The Soviet Union's Marxist leaders have traditionally regarded the economic 'base' as decisive, claiming for the socialist system certain distinct advantages over capitalism. In theory, the 'scientific management of society' not only promises that the Soviet Union can catch up with and overtake capitalism, but that it can sustain the otherwise impossible economic juggling act of continued growth, full employment and no inflation, thus leading to a society of material abundance.

In practice, despite considerable achievements, the Soviet economic system has proved in recent years to be one of declining effectiveness, whether measured in terms of achieving its own growth targets and thus satisfying domestic expectations, or in terms of comparison with the uneven performance of capitalist economies. By the 1980s economic growth, a key target, appeared to be inexorably declining, as Table 6.1 suggests.

Table 6.1   Growth Rates of National Income in the USSR (per cent)

1966–70	1971–5	1976–80	1981–5	1986–90	1991–5
41	28	21	16.5	22	28

Source: Aganbegyan 1988, p. 2.
Note: The 1966–85 figures are official achievements, the 1986–95 figures official projections. Aganbegyan argues that in reality the more accurate figures would be only about 32 per cent for 1966–70, falling to about 10 per cent for 1976–80, and virtually to zero for 1981–85.

In some basic areas, such as steel and coal in 1979, or oil and gas in 1984, there were even years of actual decline in output. Admittedly there are considerable difficulties in measuring and comparing, but even the official figures quoted here point very clearly in the wrong direction. The 1985 plan achievements, for example, were essentially those intended for 1980. Growth rates had been declining from the 1950s, and particularly sharply from the mid-1970s.

The comparative evidence meanwhile suggested that in the longer run the Soviet model was not notably more efficient than many capitalist rivals. Thus, for instance, between 1951 and 1979, Soviet annual growth rates averaged 4.8 per cent, compared to 4.6 per cent in France, 4.8 per cent in Italy, 5.1 per cent in West Germany and 8.3 per cent in Japan. Much of this Soviet growth, moreover, took place in the earlier period. Per capita consumption in the USSR by the early 1980s was only one third that of the United States and about half that of most West European countries. On a basic matter – the gap with the United States – the Soviet economy was falling further behind. In 1960 Soviet GNP was 47.7 per cent that of the United States; by 1975, 57.9 per cent; but by 1983 it was down to 55.7 per cent and falling.

In short, by the end of the Brezhnev era, it was increasingly clear that the Soviet command economy was in trouble. Its past achievements were good, but in the longer run not spectacular, and its more recent performance was increasingly unsatisfactory. Reform of the economy was thus the most consistently dominant of all Soviet political priorities during the 1980s and, as discussed in Chapter 2, the essential *raison d'être* for Gorbachev's *perestroika* programme.

Let us now examine why this was so, why attempts at reform in the past have been so relatively unsuccessful, and what prospects for economic rejuvenation *perestroika* has now created.

The Stalin Command Economy

There is no necessary connection between communist rule and a centrally planned economy, as the NEP years of the 1920s showed, but in practice the command economy that evolved under Stalin has proved the most enduring part of his bequest and the most difficult to eradicate. In essence, the command economy involved the nationalising or collectivising of virtually all economic enterprise, all activity to be planned from the centre in detail and quantitatively. Such plans were binding on lower agencies. Wages and prices were thus set not by the market but by central bureaucracy, with labour, capital and materials being administratively rationed. Growth, particularly industrial and military growth, was the predominant goal, the overriding aim being to fulfil, or if possible overfulfil, the plan within the allotted period. Targets for each subsequent year were in turn based on the previously achieved level, with a few points added: the so-called 'rachet principle' (Birman, 1978).

This command model retained certain considerable strengths even into the 1980s. It had contributed greatly to the extraordinary industrialisation achievements of the 1930s and wartime victory in 1945, as discussed in Chapter 1. It provided the basis for the long-term strategic planning that enabled the Soviet Union to become a nuclear superpower, to maintain a global lead in space research, and to develop effective national fuel and energy policies. By 1980 the Soviet Union could claim to produce 20 per cent of the world's industrial output, as opposed to only 4 per cent in 1913. Even on CIA figures, the Soviet economy had grown by 4.8 per cent per annum on average between 1951 and 1979, as opposed to only 3.4 per cent in the case of the United States.

In addition, the command economy virtually eliminated unemployment. To the extent that it did exist, not least increasingly in rural Central Asia from the 1970s, it was certainly not on the scale found in capitalist economies. There was also relative economic equality regionally. Despite the imbalances discussed in the previous chapter, the absence of a market economy had allowed for a geographical expansion of the Soviet economy that might very well not have occurred otherwise, and helped minimise those variations which did exist. Furthermore, the economic system was nothing if not easily understood. It had a basic political logic to it, and simple quantitative targets that even the most unimaginative provincial bureaucrat could understand: simply to do what the central plan required and to produce somewhat more than in the previous year.

Against this, however, had to be set a litany of disadvantages whose prominence had grown with time. Four in particular stood out. First, the focus on quantitative growth was increasingly at the expense of qualitative development. Much waste was encouraged by the insistence on measuring output quantitatively – sometimes by nothing more sophisticated than weight. According to Soviet data, the economy in 1983 had to spend 2.2 times as much oil, 3.7 times as much cast iron, 3.0 times as much steel and 2.9 times as much cement as the American economy to produce a comparable unit of national income. In *The Gulag Archipelago* Solzhenitsyn instanced the timber barges that he observed on the White Sea Canal one day in 1966, one travelling north and one travelling south, each with an identical load. 'And cancelling the one load against the other we get zero' (Solzhenitsyn 1975, p. 102). Officially, however, two productive additions to the statistics of economic activity had been made.

A second and associated major cost was low productivity. The Constitution guaranteed the right to work (Article 40), but serious underemployment was in fact commonplace. By the early 1980s labour productivity was only 55 per cent that of the United States, and in agriculture it was less than 12 per cent (Bergson and Levine 1983). Successful experiments to boost productivity only showed how deep-seated was the problem. The Shchekino chemicals combine in Tula, an industrial city just south of Moscow, shook out almost one third of its labour force in five years from 1967. This was a highly publicised campaign, an attempt to show what could be done. Similar results were achieved at the Moscow ZIL truck works in 1985, but these were both showpiece enterprises that were already relatively modern and efficient. In practice some 70 per cent of all production came from just 10 per cent of the Soviet Union's industrial plant.

Third, the record on technological innovation was poor, for with quantity dominant, there were inadequate incentives to change. Thus, in large areas, such as microelectronics or plastics, the Soviet economy had become increasingly vulnerable to international comparison, there being very few areas where the Soviet Union was technologically even level with capitalism. This point was to be corroborated during the 1980s, as the Soviet economy essentially failed to compete in the extraordinary global revolution of information technology that so characterised the decade.

Fourth, the Stalin model in practice, far from being a simple affair, was a highly complex bureaucratic Leviathan, not so much planned as organised, and over-organised at that (Crouch 1979). 850 billion documents were being issued annually by the central planners by the 1980s. The economy may have been centralised, but it was not necessarily very well co-ordinated. Thus by the 1970s there were 38 different brands of washing machine and 33 makes of refrigerator manufactured by enterprises that came under the authority of nine quite separate central ministries. The traditional desire to overfulful production symbolised this fundamental lack of co-ordination. Properly speaking, in a planned, balanced economy over-fulfilment would have been as unhelpful as underfulfilment. In practice, it was often lauded as part of a socialist work ethic. Meanwhile, in the absence of the market mechanism supply and demand rarely matched, producing endemic imbalances. Thus, on the one hand, there was an excess production of highly trained engineers and scientists overqualified for the work available to them; on the other, there were basic material shortages in industrial and in consumer life, many items being in chronically short supply.

Other drawbacks could be listed almost endlessly. The pervasive secrecy or relative unreliability surrounding much official economic data meant that central planners commonly resorted to reading US Congressional reports on the Soviet economy or, for instance, CIA disclosures about Soviet oil prospects (Goldman 1980, p. 178). The military burden, discussed in Chapter 4, was a considerable and growing drain on economic resources at all levels. Poor agricultural performance nationally was a considerable problem in its own right. Between 1972 and 1982 six grain harvests fell seriously short of target, resulting in expensive and politically complex imports from the United States, Canada and Argentina. Output overall barely rose from the early 1970s to the mid-1980s, despite receiving one third of all investment and employing about one quarter of the labour force. As one Soviet commentator, Fyodor Burlatsky, pointed out in 1986, no healthy agricultural economy needed to run formal 'weeding campaigns' in the spring, or draft large numbers of urban workers to assist with the summer harvest, as seemed to be the case in the Soviet Union. The private agricultural sector produced by the 1980s approximately one third of the total output by value from less than 2 per cent of the land.

All economies have waste, and ultimately the success or failure of the Soviet economy under Brezhnev was a relative matter. As Nove put it at the time, the situation was 'neither catastrophic nor hopeful' (Nove 1982, p. 184). Soviet people ate and lived better than in the past, meat consumption per head more than doubled between 1950 and 1975, while potato consumption per head halved (Aganbegyan 1988, p. 176). People coped, not least by recourse to the black market, which on many unofficial estimates accounted for up to one third of Soviet economic activity by the 1980s. Expectations, however, although they remained quite low, did rise. 70,000 car workers at the giant Togliatti car works in Central Russia went on strike over poor food supplies in 1980. Economic results were not what they ought to have been, even on official evidence, the impression increasingly being that the Soviet command economy was out of date and had produced merely a semi-developed country.

The Reform Debates

Given these shortcomings, why has the Soviet command economy proved so impervious to reform? It is not, after all, as if reforms have not been attempted. On the contrary, schemes to improve the economic mechanism were debated or tried almost endlessly after 1953, not least with the so-called Kosygin reforms of 1965 discussed in Chapter 2. Radical economists were already criticising the excessive centralism, the absence of the market and lack of democracy in the economic system at the end of the Khrushchev era. Brezhnev, for his part, later attempted further reform, seeking to streamline the economy with a major enterprise restructuring plan in 1973. Important reforms in 1979 sought to assist innovation and productivity by introducing a 'comprehensive' overhaul of management. Major Territorial Production Complexes were also established, notably in the virgin forests of Siberia. These not only built hydro-electric schemes or ran aluminium or wood-processing plants, or oil and gas exploitation schemes, but also had vast budgets for whole ports, airfields, roads and supporting towns. There were continuing efforts to streamline agriculture with the setting up of agro-industrial enterprises which, for example, not just grew the fruit but packaged and distributed it. The Kosygin reform aim of grafting plan and market continued, too. By 1980 four of the biggest industrial ministries had switched to self-accountability (profit and loss) systems. Between 1976 and 1980 over 11,000 enterprises, following in the footsteps of the 1967 Shchekino experiment, shed a total of nearly one million jobs.

Such changes can now be seen in principle as important precursors of economic *perestroika* under Gorbachev and as an example of the evolutionary forces at work in Soviet politics. But in practice, however, at the time, like the weighted Russian doll, they always seemed to result in the traditional command economy bouncing back upright. This was partly because of opposition from within the party *apparat* to changes which were seen as undermining its power – the power to allocate resources bureaucratically – and partly because reforms were often legally imprecise and old rules were not always rescinded (Holmes 1981). As a consequence, reforms tended merely to widen the range of planned success targets for managers. It was now not just a matter of achieving more but also, and at the same time, of cutting the wages bill or introducing bonus schemes or devising new products. The result was often increased confusion rather than anything else, with both plan and market criteria uneasily co-existing. Thus by 1980, for example, although technically about 50 per cent of the industrial workforce was employed by enterprises on self-accounting principles, no enterprise was actually allowed to go bankrupt. The traditional emphasis of the plan on quantity therefore tended to dominate, as in the past.

By the 1980s, faced with this 'treadmill of reform' as it has been called, the economists began to get more outspoken. In 1980 *Pravda* published an authoritative article proposing wages cuts and planned redundancy schemes in order to focus priorities clearly on increased productivity. There were Aesopian debates, too, about the successes of the post-Mao Chinese economic reform programme, particularly in agriculture, which had seen a quadrupling of productivity between 1978 and 1982 alone. There was the celebrated so-called Novosibirsk Paper of 1983, presented by Academician Zaslavskaya to a top-level seminar in Moscow attended by Central Committee members, representatives from Gosplan and the Academy of Sciences. A member of the reformist Economics Institute at Novosibirsk, Zaslavskaya argued bluntly that the economic system was just no longer compatible with modern reality. 'The complexity of the economic structure has long since overstepped the threshold of its efficient regulation from a single centre' (Zaslavskaya 1984). The planning system's rigidities were themselves a systemic cause of corruption, idleness and dishonesty. The Soviet people were now too well educated and too well informed to be treated like 'little screws which could be manipulated at will by central management'.

In short, more market and less plan was needed although, she stressed, this would be complex and difficult and would be resisted. 'Any radical restructuring . . . will vitally affect the interests of many social groups.' Reform 'cannot be realised without conflict' with the middle ranking bureaucracy in particular who 'have sprouted like mushrooms in recent years'.

Gorbachev and Economic *Perestroika*

Gradually, such critiques took root. By 1985, the new leadership was faced with a situation of unprecedented resource stringency (guns *or* butter rather than guns *and* butter in the 1990s) and the mounting evidence that a growth strategy dependent on pouring large quantities of labour and capital into the economy was increasingly unfeasible (Bialer 1980b). Productivity had to improve dramatically if only because of the marked reduction in the growth of the labour force in the immediate future. In the 1980s it grew by less than six million, only about one quarter that of the 1970s, and almost all of this growth was in relatively unindustrialised Central Asia; European Russia experienced a net decrease in its labour force. Meanwhile, the rapid exhaustion of easily accessible natural resources in European Russia was readily apparent. By 1980, 56 per cent of Soviet energy needs was coming very expensively from east of the Urals, 700 million tons of coal, gas and oil being 'exported' to European Russia, as opposed to only 130 million tons in 1970 and a mere 10 million tons in 1953 (Taafe 1980, p. 160). By the 1980s Siberia was absorbing one quarter of the entire capital investment in the Soviet Union, despite possessing less than 11 per cent of the total population.

New leaders, unprecedented stringency, an awareness that the old methods did not work well enough and that there were ultimately strategic and security implications for a nation with an economic system of declining efficacy: all these factors produced Gorbachev's call for 'revolutionary change'. 'One is staggered to see how much has been done on the principle of "we'll muddle through somehow". But we are *not* muddling through, comrades'. Speaking in Khabarovsk in 1986, Gorbachev stressed that 'we must disclose the potential of a planned economy . . . I would equate the word *perestroika* with revolution . . . there is no other way'.

Two basic points need stressing about Soviet economic *perestroika* under Gorbachev, however. The first is that there was no detailed 1985 blueprint. Policy evolved with time, the leadership's own analysis becoming arguably more radical. At the same time its awareness of the obstacles in the way of change possibly became greater. Thus, the original focus in 1985–6 was on 'intensification' and 'acceleration' rather than on any more far-reaching restructuring. The key priorities were seen to be the need to get strategic development of new technology, with investment priorities more precisely focused. Major shifts were planned. By 1990, 50 per cent of industrial investment was to be for retooling and modernising as opposed to only 37 per cent in 1985. Some ministerial streamlining took place, and Gosplan was ordered to establish clearer economic priorities. There was a fresh wave of highly publicised experiments to free unproductive labour. The Belorussian railways shed 12,000 workers in 1985, and by the year 2000 some 15 million workers will need to be similarly redeployed or retired, probably not, in the end, without 'complications', i.e. to some extent deliberate unemployment. Virtually all growth in national income and industrial output in the 1986–90 Plan, and in subsequent plans to the end of the century, is to come from increased labour productivity.

It was only in 1987, however, that the full dimensions of economic *perestroika* became clear, with Central Committee ratification of a major document on 'Basic Provisions for the Radical Restructuring of Economic Management' and a new Law on State Enterprises which came into effect in January 1988. These set in motion the most extensive reshaping of the national economy since the 1920s, effectively ending the leadership's commitment to the Stalin command economy. Economic *perestroika* has continued to evolve and is likely to go on doing so now for the foreseeable future.

This brings us to the second key point about Gorbachev's economic *perestroika*. Even this radical package was itself a political compromise, evolving out of experience and debate. *Glasnost* encouraged much wider discussion than ever before about economic reform, but it was easier to establish consensus on what was wrong than on measures to put things right. Broadly speaking, there were three schools of thought amongst economists by the mid-1980s. The conservatives continued to argue that the system itself should be left intact: intensification and acceleration were adequate remedies. In other words, cutting plan indicators, setting more realistic plan targets and devising better plan criteria for encouraging innovation and productivity would suffice. The party would remain safely in overall control. Second were the reformers who argued for much less central planning, leaving enterprises far more scope to work out their specific production obligations through contractual arrangements with other enterprises. Most radical of all, however, were those such as Zaslavskaya and Aganbegyan who wanted to see the Soviet economy much more integrated with the capitalist economy via a fully convertible rouble, and wanted to see the effective elimination of the central planning system. All economic activity should be by way of enterprise contracts. A June 1987 article in *Pravda* asked whether it would not be 'more opportune not to fulfil the plan, but to just work. To just build houses, write books, treat patients, bake bread. To stop this flood of hollow figures, to throw off this obsession with plans.' Given this range, the Central Committee, perhaps understandably, opted for the middle way. So the 1987 reform proposals, radical though they were in intent, were a political compromise (Litvin 1987). This can be seen if we look more closely at what they involved and at their strengths and weaknesses.

Essentially, under the 1987 proposals, Gosplan and the central ministries were to continue developing Five-Year-Plans for the economy based on strategic economic 'control figures' set by the Politburo. These plans, however, were to be indicative rather than directive, that is to say, a somewhat flexible target, seeking to reflect both industrial and consumer demands. Enterprises would be allowed to construct their own plans using as a basis 'state orders' (i.e. contracts obtained from ministries). The rest of a given enterprise's productive capacity could then be available for free negotiation with customers. Enterprise performance was now to be evaluated not by crude 'from the achieved level' criteria, but by more flexible annual plans based on the entire range of resources, materials, labour and land available to the enterprise and its consequent expected productive potential. The necessary resources would be bought through bilateral contracts, not allocated by central ministries. Enterprises would be self-supporting financially, profitability (via productivity, efficiency, technological innovation) being the key criterion, and bankruptcy the alternative. By 1991 two thirds of the economy was to be geared to direct trading between enterprises, based on these principles.

From January 1988 all wage ceilings were abolished, too. This reflected an attempt to restructure the relationship between the state and individual labour, an historic development, not least in agriculture. The 1920s agricultural model of small-scale private enterprise coupled with a heavily guided market mechanism had been favourably discussed after 1985, with a new deal foreshadowed at the 1986 Party Congress, giving strengthened farm autonomy, and arrangements for work brigades, teams or even individuals to enter into contracts with farm management. In 1988 this was consolidated with legal measures that sought to encourage agricultural workers not just to take such initiatives, but to take out long leases and make firm commitments. Only in this way could such workers finally regain that sense of responsibility for the land which was destroyed by Stalin. Or, as Bukharin had put it in 1925, 'enrich yourselves.' Henceforth initiative and enterprise will not be punished as 'kulak' activity, as in the past.

Other emerging key planks of economic *perestroika* included a potentially very significant upgrading of territorial planning powers, not unlike the Khrushchev experiments, to assist coordination at regional or republican level, proposals to elect enterprise managers which were introduced in 1987, and a major upgrading of the role of banks and banking in the economy, not least with the prospect of greater international trading in the 1990s.

Economic Problems and Prospects

What, though, are the problems associated with all this? The wider implications for the entire social and political reform programme will be discussed in the concluding chapter. At this point some specifics can be noted, however. The centre, by means of state contracts, will still maintain overall strategic direction of the economy and will still largely indicate what should be produced. Prices are still set centrally, for the moment, although this was the subject of much Central Committee debate in 1987–8. The producer does not sell on an open market so much as to other enterprises (e.g. retail outlets) which are themselves still operating to a plan. The military sector is still likely to receive favourable treatment at the expense of the non-military sectors. It is not clear that productivity and technological innovation have been given sufficient scope to make the crucial qualitative differences. State orders are to take precedence, at least for the early years, to ensure that top priority needs are met, but many managers, reluctant to launch themselves on the unknown sea of freely negotiated contracts, are seeking as many of these as possible, rather than taking entrepreneurial risks. The old system thus survives in important essentials.

Meanwhile, Gosplan, ministerial and party officials have been notably equivocal even about these changes, for much is at stake and much remains unresolved. Evidence of footdragging and opposition has been well documented, not least by Gorbachev himself, who spoke in November 1987 of an 'increase in the resistance of those conservative forces that see *perestroika* as a threat to their selfish interests'. The Gosplan chief, Nikolai Talyzin, was sacked in February 1988 for failure to curb such forces adequately.

Given the sheer scale and intricacy of the Soviet economy, and the relatively fast-changing nature of events since 1985, it is only possible to offer very tentative conclusions at this stage. There has certainly been an historic tilting towards a less than wholly state-run economy, as part of the wider social and political *perestroika* of the post-Brezhnev era. Whether it will reverse the trend towards declining economic efficacy prevalent under Brezhnev is still an open question. Equally unresolved is just what combination of plan and market, if any, can be made to work in the longer run. Some economists both inside and outside the Soviet Union have considerable doubts. They believe that it is a halfway house ('like being a little bit pregnant') that cannot really be sustained. Others see it as a necessary and workable move towards achieving a more productive, efficient and innovative economy for the challenges of the twenty-first century.

The Environmental Record

Central to the achievement of a successful economy must be the basic administrative ability both to formulate and then to implement policy. It is to this question of administrative capacity that we now turn. How effective is Soviet administrative performance? Are there distinct advantages to the one-party state? Or does the record suggest that, just as the economic system had by the 1980s become excessively centralised and ineffective, so, too, the bureaucratic machine had become unnecessarily top-heavy and unresponsive? This is a widely held view, compounded by much evidence that policy implementation, as opposed to policy formulation, is often very uncoordinated (Ross 1987). On the other hand, it is difficult to envisage rule over such a vast and complex land without at least some such problems. Some writers are confident that, on the whole, Soviet administration has proved to be a success (Smith 1980, p. 213). It is 'quite flexible in meeting competing demands and adapting to changing conditions' and coping with the most pressing needs. Bearing this distinction between policy formulation and implementation in mind, we shall now look at three contrasting but related case studies of environmental issues, for this is a field that has brought into the open better than most the strengths and weaknesses of Soviet administrative performance.

I. The Chernobyl Disaster, 1986

The first case is that of the crisis surrounding the Chernobyl disaster of April 1986, when Reactor Number 3 exploded in what was at that time the world's worst civil nuclear power accident. In administrative terms this might be seen as a classically Bolshevik problem to be 'stormed', sheer political discipline and commitment counting above all else. Thirty-one people died as a direct consequence, 135,000 others were evacuated from over 60 towns and villages in the region, many for ever. At least 200,000 people were exposed to unacceptably high levels of radiation, and further Chernobyl-related deaths will certainly follow in the years to come. 368 square miles of farmland were permanently contaminated and 2 billion roubles worth of direct damage caused, quite apart from the longer term and unmeasurable costs.

Chernobyl was not the first nuclear accident in the Soviet Union. A nuclear waste explosion near Chelyabinsk on the edge of the Siberian plain in 1957–8 resulted in several hundred square miles of land being devastated and permanently abandoned. A major atomic science park near Moscow employing 28,000 highly specialised people had to be closed in 1983 after serious contamination of the surrounding water table. But Chernobyl was by far the most significant, if only because of its international implications which were compounded by the initial attempts to handle the disaster in traditional ways, with a complete news blackout. It took three days of complaints from Scandinavia before the Soviet authorities admitted the existence of any disaster. In an attempt to at least limit the political fall-out, local officials in the Ukraine had withheld information both from the local population and from Moscow. It took nine days and a visitation from Politburo members before proper evacuation of the local population was organised and a 30-mile exclusion zone and clean-up operation established. It took three weeks before Gorbachev himself went on Soviet television to discuss the full disaster.

However, once manoeuvred into action, the regime proved to be relatively effective in handling the crisis. Secrecy had bred rumour and panic and paradoxically did much to finally strengthen the hands of those within the reform leadership who were already arguing in favour of a general policy of *glasnost*. Chernobyl thus acted as an important agent in the creation of *glasnost* (Jones and Woodbury 1986). International specialists were flown in to cope not just with the survivors but with the reactor itself. 8,000 new houses were built within the first six months, mostly solid brick structures. A major clean-up operation was conducted. Responsible officials were put on trial and subsequently jailed for culpable negligence. A government commission of inquiry was held whose findings were accepted by the International Atomic Energy Authority in Vienna, namely that unauthorised experiments, human error and sloppy working practices were to blame rather than any intrinsic reactor design faults. With some success, a considerable public relations campaign was developed, aimed at international as well as domestic audiences. It highlighted not just the heroic attempts to clean up Chernobyl and resettle and rehabilitate the population, but also the wider Soviet foreign policy argument about the ecological destruction that nuclear warfare would certainly bring.

Meanwhile, the leadership reaffirmed its commitment to the Soviet civil nuclear energy programme. This was to continue regardless, the largest such programme in the world. By 1986 there were 41 working nuclear reactors and a further 26 planned or under construction. Between 1986 and 1990, nuclear energy output was planned to more than double. By 1990 nuclear power was to account for 21.2% of Soviet electricity output, as opposed to a mere 10.8 per cent in 1986 (Thornton 1986). The Chernobyl complex itself was intended to be the largest in the world, with six reactors at work by 1988, producing sufficient power to light in theory the equivalent of every home in Britain. This reaffirmation of nuclear power was in contrast to the response in the United States at the time of the far less serious Three Mile Island accident in New York State in 1979, as a consequence of which no further American nuclear power stations were commissioned.

In short, it could be argued, here was a traditional Bolshevik 'quantity' response to an unprecedented, but relatively straightforward, 'stormable' problem. And yet, as the need to introduce a measure of *glasnost* showed, that traditional response had obvious weaknesses even at the time. Not only had secrecy led to rumour and panic but it had, arguably, made it less easy before the disaster to challenge the lax working practices that had apparently existed at Chernobyl. The Moscow leadership itself, without wide public debate on this as on other policy issues, was liable to get only biased information from ministries with interests at stake, or specialists, or local political leaders. The limitations of the traditional approach became even more marked after 1986, with the steady emergence of a shocked public opinion as a significant political force. In 1987, after much public debate and pressure, not least from Ukrainian scientists, journalists and writers, the authorities decided not to proceed with commissioning the fifth and sixth reactors at Chernobyl. Similarly, plans to build new reactors in southern Russia and in Armenia were also dropped.

Chernobyl has not resulted in an abandonment of the Soviet nuclear power programme, but it has certainly put it on the defensive. In the Ukraine the press in 1988 asked whether 'each of these [new planned] power stations doesn't conceal another Chernobyl?' and, furthermore, why the Ukraine, with only 3 per cent of the land of the Soviet Union and a high population density, should have 40 per cent of its nuclear capacity. More generally, there appears to be an increased recognition in Moscow that the only way a chain reaction of 'fear, ignorance and distrust' about nuclear power can be countered is not by decrees or dismissive platitudes from the Ministry of Atomic Energy, but through essentially unfettered public debate; for the continuation of the civil nuclear power programme in the Soviet Union, as elsewhere, is no longer a simple matter of imposition from above.

The Soviet system, as Chernobyl showed, can be very effective at mobilising both physical and political resources to achieve a clearly defined goal. Policy formulation and implementation are closely intertwined. This has often been seen as one of its classic strengths and it remains an important attribute. But in a more complex modern age even a clearly defined crisis such as Chernobyl was not entirely amenable to traditional 'storming' techniques.

II. The Case of Lake Baikal

If, without stretching the point too much, Chernobyl demonstrated some of the strengths and weaknesses of the traditional mobilisation regime, our second example, Lake Baikal, has become for many Soviet people the classic instance of a modern drift towards an ineffective 'bureaucratic pluralism', where the political leadership has appeared at best as an uncertain compromiser.

Lake Baikal in Siberia is the oldest and deepest freshwater lake in the world, some 600 kilometres in length and up to 80 kilometres wide. It contains one fifth of all of the world's freshwater, and in a particularly pure form. Three quarters of all marine life in Baikal is unique to the lake. It has a resonance for Soviet people that the Grand Canyon or Yosemite have for Americans. For thirty years, however, Baikal has been the focus of an increasingly anguished national debate, not just about pollution but also about the whole decision-making process and the extent to which there is ultimately any political accountability in the Soviet Union.

In 1957 the Ministry of Timber, Paper and Woodworking proposed to build a cellulose factory on the southern shores of Baikal, to produce high-quality rayon cord for, among other things, military aircraft tyres. The defence industries required the technology, the lake would provide the water, and the nearby forests the wood. The scheme was attacked from the outset by a mixture of both institutional and informal critics, the Ministry of Land Reclamation and Water Resources being the principal bureaucratic opponent, but soon joined by ad hoc coalitions of journalists, scientists and writers. It was also opposed by the State Committee for Scientific Research and the Siberian Department of the Academy of Sciences, by mass circulation journals such as *Oktyabr*, as well as liberal ones such as *Novy Mir* (Kelley 1976). In 1966 the newspaper *Komsomolskaya Pravda* published a letter signed by a wide range of distinguished citizens, including a vice-president of the powerful and prestigious Academy of Sciences, other academicians and heroes of Socialist Labour, calling for the project to be abandoned. Gosplan set up a commission of enquiry to give 'final advice' in 1966; it reported in favour of the scheme but insisted on strict safeguards about the emission of pollutants into Baikal.

The result was that the first plant opened in 1966, but only after a lengthy delay and only with the later addition of an enormously costly water filtration system. A second plant followed in 1973. Few parties were satisfied. In 1977 the Academy of Sciences recommended the closure of both plants. Critics talked of Baikal being on the verge of 'irreparable change'. Meanwhile, ironically, the original technology was now obsolete. High-strength synthetic fibres could be manufactured anywhere to the required quality. The Angara River Basin, it was now revealed, had all along possessed suitably pure and less easily polluted water and would have made a better base.

Baikal became a national *cause célèbre* during the 1970s, part of a major environmental debate, not least at the time of the promulgation of the new Constitution in 1977. It also focused attention on the decision-making processes themselves. If subordinate agencies could feud so destructively, this implied either that the centre could not or would not intervene. The resulting 'authority leakage' became more marked with time. Between 1969 and 1987 the Central Committee passed four major resolutions aimed quite specifically at protecting Baikal from further pollution. There had been special commissions of Gosplan and the Academy of Sciences. None had had the desired effect.

It might be thought that such 'narrow departmentalism' was a product of the Brezhnev era, but the phenomenon went deeper.

The Gorbachev leadership was challenged in 1986 by the writer Rasputin, perhaps the most influential public campaigner on Baikal, to end once and for all the 'waste and damage'. Yet another commission of enquiry, this time answerable to the Central Committee, was set up with Rasputin as a member. It produced what he saw as further 'procrastination', however. The cellulose effluent was now to be piped from Baikal to a river 76 kilometres distant. Work on this was abandoned in 1987 after mass protest demonstrations in the nearby city of Irkutsk. Officially, the plants are to switch to furniture production from 1993, so the varied environmental and bureaucratic lobbies have made some progress. The dominant impression remains, however, in what *Pravda* has called this 'very instructive history', of a considerable and inbuilt degree of bureaucratic pluralism, of poor administrative co-ordination, even on an issue such as Baikal which has been a unique focus of national concern for many years.

Meanwhile, at least two options could have been implemented far sooner by a more determined leadership. One was to close down the cellulose plants altogether and redeploy the workers, a proposal that even the local party leadership, traditionally concerned to defend the economy, favoured by the late 1980s. The second was to introduce far tougher financial penalties for pollution. There were drawbacks to this option in practice, for the traditional command economy did not easily throw up ways in which the polluter could be made to pay financially (Komarov 1978). As Rasputin put it in 1986, 'as usual in our country, there will be no-one to hold responsible'. A more determined new leadership, coupled with economic *perestroika* and profit and loss accounting, ought in theory to improve this situation, although in the case of Baikal, pressures are mounting with the development of lead and zinc mining and of the new Baikal–Amur main line railway – effectively a second Trans-Siberian link – on the northern shores, both of which are likely to intensify damage to the local ecology still further.

In short, as this case illustrates, Soviet political and administrative performance can be highly indecisive and uncoordinated, not just in terms of policy implementation but in basic policy formulation as well. The centre is not always willing or able to control effectively its subordinate bureaucratic agencies, resulting in, at best, some unsatisfactory political compromises.

III. The Diversion of Siberian Rivers

In our third case, however – the proposed diversion of Siberian rivers – although similar patterns of 'narrow departmentalism' can be ascertained, we are essentially dealing with what Gustafson has termed a 'third-generation' (i.e. post-Brezhnev) issue. This is a case where, even if there is effective short-term policy formulation and implementation, the sheer scale and complexity of the matter rules out 'solutions'. Here at best political leaders can only seek to ameliorate problems, not solve them. As Gustafson has observed, in such third-generation cases 'nothing is ever finally settled. Issues keep resurfacing in different forms' (Gustafson 1983, p. 10). The controversy about diverting Siberian rivers, the so-called Sibaral project, illustrates this, for it is part of an increasingly complex resources problem facing the Soviet Union, which would tax even the most effective administrative machine.

Put at its simplest, the Soviet people are in the wrong places: 60 per cent of the nation's energy resources are to be found east of the Urals, but 75 per cent of the population lives to the west, where population densities are high. The Yakut region of Siberia, nine times the size of France, has less than 900,000 people. The rapidly rising population of the southern Muslim republics, meanwhile, discussed in the previous chapter, has created a North–South mismatch of its own, for although there are considerable labour shortages in the European part of the Soviet Union, where the bulk of the nation's industrial capacity is sited (20 per cent of all industrial output comes from the central economic region, within a radius of some 400 kilometres of Moscow), there is already substantial underemployment in much of Soviet Central Asia. By 1987 there were officially one million underemployed in Uzbekistan, in a population of 6.8 million, and 234,000 in Tadzhikistan, with a population of 4.8 million. On the outskirts of the Caspian oil city of Baku alone there were up to 200,000 people living in rough-and-ready shanty towns, driven there by the prospect of work, a vast and unregulated community growing at the rate of 20,000 a year.

What policy options are available to cope with this? Migration of Muslims on any scale out of Central Asia has not so far been considered one of them. Muslims, for cultural, economic and climatic reasons, are not migratory, and most do not speak Russian. Importing work to the region is a real but limited alternative. Some shifts in resource allocation, not least of labour-intensive industries such as food processing, have occurred in recent years, but at the expense of other regions and, to some extent, they only exacerbate existing transport bottlenecks, for much of the industrial output of Central Asia has inevitably to be directed at that great majority of the population that still lives in the European part of the country. Active family planning programmes were introduced in some Central Asian republics in 1987, but between 1984–7 alone the population of Soviet Central Asia rose from 44.5 million to 47.5 million, and is still likely to reach over 60 million by the year 2000.

Here, therefore, is a complex phenomenon requiring the coordination of a considerable range of policies, not least to provide adequate water supplies. 84 per cent of Soviet water resources flow north and east into the Arctic or Pacific Oceans across often very desolate and economically underdeveloped territory, only 16 per cent flowing across the south and west of the country, where the vast bulk of people, industry and agriculture are situated. Hence Sibaral, the 'project of the century', a huge engineering scheme to divert the flow of the Siberian rivers Ob' and Yenesei south, with dams, locks and huge new earthen canals, towards the Aral Sea and the surrounding rivers on the borders of Uzbekistan and Turkmenistan. Irrigation systems would then convey water elsewhere to the whole region. Other associated schemes included a new Volga–Don canal system to irrigate the south and west of the European part of the country.

The Siberia–Aral Sea canal project would have been the largest engineering scheme in history. Its potential had been recognised even in Tsarist times, but in the 1970s it gained a fresh momentum as Central Asian water demands increased. It immediately ran into controversy, however, as critics questioned the necessity, the cost and the environmental consequences. In the widely read and influential weekly *Literaturnaya Gazeta*, the journal of the Writers' Union, a debate took place in 1982 which turned the whole question into a major controversy on the lines of the Baikal affair. The chief project engineer, Igor Gerardi, was forced to defend the scheme, arguing that it had been thoroughly investigated and carefully designed, that it would produce economic benefits and would pay for itself within a decade. The environmental hazards were not severe and the deteriorating water situation in the south made such a project necessary anyway. A leading critic, the economist Viktor Perevedentsev, categorically rejected these conclusions, questioning the adequacy of the environmental research and the economic justification for the project. He calculated that it would prove to be twice as expensive as had been claimed, and that more effective options existed to increase food production, such as water consumption controls, improved irrigation in Western Siberia and Northern Kazakhstan, the reconstruction of old waterways in central Asia, and better crop rotation and anti-soil erosion schemes. Such views, however, were hotly criticised, and in 1983 Andropov confirmed that the plan was to go ahead, and preliminary design and construction work continued. The first phase was to be under construction by 1988 and completed early in the twenty-first century.

Then, in a dramatic and unexpected reversal in 1986, the Politburo scrapped the whole scheme, including the European variants. The project was to stop forthwith. What had happened? Most notably, a new leadership had come to power, persuaded that 'hero projects' were an anachronism, and that, in the context of economic 'intensification', potentially wasteful schemes of this kind had to take a lower priority. The economic case against was also very persuasive, particularly as it was argued by reform economists such as Aganbegyan (a former colleague of Perevedentsev) who were personally very close to Gorbachev. The foremost scientific 'diverter', the President of the Academy of Sciences, Anatoli Alexandrov, was retired in 1986 and replaced by a reformist from the Institute of Economics at Novosibirsk, Georgi Marchuk. In addition there were 'broad public circles' of opinion to take into account, as the Politburo specifically put it at the time. In the context of Chernobyl and *glasnost,* public debate about Sibaral had eventually culminated in 1986 in an unusually bitter public feud involving ministries, journalists, writers and scientists. At the Russian Writers' Congress in 1985 the writer Bondarev had described it as 'a dangerous project . . . when will patient reason come to replace technocratic impatience and parochial ambition?' The poet Vosnesenski described Sibaral as a 'criminal' plan in 1986, and there were authoritative criticisms even in *Pravda* and the party's theoretical journal, *Kommunist.* Some scientists argued that the ecological consequences for the entire Arctic Ocean were incalculable. Such outcries, including reportedly the threat by several celebrated writers such as Rasputin to go on hunger strike until the project was abandoned, were undoubtedly powerful factors, although the economic arguments were probably paramount in the Politburo's decision (Micklin 1987, p. 81).

Some of the opposition to Sibaral was fuelled by the recent environmental disaster in the Kara-Bogoz-Gol (Black Throat Gulf), officially acknowledged in 1983 to have been a 'blunder'. This salty marsh the size of Belgium is linked to the Caspian Sea – itself the equivalent in size of Italy. The level of the Caspian had fallen sharply in recent years and to prevent this accelerating, as water was drained off into the marsh, the strait between it and the Kara-Bogoz-Gol was dammed in 1980. Within three years, however, not only had two thirds of the marsh evaporated altogether, destroying the major salt and chemicals industries along its shoreline as well as the livelihoods of many thousands of people, but it was realised that the Caspian was rising and doing so for other reasons, indeed rising excessively because of the dam. It was flooding fishing ports and oilfields around the Caspian. The obvious solution, a permanent regulating lock, had still not been agreed to even by 1988, infighting between the Ministry of Land Reclamation and Water Resources and the Ministry for the Chemicals Industry about who should shoulder the cost and responsibility of the disaster having remained unresolved. Twelve organisations in 1988 were reportedly 'studying the problem'.

There was also a widespread reaction against 'hero projects'. As a case in point, *Izvestia* in 1987 roundly condemned the Baikal–Amur Mainline (BAM) project of the 1970s. What had seemed a 'crystal-clear' scheme, due to open in 1982, costing 4.5 billion roubles and carrying 35 million tons of freight annually, an earlier 'hero project of the century', had still not fully opened in 1988. It had meanwhile cost twice the original budget and had generated less than a million tons of traffic in the first, admittedly irregular, year of operation.

Perhaps the most remarkable aspect of the Sibaral affair, however, was the subsequent reaction to the 1986 decision to abandon the project. Here, after all, was a cutting of the Gordian knots of bureaucratic pluralism, by an energetic new leadership, and after at least some consideration of the evidence. But 'broad public circles' were by now thoroughly aroused, notably in Central Asia, where writers including Aitmatov, as well as journalists and party officials, mounted a public campaign to reopen the question. Unless dramatic action was taken, not only would regional water resources be fully exploited by the 1990s, but a major ecological catastrophe would ensue.

A key exhibit was the Aral Sea itself, the fourth largest salt-water lake in the world and the size of Wales, which was now drying up at such a rate that by the year 2010 it would have disappeared altogether. Demands on the Aral Sea, from the cotton industry above all, are now so great that its level has dropped ten metres in 25 years, some 'ports' now being 30 miles from water. By the late 1980s a vast new salt desert was being created, with salt dust storms stretching up to 25 miles wide and over 200 miles in length scouring the region ten or twelve times a year, and causing serious and complex ecological damage, including climatic change, over an enormous area. The Aral Sea, in the view of the Uzbek Academy of Sciences 'is a decisive catalyst for the climate of the whole of Asia. This is going to affect the weather, the rainfall and eventually the food supply of India too . . . the catastrophe is global.'

Considerable bitterness between national élites has ensued, with Uzbeks accusing Russians of being 'saturated with touching concern for preserving northern nature' but having not a word to say about the life and economy of the southern republics, and the 'diverters' being accused in *Izvestia* of planning 'a large-scale ecological and economic crime', based on 'mathematically illiterate research'. *Pravda* has argued that the Uzbeks must restructure their economy, not least by ending the massive and water-hungry reliance on cotton, and by imposing proper administrative discipline on a 'badly organised system'. Even 'redistribution of the population' should not be ruled out.

Thus, by 1988, the Politburo found itself trapped between competing disaster scenarios with no easy way out. In short, here was a genuinely 'third-generation' issue, very complex, touching ecological, economic, nationalist and other nerves, and an example of Gustafson's point that political problems cannot be 'finally settled', for they merely resurface in other forms.

Conclusion

What, then, more widely, do these examples suggest about the ability of the Soviet system to handle complex political and administrative questions? There is no single answer. As Chernobyl showed, the Soviet system certainly can on occasion mobilise resources effectively, but it can also be prone to the ineffectuality demonstrated by the Baikal and Kara-Bogoz-Gol cases. New leadership may now make some difference to this record. In 1988 a new State Committee on Environmental Protection, merging the responsibilities previously shared by nine different state committees and seven ministries, was created complete with tough new powers to tackle the newly acknowledged environmental pollution crisis. But this may be a case of running in order to stand still. As Sibaral has shown, the complex pressures to which the regime is now subject, together with heightened popular expectations for 'solutions', would tax the capacity of even the best-run administrative system.

Further Reading

On the Soviet economy, Nove (1969) provides a comprehensive economic history. Buck and Cole (1987) look specifically at modern economic performance, as do Bergson and Levine (1983). Both Goldman (1987) and Aganbegyan (1988) consider the problems and prospects for Gorbachev's economic *perestroika*.

There are several studies of Soviet administrative performance, including Smith (1980), Ross (1987) on the record in housing, Holmes (1981) and Lampert (1985) on industrial policies, and Gustafson (1981, 1983) on environmental and energy questions. Zeigler (1987) is also a full-length study of environmental policy whilst, in contrast, Komarov (1978) is a short but well informed polemic on the regime's failures in this area. There are several studies of the Chernobyl affair including Marples (1986) and Gale and Hauser (1988).

As with previous chapters, it should also be noted that the research reports of Radio Free Europe and Radio Liberty and the Soviet press itself are invaluable on recent developments.

7

Models and Overviews of Soviet Politics

The economic and political effectiveness of the Soviet system has clearly been questionable, as previous chapters have suggested. What has been less in dispute, however, is the basic stability of the system. Soviet politics is obviously, like any other, in a permanent state of 'transition' and overall stability cannot always be taken for granted but, despite all the ups and downs of Soviet history, the record to date has been a remarkable one. Few regimes in the twentieth century have survived as long. How and why has this been so? There are many schools of thought which have between them produced a wide range of basic 'models' – abstract, systematised pictures – of Soviet politics. These, quite apart from throwing light on questions of stability and change, also help to put Soviet politics into a wider perspective. They thus provide an appropriate coda to much that has been dealt with in previous chapters. We shall now take the six most widely discussed models and consider each in turn. In practice they can be divided into two groups: those that focus on regime power and coercion and those that, in contrast, stress the importance of consensus and evolution as the principal explanation for system stability.

Stability through Power

1. The Totalitarian Model

The most common starting point for any analysis of Soviet politics remains the Totalitarian model, outlined in Chapter 1. The combined effects of an official ideology, a single party, a planned economy, a dictatorial leadership, propaganda and police controls and the weapons of terror create, it is argued, a syndrome of absolutism, of total regime power. This ultimately puts the Soviet system into a separate political category from other autocracies, let alone democracies. Some, such as Solzhenitsyn, contend that totalitarianism derives from above, an imposition by a cruel and rapacious state machine on an innocent people (Solzhenitsyn 1973). Others, such as the iconoclastic dissident writer Zinoviev, see it as a cultural and political phenomenon springing from below, a product of a deeper collectivist tradition. As Zinoviev has put it, the Soviet Union is a 'self-regulating concentration camp' (Zinoviev 1978, p. 258).

There are important weaknesses in this model, even as applied to the Stalin years, as discussed in Chapter 1. These are much more marked when applied to the subsequent era. Society may to a large degree have been atomised and terrorised under Stalin, but that has not been the case subsequently, as the rise of protest and dissent and the growth of a form of civil society has shown. Moreover, although the totalitarian model does not exclude élite conflict, it does not assign to it a very high priority, despite the evidence, for example – discussed in Chapter 2 – of continuing élite conflicts since Stalin over change and development. Most fundamentally it underplays the dynamics for change, implying that political development has reached an historical cul-de-sac of total regime power, from which there is no escaping.

There are, however, distinct strengths to the approach, for all this. As Schapiro has argued, the basic 'contours' were still present even in the 1970s to a considerable degree (Schapiro 1972). The Soviet state still possessed an ambition and a power that was rarely to be found abroad, and system distinctions were still worth making.

Either way, the totalitarian analysis provides a powerful explanation for continued system stability as essentially a product of coercion, and it remains a widely held mental starting point. Thus the US Congress decided not to allow Gorbachev, 'the leader of a totalitarian power' to address it on his visit to Washington in 1987. *Perestroika* was merely a blind, to lull the West into a false sense of security, while the Soviet system reassembled itself as a far more formidable adversary.

II. The State Capitalist Model

A second approach, the State Capitalist model, stresses that a broader élite or 'new class', not a single dictator, controls the state and party apparatus. Like totalitarianism, it is generally an approach highly critical of Soviet reality. The new class is functionally tantamount to the bourgeoisie under capitalism, exploiting for its own interests what are nominally public assets, for control of the economy under Soviet socialism is equivalent to ownership under capitalism. There have been many variations on this theme. Trotsky classically saw the new élite as a bureaucratic 'caste' acting in conflict with the interests of the party and the proletariat, this new stratum being a 'degenerate' product. Others, such as Milovan Djilas, once a member of the Yugoslav Communist leadership, saw a fully fledged new class in the Marxist sense, because of its relation to the means of production. The result is possibly a degenerate form of neo-capitalism, possibly a new form of 'bureaucratic state', a sort of third way (Lane 1982).

In any event, such approaches have focused on exploitation and privilege by a central political bureaucracy or *nomenklatura* which, as Nove put it, exhibited something close to class consciousness, being very aware of its status and of the need to refuse, via censorship, proper discussion of its rights and privileges. This, argued Voslensky, had 'led ultimately to the establishment of a new antagonistic class society', one in which the élite had sought to stupefy the oppressed by adapting the ideology of Marxism–Leninism to stress class consensus rather than conflict as a defining characteristic of socialism (Voslensky 1984). Writers from Orwell to Sakharov, Bahro, Kuron and Modzelewski, Medvedev and others have argued along similar lines over a period of several decades (Nove 1975).

The weakness of such approaches is that they tend to minimise élite infighting, for example over resource allocation or specific policies, as well as over major strategic goals such as *perestroika*. It is also arguable whether in any real sense there was ever a degeneration from a time when the proletariat was not exploited. The concepts of 'exploitation' and of 'class' are not crystal clear either. How is exploitation proved empirically? Are rulers exploiters merely because they rule? Are 'the rulers' merely the party *apparat*, or the wider *nomenklatura*, or even simply the Politburo?

The strength of this type of approach, however, is considerable. It focuses attention on the economic basis of political power and particularly on the fact that power over the planned economy is a political power. It has also questioned the extent of political stability. Has state capitalism resulted in an ultimately wasteful and dysfunctional economy leading inexorably to political crisis at some point? Is *perestroika* therefore merely a rearranging of the deckchairs on the socialist Titanic which will stave off nothing because the élite will cling to its bureaucratic and economic powers and thus thwart all attempts at fundamental reform? Or does *perestroika* indicate the continuing vitality of the ruling élite's hold on power? The answers may not be simple, but the questions are highly pertinent.

III. The Neo-Traditionalist Model

A third type of approach, meanwhile, which can be described as the Neo-Traditionalist Model, focuses on the unchanging traditions of Soviet and Russian political behaviour. A society in which peasants still cross themselves, as some do, when in front of the wax-like image of Lenin in the Red Square Mausoleum is not a 'modern' one. The rites and rituals of Soviet life such as the secular idolatry of Lenin or the 'petition culture' (discussed in Chapter 3) suggest a Third World, not a First World, polity. As Pipes has pointed out, for example, the parallels between the Criminal Code of 1845 and of 1960 are at least as marked as the differences.

Code of 1845:

Persons guilty of writing and spreading written or printed works or representations intended to arouse disrespect for Sovereign Authority, or for the personal qualities of the Sovereign, or for his government are on conviction sentenced, as offenders of Majesty, to the deprivation of all rights of property and exile for hard labour in fortified places from ten to twelve years.

Code of 1960:

Agitation or propaganda carried on for the purpose of subverting or weakening Soviet authority . . . or circulating for the same purpose slanderous fabrications which defame the Soviet state and social system . . . shall be punished by the deprivation of freedom for a term of six months to seven years, with or without additional exile for a term of two to five years . . .'

(Pipes 1977, p. 294)

Jowitt has taken the point further, arguing that the Soviet state of the 1980s has degenerated from a once 'heroic' modernising age into an essentially pre-modern and corrupt system, a 'status society' closer to traditional charismatic and feudal regimes than to modern legal rational societies. Political barons extracted 'tribute' or 'booty' and planned heroic projects, all at the expense of methodical planning, proper scientific and industrial development, or basic system integrity (Jowitt 1983).

There are weaknesses in the approach. Corruption is hardly the defining characteristic of the system, however ineradicable it might be. It occurs to a greater or lesser extent in all societies. Moreover, it underplays the real evidence of modernisation which does exist, such as élite commitment to economic and technological progress and to social development through education, urbanisation, and the specialisation inherent in a modern industrial economy. To the extent that it conceptualises the phenomenon of widespread corruption, however, neo-traditionalism is a useful approach. After all, as Amann has put it, it is difficult to see why the élite (however defined) would need to engage in corrupt practices if it systematically exploited the masses as an established class or stratum (Amann 1986, p. 482). It also suggests that system stability derives at least in part from secrecy and censorship; for secrecy is seen as a defining feature of the Soviet policy. A neo-traditionalist political order 'is concerned more with public awe than public legitimacy'. The 'public dissemination of information independent of party control' is seen as destabilising, at least to pre-*glasnost* era rulers.

All these approaches see Soviet politics essentially as concerned with élite power, not popular welfare. They stress the view that politics is about the maximisation of such power and privilege. Public welfare is at best a 'grudging concession made in order to ensure social stability' (Amann 1986, p. 478). Those in the West who take such views tend to argue that the Soviet system is therefore profoundly anti-democratic, anti-Western in its culture. Furthermore, it is inherently unpredictable because of the perpetual and often secret struggle for power. Its long-term ideological aims and objectives are immutable, and geared to global expansionism. Given the pervasive nature of state power over society, even domestic economic weaknesses can be transcended, for what cannot be gained by technological superiority can be achieved by nurturing traditional Russian stoicism and tolerance in the face of material deprivation.

In these terms, then, Soviet system stability is a matter of rapacious élite power wielded through ideology or myth and secrecy and through control of the state bureaucracy, as much as through physical coercion or terror. The results can be seen in the continued history of global expansionism, military might and mass acquiescence.

There are three other basic models, meanwhile, which see system stability deriving essentially from the élite's use of power as a means to an end, namely, achieving security, consumption or welfare goals. The regime is thus concerned – like others – with the costs of the arms race, the search for security, and the problems of how to maintain stability and control in a rapidly changing world. Such approaches tend to stress that stability has stemmed from the ability to evolve and adapt to change and, as it were, provide both guns and butter. Breslauer has termed such a regime one of 'welfare state authoritarianism': power and stability through consensus (Breslauer 1978). Let us now consider these three models.

Stability through Consensus

1. The Modernisation Model

The Soviet Union can be seen as a 'modernisation' regime, that is to say, one that has been characterised above all by an emphasis on urbanisation, industrialisation, and bureaucratisation. Modernisation approaches stress this aspect of Soviet experience. Modernisation is a global phenomenon of the twentieth century, history being ultimately propelled by technological change. Such change, runs the argument, must lead to at least a degree of social pluralism, economic decentralisation and political democratisation. In a word, dictatorship and the micro-chip are incompatible.

Some modernisation theorists such as Shils have seen such development as a 'universal aspiration', implying, as Brzezinski and Huntingdon put it, a long-term 'convergence' of political systems (Brown 1974). Such views have their critics. The Soviet Union remains a one-party state deriving from a very specific history and tradition. Moreover, there is still a substantial gap between Soviet reality and the modernisation ideal of legal-rational government in which the rule of law is dispensed independently of the party *nomenklatura*. As Jowitt has argued, the Soviet system retains strong pre-modern features, not least political and legal arbitrariness. Thus, whereas the Jewish dissident campaigner Anatoli Shcharansky spent the years 1978 to 1986 in prison after applying for an exit visa to Israel, Stalin's daughter Svetlana Allilueyva, who defected to the West in 1967 and became a major critic of the Soviet system in the 1960s and 1970s, was allowed to return to Georgia in 1984, where she was allocated a large flat, a pension, a chauffeur and private tuition for her daughter. She was then allowed to emigrate to the West, despite repeated public criticism of the Soviet system.

The modernisation approach has its merits, however. It helps account not just for *perestroika* and its underlying imperatives, but for the sheer persistence over more than thirty years of economic and technological pressures for reform, despite deep-rooted bureaucratic opposition. It is a reminder that many of the issues that the Soviet Union faces are to be found elsewhere, such as alcoholism and drugs, the need for industrial renewal, the search for strategic security, or rising ethnic consciousness. Political development approaches also provide a clue to system stability, seeing it as derived from the commitment to change (Almond and Powell 1966). A strong state in itself is not an adequate goal, for there must also be some mass welfare which ultimately can only come through a secure economic base.

II. The Institutional Pluralism Model

An alternative approach is what has often been termed as the model of Institutional Pluralism. This highlights the tensions that do exist within the élite, and which are in a sense the necessary product of modernisation. The ruling group in itself now lacks sufficient expertise in decision making, and thus has allowed a degree of institutional pluralism, or licensed élite debate. In a sense it has no choice but to hold the ring, for the ruling group itself, although it may define the goals, does not have 'the answers' about how to achieve those goals (Skilling and Griffiths 1971). Such a phenomenon can be seen as a rational development. Leaders are no longer in the heroic mould but merely, and quite legitimately, attempting 'system maintenance', as Gehlen put it (Gehlen 1969). Others see it as a form of degeneracy; Downs has called such pluralism 'authority leakage', weakening the integrity of central authority and policy implementation (Smith 1980, p. 7). The 1983 Novosibirsk Report, using another metaphor, described such 'braking mechanisms' as fundamentally inimical to reform.

Either way, such approaches run the risk of overstating the coherence and power of any institutional groups and, as with the corrupt neo-traditionalist model, may be more applicable to the Brezhnev era than before or since. The leading and co-ordinating role of the party apparatus is not to be underestimated, argue the critics, nor is the continuing coercive power of the state.

Institutional pluralism, however, helps explain the complexities of reform. The ruling group is subject to real institutional constraints, in practice locked into a 'circular flow of power' with the wider party and state *apparat*, all being mutually interdependent. Thus, to take an example referred to earlier, the collapse of détente in the late 1970s could, at least in part, be attributed to the necessary compromise that Brezhnev had struck with the military on expenditure levels, the result being a widespread perception in Western chancelleries that Soviet military power was excessive and incompatible with the professed diplomatic and political aims of détente, i.e. a lessening of tensions in Europe. One policy cancelled out the other.

Institutional pluralism suggests that this form of 'authority leakage' is the necessary price paid for basic élite stability. The ruling group retains control because of a 'trust in cadres' which allows sufficient latitude to the newly confident professional and institutional groups. Institutional conflict and competition are inevitable but can be adequately channelled and controlled by the ruling group. The alternatives, uncontrolled pluralism or dictatorial rule, are either unacceptable or unworkable.

III. The State Corporatist Model

The pluralist model emphasises conflict and competition within the élite. An alternative is the State Corporatist model approach with an emphasis on élite consensus. The principal institutional élites have been 'incorporated' into a mutually acceptable framework (Bunce and Echols 1980). So, too, have the masses in the sense that, in return for socio-economic security, the masses support the existing order. In the corporate state the élite and the masses strike a tacit deal which meets many of their respective needs. Such a model, implying patterns of coalition building by the ruling group, may be again more applicable to the Brezhnev era than before or since. The ending of Brezhnev's 'stability of cadres' policy, the redeployment of thousands of bureaucrats, and the exposure of élite corruption, all suggest conflict rather than consensus.

Nonetheless, the corporatist model has some strength. The collapse of détente may have been unwelcome to the Soviet leadership, but the apparent tension between diplomatic and military policy under Brezhnev was not an unintended consequence of the state being merely a passive middleman surrounded by competing élites. On the contrary, this tension was an acceptable price paid for basic 'coalition maintenance'. The ruling group broadly does retain control over basic priorities. Environmental problems have simply not had a high priority, but satisfying the military élite has. The political agenda itself is thus under the control of the ruling group, and system stability is achieved through a mix of institutional and social consensus.

The Uncertain Future

Both groups of models provide clues to the question of political stability. As Amann has argued, it may be that a new synthesis is now needed which stresses the sheer complexity of Soviet reality, a model that merges 'coercion and consensus' as it were. On the one hand, the Soviet system is 'coercive' in its treatment of dissidence, and has a ruling élite that has traditionally taken a very proprietorial attitude towards state assets, believing firmly in its own 'leading role'. On the other hand, there is evidence of 'consensus', of genuine commitment to economic and social development and to both the necessity and the desirability of expanding the bounds of permissible public debate. The élite appears to have practiced a combination of idealism and self-preservation which has helped maintain overall system stability, at least until now.

Is this still the case? In the context of the very fast-moving Gorbachev era, it is far from clear that old assumptions about system stability still apply with the same force. Political leaders since 1985 have more than once warned that stability can no longer be taken for granted. Hitherto, system performance has been adequate to maintain economic growth, social cohesion and national security, but the 1980s saw issues grow more complex, and margins tighter, a fact now openly accepted. Arguably, political problems are no longer non-cumulative, and the factors that contributed to stability in the past are now of decreasing salience. Certainly the radical economist Nikolai Shmelev, writing in the widely read monthly Soviet journal *Novy Mir*, takes this view. In 1988 he wrote that 'without dramatic transformations half-way into the 1990s, our economy will collapse, along with our society and our foreign relations, our army and so on. It will be too late then to worry about democracy; such a collapse is more likely to produce a dictatorship.'

How realistic is such a vision? What overall assessment of the strengths and weaknesses of the *perestroika* process can be made at this stage? Can the potentially revolutionary consequences of *perestroika* be harnessed in an evolutionary way? It is to these questions that we now turn in the concluding chapter.

Further Reading

The most comprehensive short overview of political models and Soviet politics is Amann (1986) on whom this chapter draws quite heavily. More detailed studies include Brown (1974) and Breslauer (1978). Specific cases for particular approaches are made by Brzezinski (1969), Schapiro (1972), Nove (1975), Bunce and Echols (1980) and Jowitt (1983).

8

Perestroika and the Prospects for the 1990s

Recent events have moved very fast indeed. The Soviet Union is now undergoing a degree of economic, cultural and political ferment unseen since the 1920s. This book has sought to show that this ferment is, at least in part, an evolutionary development. *Perestroika* did not spring fully formed from the new leadership in 1985. It can be traced back in part to Andropov and even to the now much maligned Brezhnev years which never entirely stifled pressures for reform. (Let it not be forgotten that Gorbachev was, after all, first appointed to the ruling Politburo by Brezhnev.) Moreover, *perestroika* has continued to evolve since 1985. There has never been a single blueprint for change, the process being a continuing political response to rapidly changing social and technological pressures. This evolutionary thrust could well be maintained in the future if present attempts to make *perestroika* in some way 'irreversible' prove successful.

However, as the chronology of events at the end of this book indicates, events have not only moved very fast but at an accelerating pace. Strikes, riots and mass uprising over nationalist grievances, food supplies and environmental pollution, have suddenly become commonplace. The 1988 Party Conference was an occasion for genuinely open and unscripted political debate of a kind not seen since the chaotic times of the 1917 Revolution. Have *glasnost* and *perestroika* turned into a revolutionary process, the shock too great for the political system?

It is to the overall prospects for *perestroika* in the 1990s that we now turn in this final chapter. We offer some tentative guidelines that need to be borne in mind when attempting any such forward view. These guidelines are anchored in the belief that, although there is much promise in the *perestroika* process, it does face very considerable difficulties.

Let us start with the case that an optimist would make – an optimist here being defined as one who sees *perestroika* not just as a major and positive development of historic significance, but as a broadly successful and irreversible process.

Perestroika: The Optimist's View

1. The first point to make is its sheer necessity. Rigid Marxist one-party states have simply outlived their usefulness, as China's leaders discovered in the 1970s. Soviet leaders are now also convinced that, without successful and radical economic reform, the Soviet Union's claim to superpower status will become increasingly threadbare by the end of the century, for it will rest, at the most, on merely an arid military strength. It is not even a matter now of catching up with the Japanese economy and its record of growth and innovation. The real urgency is not to fall even further behind, for as mentioned earlier, the Soviet economy missed out almost entirely on the crucial global revolution of information technology in the 1980s, and the comparative situation is if anything even worse then when *perestroika* was first mooted. The gaps are likely to get even more marked in the 1990s. As Gorbachev reputedly said to the Writers' Union as early as 1986, 'if not us, who? if not now, when?'

This crisis therefore requires a radical restructuring at home and some fundamental new thinking abroad. It includes a scaling down of military commitments, not least in Afghanistan, and in the ruinously expensive and outdated Cold War with the United States. Gorbachev has described the two superpowers as 'two dinosaurs circling each other in the sands of nuclear confrontation.' While the rest of the world has evolved, the two superpowers have become stuck in an obsessive confrontation that has shown little rational regard for their survival as great powers. Both superpowers thus were, and are, heavily overmilitarised. In the case of the Soviet Union this process has deepened the stagnation of the 1980s; in the case of the United States, it has undermined the nation's economic competitiveness and its financial solvency. In their very different ways, both nations have come to recognise this. No coherent political alternative to *perestroika* that addresses these unavoidable issues has existed now in the Soviet Union for several years.

2. *Perestroika* is not a one-off policy, but a process, and, though it is still evolving, there is an intellectual and political coherence to it. The connections have been made, as Khrushchev or Andropov never made them, between political, social and economic life, domestic and foreign policy. All are interwoven. The very scale and ambition of *perestroika* is a major strength. Economic reform cannot be undertaken in isolation from political, constitutional, cultural and social questions. Equally, isolated reversals or changes in policy direction need not necessarily derail the deeper processes now in motion, a point that can be reinforced by considering the larger, but somewhat switchback, experience of China's modernisation programme since the death of Mao Tse Tung in 1976.

3. The Soviet political leadership is collectively and publicly committed to *perestroika*. It has persuaded itself that a 'pre-crisis situation' existed by the mid-1980s. Political and social stability, as the Polish Solidarity crisis of 1980–82 reminded them, could not be taken for granted, nor could their own political immortality. Though there are leadership divisions, they are about the pace and scope of change, not about its necessity. Gorbachev's presumed opponent Ligachev, the focus for conservative opposition to *perestroika* within the party apparatus, does not want to stop *perestroika*, but only to slow it down to a less hectic pace, preserving élite privileges, for example, along the way. Such divisions are, in any case, signs of political life: as one party spokesman put it in 1987, 'you only find complete unanimity in a cemetery.'

4. Revolutions from above are not to be underestimated. *Perestroika* and *glasnost* came originally from above, in 1985–86, and the political weapons that Soviet leaders possess to achieve their objectives are still formidable, as the significant leadership changes of September 1988 illustrated. Of course an autonomous

civil society is beginning to emerge and so far *perestroika* is opposed by vested interests that are skilled at undermining any reforms. Nonetheless, traditions of power and patronage remain, and the leadership essentially still controls the political agenda, not least through its continuing hold over the media, and its ability to think and plan strategically. For instance, the main Soviet press has carried very little coverage of the upsurge in nationalist activity in the Baltic States since 1987. Similarly, new party schools to create a fresh stratum of young, highly skilled and thoroughly restructured officials have been established in Tashkent, Baku, Volgograd and Moscow since 1986. Just as Stalin's party schools produced a 'thrust forward' generation in the early 1930s, so *perestroika* intends to do in a very different context in the 1990s.

Meanwhile, the changes now underway to democratise political institutions come essentially from above, and are a considered attempt to break ingrained past habits. Instead of an appointed, secure stratum of officials, there are now to be, at least in principle, competitive elections for all party secretaries and all members of soviets. Public accountability to the electorate is the new watchword, with 'stability of cadres' to be avoided at all costs, no-one being eligible to serve for more than two five-year terms of office, either in party or soviet posts. Such changes are potentially of enormous and lasting political significance for they imply a quite new relationship between the ruling party *apparat* and the people.

5. Underlying social trends both helped create and now reinforce *perestroika*. The traditional relationship between state and society, with few if any constraints on state power, has simply had to be rethought. Soviet leaders now preside over a highly educated society that is ready for a degree of self-management, and is less prepared than before to accept authority uncritically. A small but revealing trend which illustrates this point has been the series of successful popular local campaigns since 1985 to persuade the authorities to give back old names to streets, districts or even whole cities that in the past have been unilaterally renamed after political leaders, often when they were still in power. This could be seen simply as another attack on the Brezhnev era, the scores of towns or settlements named after him having been particularly

vociferous, but circumstances have changed and expectations are now different. It is unlikely that this 'renaming mania' will ever again be applied as part of a cult around a Soviet politician still in power.

6. *Glasnost* is a revolutionary and irreversible development, one of major significance. The intelligentsia always knew more than it should, but most ordinary people now do as well. Journalism, literature, film, radio and television cannot simply be forgotten once seen or read; an entire nation cannot regain what has been described by the Soviet press as its 'ideological virginity', and taught to forget what it knows.

The public reassessment of Soviet history that has taken place since 1987 is a case in point. Seventy years are now being reassessed: communist saints uncanonised, the damned redeemed, old heresies turned into new orthodoxies. Even Lenin himself is not entirely sacred: the prophetic attack by the revolutionary Rosa Luxemburg as far back as 1918 on Lenin's vanguard party has been openly debated by the playwright Mikhail Shatrov. ('With the repression of political life in the land as a whole . . . public life gradually falls asleep . . . only the bureaucracy remains. The few dozen party leaders of inexhaustible energy and boundless experience direct and rule . . . at bottom then a clique affair. A dictatorship to be sure; not the dictatorship of the proletariat, but only a dictatorship of a handful of politicians.')

Stalin's 'genocide' against the peasants, in which '5–10 million died', has been discussed, and the show trials of the 1930s have been described as making 'Shakespeare's tragedies look like children's stories'. Even Stalin's war record has come under fiercer attack than ever before. The 1939 Pact with Hitler has hitherto been seen as a tactical necessity, even if Stalin subsequently wasted the time that he gained by it. But it has now been characterised as a 'criminal mistake' which 'nearly destroyed' the Soviet Union.

The cumulative shock of all this is undeniably great, but significantly, it does not appear to have polarised the nation in the way that Khrushchev's denunciations and Solzhenitsyn's writings did a quarter of a century ago. The events themselves are much more distant, and society in any case much less ideologically fixated and less easily shocked than before. Indeed, the entire *glasnost* phenomenon has been remarkably well absorbed, a sign of a more mature society, determined to think for itself.

7. A government of laws, not of men – the party's political power constrained by the rule of law – is now a stronger possibility than at any time in the past. The party leadership intends to create a 'socialist legal state' that would seek not only to enshrine *glasnost* and *perestroika* in a constitutional and legal code, but would – perhaps more significantly, for the mere passing of laws does not guarantee their observance – attempt to subordinate the powers of the party to due legal processes. Calls have been made for a judiciary independent of the party *apparat*, quite unlike the practice of the past seventy years; for the assumption of innocence before trial; for the ending of all anonymous denunciations as a basis for prosecution; and for the public accountability of the KGB to the Supreme Soviet.

8. Last, but not least, is the 'Gorbachev factor' itself. History will no doubt paint a more subtly shaded picture, but the reputation currently enjoyed by the Soviet leader is extraordinarily high, and a significant political factor in its own right. Gorbachev is seen by many in the Soviet Union as their 'last, best hope', a powerful, clever and imaginative reform leader. The charisma has a global dimension, too, for Gorbachev is more widely approved of and trusted in the West than many western leaders.

This array of optimistic arguments is highly persuasive, but there are several opposing factors that must be borne in mind, some of considerable weight. What does the pessimist say?

Perestroika: **The Pessimist's View**

1. Economic *perestroika* – the real key to success or failure – is proving to be far more difficult than had been anticipated. The obstacles appear almost insurmountable. This is in part because vested interests opposed to reform are simply not implementing agreed changes. As *Novy Mir* remarked in January 1988, in an analogy with the 1917 Revolution, there is a situation of 'dual power', the radicals in the leadership often thwarted by the conservatives in the country at large. But even if this were not the case, the sheer scale and complexity of economic *perestroika*

could well prove self-defeating. It is not the most radical set of reforms in the communist world – those in China and Hungary should probably share such a prize – but in the Soviet context it is not far short of revolutionary. It is a simply enormous task to change the economic habits of a lifetime, to replace the Stalinist legacy of centralised, authoritarian control with a partially decentralised economic market system – almost desperately so.

In the short run, many central ambiguities remain, not least because of the piecemeal advance of *perestroika*. What really counts: quality or quantity? Gorbachev implies quality: 'we don't need millions of tons of steel, millions of tons of cement, millions of tons of coal as such . . . what we need are tangible end results.' Yet sheer quantity, high growth rates, are politically desirable. Low growth looks like failure and is easily interpreted as such by conservative critics.

2. Popular support for economic *perestroika* is in reality quite limited. Support certainly exists amongst skilled workers, lower level managers and members of the intelligentsia, but this is a fairly confined range. Most people are much less sure about the virtues of *perestroika* for them, particularly if it means higher prices, unemployment, and unsettling changes. For many, in any case, *perestroika* has yet to progress beyond political speeches and slogans. There are few signs that the endemic shortages and queues are withering away, or that ordinary daily economic life is changing for the better. The reform leaders have been saying, in effect 'work hard and life will be better'. Many people appear to be replying, 'when life is better, then we shall work harder. Meanwhile, we shall wait and see.' What does a true *perestroikist* do to gather support, therefore? He could loudly attack the bureaucracy, as Yeltsin did. The Yeltsin affair of 1987–88, however, ended rather unsatisfactorily. Yeltsin, the very model of a dynamic and committed *perestroikist*, who had been much praised in the Soviet media, was unceremoniously sacked from the leadership amidst very limited public explanations, and accusations of 'demagoguery'. Many ordinary party workers in favour of reform were left confused and dispirited.

Ironically, despite all the obloquy now heaped upon the Brezhnev era, its economic record was not bad enough to result in any real collapse, and at the grass roots many people therefore remain to this day unconvinced about the overall necessity for economic *perestroika*, let alone about its specific side effects.

3. Thus, there have been clear signs that economic *perestroika* is bogged down. Gorbachev at the 1988 Party Conference said that 'we could have accomplished far more than we have'. Income growth in 1987 was only 2.3 per cent, the second lowest since 1945. The previous lowest was 2.2 per cent under Brezhnev in 1979. Farm output, a key factor, remains virtually stagnant. The gap between political promise and economic reality remains worryingly wide. Unless there is real and tangible improvement in living standards within the next year or two, argues the pessimist, the entire *perestroika* process will be damagingly discredited. As in the past, the impetus for economic reform could disappear, victim to party opposition and popular apathy. An enterprise manager in a Soviet television play by Fyodor Burlatsky pessimistically made just this point in 1986:

> Nothing will come of this [*perestroika*], nothing . . . the reason is simple. We are tackling these questions for the third time in our lives. The first was after Stalin . . . we talked of nothing else but reforms, democracy, public self-management. And what came of it? The second time was in 1965 [The Kosygin economic reforms]. Again nothing happened. Everything disappeared without trace, like water into the sand . . . It's not our way. It contradicts the whole system.

Admittedly, Burlatsky's chosen conclusion was more optimistic, but the pessimist made a good case.

4. *Glasnost* may be a necessity, but a very destabilising one, both for society and for the party. *Glasnost* evolved as a deliberate political strategy designed to strengthen the hand of the party radicals. It sought to encourage enthusiasm for change by allowing conservative vested interests to be openly challenged from below. *Glasnost* therefore has political parameters. It is not – at least in theory – total or unqualified, but a strategy designed to allow public discussion of 'socially significant matters' and to provide protection against civil abuses by law enforcement agencies. It is not a charter for 'cliques, demagogues and nationalists' to agitate 'to the detriment of the Soviet state and society'. All this has been officially spelt out, and can be seen for instance in the way in which the Brezhnev era is now politically re-written under *glasnost* in an almost wholly negative way – far more than the record justifies.

Despite this, many conservative critics within the party have suggested that this is exactly what has happened. *Glasnost* breeds chaos, as events in the southern republics and in the Baltic have shown only too clearly. *Glasnost* breeds disillusion. What is achieved by suggesting that the Stalin era was not socialist in any sense? Is it constructive for legal experts in *Literaturnaya Gazeta* to argue that the Soviet Union 'has not been a lawful state in the true sense for a single day in the whole history of its existence' because the ruling 'nucleus' (the party) controls the legal system? *Glasnost* breeds political disorientation, with misguided publicity for 'neo-liberals', 'militant cosmopolitans' and 'peasant socialists'. A strongly worded and articulate denunciation of *glasnost* on these lines attracted much attention when published in *Sovietskaya Rossiya* in March 1988. *Pravda* denounced it as a 'manifesto' against *perestroika*.

Glasnost is not, as one cynical émigré has suggested, 'Russian for a shortage of barbed wire'. It evolved for coherent political reasons. But, for all its attractions, it can be argued, it has its opponents, is difficult to control and threatens to undermine the stability of the Soviet system sooner or later.

5. There are major political strains associated with *perestroika*. It is an exceptionally difficult, if not impossible, task for the party leadership to carry through successfully such fundamental changes without losing control on the way. Far too much responsibility rests on the shoulders of one, admittedly charismatic, figure, Gorbachev. His support within the party is limited. Few of the 18 million party and state bureaucrats welcome radical change and, if nothing else, this could fatally slow down the pace of *perestroika*.

Moreover, there is a deeper political paradox that remains unresolved. The Gorbachev leadership wants, in effect, two incompatible things: a retention of central control ('the re-affirmation of the party's role') and greater democracy ('socialist pluralism'). Can the Soviet one-party state properly reform itself and the economy and still remain a one-party state? Can it direct and control *demokratizatsiya* in such a way that political life is rejuvenated but opposition parties are still banned? History suggests few comforting answers, as implied by the Russian saying, 'a pessimist is an optimist with a sense of history'.

Conclusion

Only time will tell who has the better arguments. If *perestroika* succeeds, the transformation of Soviet politics will be enormous and the global impact immeasurable. If it fails unambiguously, or even just disappears into the sand, then a real and perhaps terminal crisis of legitimacy and effectiveness could overtake the Soviet system. The stakes are indeed very high. This author sides with the optimists in believing that the *perestroika* process will leave deep and lasting change on Soviet politics. But at the same time it may well be misplaced to think in terms of outright success or failure. The Soviet Union is unquestionably in a new and possibly lengthy era of change and struggle, in genuinely 'interesting times'. *Perestroika*, however, like Thatcherism or Reaganism, may be seen eventually as a phase with successes as well as failures, a programme which changed its priorities over time, and had its fair share of unintended consequences. Thatcherism's priorities, after all, changed from monetarism to privatisation during the 1980s. Reagan's rearmament programme produced the formidable unintended consequence of turning the world's largest creditor nation into its largest debtor. But those who see the British or American political, social and economic systems in the 1980s either as unqualified success stories or as complete disasters are relatively few and far between, and for good reasons. Perhaps we would be wise to begin any assessment of *perestroika* in the 1990s in a similar light: not as a success, not as a failure, but as a continuing process; in this instance evolutionary in its development, but potentially revolutionary in its consequences.

A Selected Chronology of Soviet Politics, 1985–89

March 1985	Death of Chernenko; Gorbachev elected General Secretary, CPSU.
April 1985	Ligachev appointed CC Secretary for Ideology and, in effect, number two in the leadership. Subsequently becomes the spokesman for *apparat* conservatives worried at the pace of reform.
June 1985	Gorbachev publicly criticises Council of Ministers for failing to establish clearer economic and political priorities. The Five-Year Plan for 1986–91 only finally accepted after four rejections by Politburo.
July 1985	Romanov, a one-time competitor for the leadership, dropped from the Politburo; Gromyko, one of the 'old guard', elevated to State President. The Georgian Shevardnadze appointed Foreign Minister in place of Gromyko.
September 1985	Gorbachev tours West Siberian oil and gas fields. Major criticisms made; relevant ministers sacked.
October 1985	Ryzhkov succeeds the 80-year-old Tikhonov as Chairman of the Council of Ministers. Creation of a new State Committee for the Agro-Industrial complex, replacing five ministries and one state committee for agricultural matters. Geneva summit between Reagan and Gorbachev.
December 1985	Navy Chief Admiral Gorshkov retired. Other key military leaders also replaced by Gorbachev appointees, 1985–86.

January 1986

Pravda criticises élite privileges. Grishin, a one-time competitor for the leadership dropped from Politburo, replaced as Moscow city chief by the radical Yeltsin who argues 'we must not assume the continued social stability of this country'.

February 1986

27th CPSU Congress. CPSU sets itself the task of 'perfecting socialism'. On the economy, commits itself to 'a radical reform; there is no other way', after the inertia and drift of the late 1970s and early 1980s. Productivity a key target. Agricultural and industrial enterprises to sell on the open market output that is surplus to the state plan requirement. Profits to be retained. Enterprises that make losses not to be bailed out. On ideology, 'life itself forces us to take a new look . . . we cannot escape the fact that our philosophy and our economics are in a state that is some distance removed from real life . . . Fidelity to the Marxist–Leninist doctrine lies in creatively developing it on the basis of our own experience'. In international relations, polycentralism and interdependence stressed rather than a bi-polar confrontational analysis (USA v. USSR).

March 1986

One year after Gorbachev's election; 12 of 27 top leaders promoted within the previous twelve months. As well as one third of ministers, one third of regional and republic leaders, 8 out of 11 central committee secretaries. Purges replacing half or more of *nomenklatura* appointees in most of the Central Asian republics.

April 1986

The Chernobyl nuclear disaster. 31 die; 92,000 evacuated, many for ever. Some estimates suggest 10,000 Chernobyl-related deaths in the USSR in future decades. It is announced that the Soviet nuclear energy programme is to continue, however.

May 1986

'Change is not coming easily . . . its pace is being slowed to a considerable degree by the unwieldiness and inefficiency of the administrative apparatus.' (Gorbachev)

June 1986
: Writers' Union 8th Congress. Glavlit (censorship organ) to be disbanded. Pasternak to be posthumously rehabilitated.

July 1986
: Gorbachev speaks of improving relations with China and Japan; 6 divisions to be withdrawn from Afghanistan, a 'bleeding wound'.

August 1986
: Pioneering anti-drugs campaigns in the press, as well as increased anti-alcoholism and anti-corruption drives.

September 1986
: The newspaper *Literaturnaya Gazeta* calls for electoral reform: open and contested elections. Gorbachev visits Khabarovsk in the Soviet Far East. 'We need . . . little short of a revolution in the Soviet Union . . . people unwilling to make the change will have to go.'

October 1986
: Reykjavik summit with Reagan. Failure to agree on radical arms reductions.

November 1986
: Supreme Soviet passes new law encouraging private enterprise.

December 1986
: Academician Sakharov released from internal exile in Gorky. Riots in Kazakhstan following the replacement of Kunaev, the native First Secretary, by the Russian Kolbin.

January 1987
: Gorbachev makes major speech to Central Committee Plenum, criticising Brezhnev, and calling for more democracy. 'Some comrades apparently find it hard to understand that democratisation is not just a slogan, but the essence of our reorganisation.' Proposals include: new electoral procedures, with the possibility of secret ballots, for Communist Party apparatus posts; contested elections for soviets; a special national Conference in 1988 to discuss economic reform and the further democratising of Soviet society. Senior KGB officials sacked for trying to silence a campaigning Soviet journalist with concocted charges.

February 1987
: 140 dissidents freed from prison. Pasternak's

Dr. Zhivago to be published in 1988 in the journal *Novy Mir.*

March 1987

Thatcher visits Moscow and declares Gorbachev's reform programme to be 'no threat to the West'. Meets, among others, Gorbachev and Sakharov. Anna Akhmatova's epic poem on the Stalin terror, *Requiem*, published in the Soviet Union for the first time, nearly 50 years after it was written; *Pravda* warns not to go 'too far' in the search for *glasnost.* Both AIDS and homosexuality in the Soviet Union discussed for the first time in the press.

April 1987

Gorbachev in Prague calls for the elimination, in stages, of all nuclear weapons from Europe (i.e. intermediate range Cruise, Pershing, SS-20s; shorter range Pershing, SS-23s and battlefield missiles). Soviet strategists discuss the option of only 'reasonable sufficiency' rather than strategic parity with the West.

May 1987

Defence Minister and head of air defence sacked after the Rust affair, in which a 20-year-old West German successfully pilots a light plane into Moscow's Red Square.

June 1987

At the Central Committee Gorbachev calls for an end to the Stalinist command economy and a 'radical transformation' to 'democratic forms of economic management', pricing reforms and 'no upper limits on the amount of honest money' a Soviet worker should earn. Enterprises to be paid only for goods sold; 'taking our economy out of the pre-crisis situation . . . within the next two to three years . . . demands a truly revolutionary transformation'. Enterprise managers to be elected; if not profitable, enterprises to be declared bankrupt. Annual economic plans to be replaced by strategic 5- and 15-year guidelines. We are in a 'pre-crisis situation; history has not left us much time to face this task'. First new-style contested Soviet elections held. Yakovlev, a major advocate of *glasnost*, elected to Politburo.

July 1987

Citizens given the legal right to take officials to court for maladministration. Former head of Chernobyl nuclear power station sentenced to 19 years' hard labour.

August 1987

Unofficial rallies and demonstrations in the Baltic States protesting at the 1939 Nazi-Soviet Pact; Crimean Tartars protest in Red Square over their continued exclusion from the Crimea. The first conference of independent left-wing reformers in 60 years to be officially sanctioned, held in Moscow: The Federation of Socialist Clubs. Its manifesto accepts the hegemony of the CPSU but calls for greater democracy.

October 1987

The Yeltsin affair: sacked from Moscow post and dropped as a Politburo candidate after criticising Ligachev and other leaders for hampering *perestroika*. The Azerbaidzhani Aliev retired from the Politburo, reportedly on health grounds.

November 1987

The youth paper *Komsomolskaya Pravda* attacks past abuses in Soviet psychiatry in which sane dissidents were incarcerated in mental hospitals. *Izvestia* attacks the original decision to site SS-20 missiles in Europe, arguing that the Brezhnev–Gromyko foreign policy of the time was partly responsible for the ending of détente. 70th Anniversary of the Russian Revolution; Gorbachev calls Stalin's guilt 'enormous and unforgivable'. Meanwhile there is an 'increase in the resistance of the conservative forces that see *perestroika* as a threat to their selfish interests'.

December 1987

Gorbachev and Reagan sign INF Treaty in Washington, committing the two to destroying such weapons over a three-year period.

January 1988

Stalin's chief prosecutor of the 1930s, Vyshinsky, pilloried publicly as a 'monster whose claws still defile our criminal procedure and legal system'. *Pravda* accuses the Armenian political élite of corruption and failure to carry out reform, and attacks the 'mafia' of organised criminals that dominated Uzbekistan and had links with Brezhnev in recent years. *Pravda* also accuses the independent political clubs of 'political extremism, petty bourgeois outburst and anti-Sovietism'.

February 1988
Bukharin formally rehabilitated, fifty years after the show trial that led to his political disgrace and death. Talyzin sacked as Gosplan chief after less than three years. Major nationalist disturbances in Armenia in sympathy with unrest in the largely Armenian enclave of Nagorno-Karabakh in neighbouring Azerbaidzhan.

March 1988
The newspaper *Sovietskaya Rossiya* carries outspoken attack on *perestroika* and a defence of Stalin and his times. *Pravda* attempts a rebuttal. 'The time has come for a clear-cut distinction between the essence of socialism and the historically limited forms of its implementation . . . the old authoritarian methods have exhausted themselves.' Further upheavals in Nagorno-Karabakh; 31 dead (officially; but 500 or more on unofficial figures). The Armenian capital Yerevan is scene of the largest popular demonstrations anywhere in the USSR since 1917.

April 1988
United Nations agreement on the phased withdrawal of all Soviet troops from Afghanistan. Zamyatin's celebrated anti-utopian novel *We* (1920) published in the Soviet Union for the first time. Press discussions about the 'dreadful' working conditions of women in the textile industry.

May 1988
Reagan in Moscow praises *perestroika* as 'momentous' and Gorbachev as 'engaged in serious reform . . . expansionism is receding around the world'.
Gorbachev admits *perestroika* has caused turmoil even in the top echelons of the party. Yeltsin calls in a BBC TV interview for the sacking of Ligachev. Attempts by dissident groups to form an opposition political party, the Democratic Union, thwarted by the KGB. A non-party Popular Front or Union for the Promotion

of *Perestroika* meanwhile publicly advocated by party reformists. Gorbachev meets Orthodox Church leaders. New Church-State laws to be drafted. It is announced that over 13,000 Soviet troops died in Afghanistan 1979–88.

June 1988

Celebrations mark the millennium of Orthodox Christianity in Russia. Special Party Conference in Moscow, the first since 1941, passes resolutions calling for major political and constitutional changes: an executive-style presidency; no more than two 5-year terms for party officials; greater powers to the soviets; a memorial to the victims of Stalin to be built. Gorbachev, addressing the conference, calls for a fully convertible rouble; Soviet farmers to be 'genuine masters of the land they work'; the Soviet people 'want full-blooded and unconditional democracy. *Glasnost* in all things big and small.' But 'we do not abandon the role of the ruling party. On the contrary, we want to reaffirm it.' Calls for KGB to be publicly supervised by and accountable to a standing commission of the Supreme Soviet. Kamenev and Zinoviev formally rehabilitated; Bukharin posthumously readmitted to the Party; Suslov, Brezhnev's leading ideologist, criticised for the 'dogmatism and stagnation' of the Brezhnev era.

July 1988

Mass strikes and demonstrations continue in Armenia over the Nagorno-Karabakh issue. Armenian Supreme Soviet votes for the Armenian enclave's transfer to Armenia; Azerbaidzhan Supreme Soviet votes to retain the enclave under Azerbaidzhani rule. The Supreme Soviet in Moscow rules against any redrawing of boundaries. Gorbachev denounces Armenian activists as 'corrupt, enemies of *perestroika*'.

August 1988

Mass demonstrations in the Baltic States calling for full sovereignty over economic and political affairs, the restoration of pre-1940 national flags and citizenship rights, and the creation of a Soviet Union that is 'a genuine union of free peoples.' The Estonian press officially describes the arrival of Soviet troops in the Baltic States in 1940 as 'an occupation'.

September 1988   Major leadership changes announced at an extraordinary meeting of the Central Committee. The Soviet President and former Foreign Minister Gromyko (first appointed to high office by Stalin) retired, along with four other survivors from the Brezhnev era: Solomontsev, Demichev, Dolgikh and Dobrynin. Gorbachev assumes the Presidency. The conservative Ligachev downgraded from Ideology Secretary and *de facto* Number 2 to an agriculture portfolio. New Central Committee Commissions, intended to be important policy-making bodies, established.

October 1988   Popular Front movements in the three Baltic States hold founding Congresses, endorsing earlier demands and calling for an end to Russian as the local official language. The Party encourages ideas for greater economic autonomy in the Baltic, but rules against complete economic independence as 'impermissible'.

November 1988   Supreme Soviet approves constitutional reforms designed to create a streamlined new Supreme Soviet meeting in regular legislative session, a new Congress of Peoples' Deputies meeting annually and an executive Presidency with heightened powers.

December 1988   Gorbachev delivers major policy speech to the United Nations in New York calling for 'a new world order through a universal human consensus'. A 20 per cent cut in Soviet conventional forces and a writing-off of Third World debts to the Soviet Union also announced. Major earthquake in Armenia.

January 1989   Economic results for 1988 reveal a budget deficit officially put at 36bn roubles and a grain harvest the lowest since 1985, 40m tonnes short of the planned target. Price reforms postponed 'for the next two or three years'.

February 1989 Last Soviet troops withdraw from Afghanistan. Nomination meetings held for elections to the new Congress of Peoples' Deputies amidst some complaints that the Party conservatives are blocking the nomination of radicals.

March 1989 Elections to the new Congress of Peoples' Deputies.

Bibliography

Aganbegyan, A. (1988) *The Challenge: Economics of Perestroika*, Hutchinson.

Alexeyeva, L. (1985) *Soviet Dissent: Contemporary Movements for National, Religious and Human Rights*, Wesleyan University Press.

Allworth, E. (1980) *Ethnic Russia in the USSR*, Pergamon.

Almond, G. and Powell, G. (1966) *Comparative Politics: A Developmental Approach*, Little, Brown.

Amalrik, A. (1970) *Will the Soviet Union Survive until 1984?*, Allen Lane, The Penguin Press.

Amann, R. (1986) 'Searching for an Appropriate Concept of Soviet Politics', *British Journal of Political Science*, vol. 16, no. 4, pp. 475–94.

Azrael, J. (1978) *Soviet Nationalities Policies and Practices*, Praeger.

Bell, D. (1965) 'Ideology and Soviet Politics', *Slavic Review*, vol. XXIV, pp. 591–603.

Bennigsen, A. and Lemercier-Quelquejay, C. (1967) *Islam in the Soviet Union*, Pall Mall.

Bergson, A. and Levine, S. (1983) *The Soviet Economy: Toward the Year 2000*, Allen and Unwin.

Bialer, S. (1980a) *Stalin's Successors: Leadership, Stability and Change in the Soviet Union*, Cambridge University Press.

Bialer, S. (1980b) 'The Politics of Stringency in the USSR', *Problems of Communism*, May–June, pp. 19–33.

Bialer, S. (1986) *The Soviet Paradox: External Expansion, Internal Decline*, Knopf.

Bidelux, R. (1985) *Communism and Development*, Methuen.

Birman, I. (1978) 'From the Achieved Level', *Soviet Studies*, vol. XXX, no. 2, pp. 153–72.

Breslauer, G. (1978) *Five Images of the Soviet Future: A Critical Review and Synthesis*, University of California Press.

Breslauer, G. (1982) *Khrushchev and Brezhnev as Leaders: Building Authority in Soviet Politics*, Allen and Unwin.

Brown, A. H. (1974) *Soviet Politics and Political Science*, Macmillan.

Brown, A. H. (1980) in Rigby, T.H., Brown, A. H., and Reddaway, P., *Authority, Power and Policy in the USSR*, Macmillan.

Brown, A. H. (1985a) 'Gorbachev', *Problems of Communism*, May–June, pp. 1–23.

Brown, A. H. (1985b) *Political Culture and Communist Studies*, Macmillan.

Brown, A. H. (1988) 'The Soviet Leadership and the Struggle for Political Reform', *The Harriman Institute Forum*, vol. 1, April, pp. 1–8.

Browning, G. (1987) *Women and Politics in the USSR*, Wheatsheaf.

Brzezinski, Z. (1969) *Dilemmas of Change in Soviet Politics*, Columbia University Press.

Buck, T. and Cole, J. (1987) *Modern Soviet Economic Performance*, Basil Blackwell.

Buckley, M. (ed) (1986) *Soviet Social Scientists Talking: An Official Debate About Women*, Macmillan.

Bukovsky, V. (1978) *To Build a Castle: My Life as a Dissenter*, Deutsch.

Bunce, V. and Echols, J. (1980) in Kelley, D. R. (ed) *Soviet Politics in the Brezhnev Era*, Praeger.

Bushnell, J. (1980) in Cohen, S., Rabinowitch, A., and Sharlet, R. (eds) *The Soviet Union Since Stalin*, Macmillan.

Carr, E. H. (1964) *What is History?*, Penguin Books.

Carrere D'Encausse, H. (1979) *Decline of an Empire: The Soviet Socialist Republics in Revolt*, Newsweek Books.

Chamberlin, W. H. (1935) *The Russian Revolution 1917–21*, vols 1–2, Macmillan.

Churchward, L. G. (1973) *The Soviet Intelligentsia*, Routledge and Kegan Paul.

Churchward, L. G. (1987) *Soviet Socialism*, Routledge and Kegan Paul.

Cohen, S. F. (1971) *Bukharin and the Bolshevik Revolution: A Political Biography 1888–1938*, Oxford University Press.

Cohen, S. F. (1977) in Tucker, R. C. (ed) *Stalinism: Essays in Historical Interpretation*, Norton.

Cohen, S. F. (1980) in Cohen, S. F., Rabinowitch, A. and Sharlet, R. (eds) *The Soviet Union Since Stalin*, Macmillan.

Colton, T. J. (1979) *Commissars, Commanders and Civilian Authority*, Harvard University Press.

Colton, T. J. (1986) *The Dilemma of Reform in the Soviet Union*, Council on Foreign Relations, Washington, USA.

Crankshaw, E. (1976) *The Shadow of the Winter Palace: The Drift to Revolution 1825–1917*, Penguin Books.

Crouch, M. (1979) 'Problems of Soviet Urban Transport', *Soviet Studies*, vol. XXX I, no. 2, pp. 231–56.

Crouch, M. (1985) in Ambler, J., Shaw, D. and Symons, S. (eds) *Soviet and East European Transport Problems*, Croom Helm.

Crouch, M. and Porter, R. (eds) (1984) *Understanding Soviet Politics Through Literature*, Allen and Unwin.

Daniels, R. V. (1967) *Red October: The Bolshevik Revolution of 1917*, Secker and Warburg.

Daniels, R. V. (1971) in Strong, J. W. (ed) *The Soviet Union under Brezhnev and Kosygin*, Van Nostrand.

Dellenbrandt, J. A. (1986) *The Soviet Regional Dilemma: Planning, People and Natural Resources*, M. E. Sharpe.

Dewhirst, M. and Farrell, R. (1973) *The Soviet Censorship*, Scarecrow.

Dibb, P. (1986) *The Soviet Union: The Incomplete Superpower*, Macmillan.

Djilas, M. (1963) *Conversations with Stalin*, Penguin Books.

Dunham, V. (1976) *In Stalin's Time: Middle Class Values and Soviet Fiction*, Cambridge University Press.

Dunlop, J. (1985) *The New Russian Nationalism*, Praeger.

Dutt, C. (1961) *Fundamentals of Marxism–Leninism*, Foreign Languages Publishing House.

Edmonds, R. (1983) *Soviet Foreign Policy: The Brezhnev Years*, Oxford University Press.

Etkind, E. (1978) *Notes of a Non-Conspirator*, Oxford University Press.

Evans, A. J. (1977) 'Developed Socialism in Soviet Ideology', *Soviet Studies*, vol. XXIX, no. 3, pp. 409–28.

Fainsod, M. (1959) *Smolensk under Soviet Rule*, Macmillan.

Ferro, M. (1980) *October 1917: A Social History of the Russian Revolution*, Routledge and Kegan Paul.

Feshbach, M. (1982) *The Soviet Economy in the 1980s: Problems and Prospects*, Part 2, USGPO, Washington DC.

Feshbach, M. (1983) in Bergson, A. and Levine, H. S. (eds) *The Soviet Economy: Toward the Year 2000*, Allen and Unwin.

Fitzpatrick, S. (1982) *The Russian Revolution*, Oxford University Press.

Fortescue, S. (1986) *The Communist Party and Soviet Science*, Macmillan.

Frank, P. (1985) in Keeble, C. (ed) *The Soviet State: The Domestic Roots of Soviet Foreign Policy*, Gower.

Frankland, M. (1987) *The Sixth Continent*, Hamish Hamilton.

Friedgut, T. H. (1979) *Political Participation in the USSR*, Princeton University Press.

Gale, R. and Hauser, T. (1988) *Chernobyl: The Final Warning*, Hamish Hamilton.

Gehlen, M. (1969) *The Communist Party of the Soviet Union*, Indiana University Press.

Gelman, H. (1984) *The Brezhnev Politburo and the Decline of Détente*, Cornell University Press.

Getty, A. (1985) *The Origins of the Great Purges: the Soviet Communist Party Reconsidered 1933–38*, Cambridge University Press.

Ginsberg, Y. (1967) *Into the Whirlwind*, Collins Harvill.

Goldman, M. (1980) *The Enigma of Soviet Petroleum*, Allen and Unwin.

Goldman, M. (1987) *Gorbachev's Challenge: Economic Reform in the Age of High Technology*, Norton.

Gorbachev, M. S. (1987) *Perestroika: New Thinking for our Country and the World*, Collins.

Gustafson, T. (1981) *Reform in Soviet Politics: Lessons of Recent Policies on Land and Water*, Cambridge University Press.

Gustafson, T. (1983) *The Soviet Gas Campaign: Politics and Policy in Soviet Decision Making*, Rand Corporation.

Gustafson, T. and Mann, D. (1986) 'Gorbachev at the Helm', *Problems of Communism*, May–June, pp. 1–19.

Haimson, L. H. (1964) 'The Problem of Social Stability in Urban Russia 1905–17', *Slavic Review*, vol. 23, pp. 619–42; vol. 24, pp. 1–22.

Halliday, F. (1986) 'Islam and Soviet Foreign Policy', Paper presented to NASEES Conference, Cambridge.

Hanson, P. (1987) in McCauley, M. (ed) *The Soviet Union under Gorbachev*, Macmillan.

Harasymiw, B. (1984) *Political Elite Recruitment in the Soviet Union*, Macmillan.

Harding, N. (1977) *Lenin's Political Thought*, vol. 1, Macmillan.

Harding, N. (ed) (1984) *The State in Socialist Society*, Macmillan.

Hazan, B. (1987) *From Brezhnev to Gorbachev: Infighting in the Kremlin*, Westview, Boulder, Colorado.

Helgeson, A. (1982) in Brown, A. H. and Kaser, M. (eds) *Soviet Policy for the 1980s*, Macmillan.

Hill, R. (1980) *Soviet Politics, Science and Reform*, Martin Robertson.

Hill, R. and Frank, P. (1987) *The Soviet Communist Party*, Allen and Unwin.

Holmes, L. (1981) *The Policy Process in Communist States: Politics and Industrial Administration*, Sage.

Hosking, G. (1980) *Beyond Socialist Realism: Soviet Fiction since Ivan Denisovich*, Granada.

Hough, J. F. (1969) *The Soviet Prefects: Local Party Organs in Industrial Decision Making*, Harvard University Press.

Hough, J. F. (1980) *The Soviet Leadership in Transition*, Brookings Institution.

Hough, J. F. and Fainsod, M. (1979) *How the Soviet Union is Governed*, Harvard University Press.

Joint Economic Committee, US Congress (1982) *Soviet Economy in the 1980s: Problems and Prospects*, US Government Printing Office.

Jones, E. (1985) *Red Army and Society: a Sociology of the Soviet Military*, Allen and Unwin.

Jones, E. and Woodbury, B. L. (1986) 'Chernobyl and Glasnost' *Problems of Communism*, Nov–Dec., pp. 17–27.

Jowitt, K. (1983) 'Neo-traditionalism: the Political Corruption of a Leninist Regime', *Soviet Studies*, vol. XXXV, no. 3, pp. 298–312.

Karklins, R. (1986) *Ethnic Relations in the USSR: the Perspective from Below*, Allen and Unwin.

Kelley, D. R. (1976) 'Environmental Policy Making in the USSR: the Role of Industrial and Environmental Interest Groups', *Soviet Studies*, vol. XXVII, no. 4, pp. 570–89.

Kerblay, B. (1983) *Modern Soviet Society*, Methuen.

Khrushchev, N. S. (1971) *Khrushchev Remembers*, Sphere Books.

Khrushchev, N. S. (1977) *Khrushchev Remembers*, vol. 2, Penguin Books.

Kissinger, H. (1979) *The White House Years*, Weidenfeld and Nicolson.

Kolkowicz, R. (1967) *The Soviet Military and the Communist Party*, Princeton University Press.

Komarov, B. (1978) *The Destruction of Nature in the Soviet Union*, Pluto.

Kopelev, L. (1977) *No Jail for Thought*, Secker and Warburg.

Labedz, L. and Hayward, M. (eds) (1967) *On Trial: The Case of Sinyavsky and Daniel*, Collins Harvill.

Lakshin, V. (1980) *Solzhenitsyn, Tvardovsky and Novy Mir*, MIT Press.

Lampert, N. (1985) *Whistleblowing in the Soviet Union: Complaints and Abuses under State Socialism*, Macmillan.

Lane, D. (1968) *The Roots of Russian Communism*, Martin Robertson.

Lane, D. (1982) *The End of Social Inequality: Class, Status and Power Under State Socialism*, Allen and Unwin.

Lane, D. (1985a) *State and Politics in the USSR*, Basil Blackwell.

Lane, D. (1985b) *Soviet Economy and Society*, Basil Blackwell.

Lewin, M. (1968) *Russian Peasants and Soviet Power*, Allen and Unwin.

Lewin, M. (1973) *Lenin's Last Struggle*, Pluto

Lewin, M. (1985) *The Making of the Soviet System: Essays in the History of Interwar Russia*, Methuen.

Lewin, M. (1988) *The Gorbachev Phenomenon*, Radius.

Linden, C. (1966) *Khrushchev and the Soviet Leadership 1957–1964*, Johns Hopkins University Press.

Litvin, V. (1987) 'Reforming Economic Management', *Problems of Communism*, July–Aug., pp. 87–92.

Litvinov, P. (1969) *The Demonstration in Pushkin Square*, Gambit, Boston, USA.

Lubin, N. (1984) *Labour and Nationality in Soviet Central Asia*, Macmillan.

McAuley, A. (1984) in Roi, Y. (ed) *The USSR and the Muslim World*, Allen and Unwin.

McAuley, A. (1988) *Religion, Nationalism and Economic Development in Soviet Central Asia*, University of Essex Russian and Soviet Studies Discussion Paper No. 9.

McCauley, M. (1976) *Khrushchev and the Development of Soviet Agriculture*, Macmillan.

McCauley, M. (ed) (1987) *Khrushchev and Khrushchevism*, Macmillan.

McNeal, R. H. (1988) *Stalin: Man and Ruler*, Macmillan.

Malcolm, N. (1984) *Soviet Political Scientists and American Politics*, Macmillan.

Mandelstam, N. (1975) *Hope Against Hope*, Penguin Books.

Marples, D. (1986) *Chernobyl and the Nuclear Power in the USSR*, Macmillan.

Marsh, R. (1986) *Soviet Fiction since Stalin: Science, Politics and Literature*, Croom Helm.

Matthews, M. (1978) *Privilege in the Soviet Union: A Study of Elite Life-Styles under Communism*, Allen and Unwin.

Matthews, M. (1986) *Poverty in the Soviet Union*, Cambridge University Press.

Medvedev, R. (1971) *Let History Judge*, Macmillan.

Medvedev, R. (1975) *On Socialist Democracy*, Knopf.

Medvedev, R. (1982) *Khrushchev*, Basil Blackwell.

Medvedev, Z. (1969) *The Rise and Fall of T. D. Lysenko*, Columbia University Press.

Medvedev, Z. (1983) *Andropov*, Basil Blackwell.

Medvedev, Z. (1986) *Gorbachev*, Basil Blackwell.

Micklin, P. (1987) 'The Fate of "Sibaral": Soviet Water Politics in the Gorbachev Era', *Central Asian Survey*, vol. 6, pp. 67–88.

Millar, J. R. (ed) (1987) *Politics, Work and Daily Life in the USSR: a Survey of Former Citizens*, Cambridge University Press.

Miller, J. H. (1987) in Miller, R. F., Miller, J. H. and Rigby, T. H. (eds) *Gorbachev at the Helm*, Croom Helm.

Morton, H. (1980) 'Who Gets What, When and How? Housing in the Soviet Union', *Soviet Studies*, vol. XXXII, no. 2, pp. 235–59.

Narkiewicz, O. (1970) *The Making of the Soviet State Apparatus*, Manchester University Press.

Nekrich, A. (1978) *The Punished Peoples*, Norton.

Nelson, D. (1988) *Elite-Mass Relations in Communist Systems*, Macmillan.

Norman, H. (1902) *All the Russias*, Heinemann.

Nove, A. (1964) *Was Stalin Really Necessary? Some Problems of Soviet Political Economy*, Allen and Unwin.

Nove, A. (1969) *An Economic History of the USSR*, Penguin Books.

Nove, A. (1975) 'Is there really a Ruling Class in the USSR?' *Soviet Studies*, vol. XXVII, no. 4, pp. 615–38.

Nove, A. (1982) in Brown, A.H. and Kaser, M. (eds) *Soviet Policy for the 1980s*, Macmillan.

Odom, W. (1973) 'The Soviet Military: The Party Connection', *Problems of Communism*, Sept.–Oct. pp. 12–26.

Pethybridge, R. W. (1962) *A Key to Soviet Politics: the June Crisis of 1957*, Allen and Unwin.

Pethybridge, R. W. (1972) *The Spread of the Russian Revolution*, Macmillan.

Pethybridge, R. W. (1974) *The Social Prelude to Stalinism*, Macmillan.

Pipes, R. (1977) *Russia Under the Old Regime*, Penguin Books.

Potichnyi, P. (ed) (1988) *The Soviet Union: Party and Society*, Cambridge University Press.

Rigby, T. H. (1968) *Soviet Communist Party Membership 1917–69*, Princeton University Press.

Rigby, T. H. (1970) 'The Soviet Leadership: Towards a Self-Stabilising Oligarchy?' *Soviet Studies*, vol. XXII, no. 2, pp. 167–91.

Rigby, T. H. (1979) *Lenin's Government: Sovnarkom 1917–22*, Cambridge University Press.

Ross, C. (1987) *Local Government in the Soviet Union*, Croom Helm.

Ryan, M. and Prentice, R. (1987) *Social Trends in the Soviet Union from 1950*, Macmillan.

Rywkin, M. (1982) *Moscow's Muslim Challenge*, Hurst.

Sakharov, A. (1969) *Progress, Coexistence and Intellectual Freedom*, Penguin Books.

Sakharov, A. (1975) *My Country and the World*, Collins Harvill.

Schapiro, L. (1965) *The Origins of the Communist Autocracy*, Praeger.

Schapiro, L. (1972) *Totalitarianism*, Macmillan.

Schmidt-Hauer, C. (1986) *Gorbachev: The Road to Power*, Tauris.

Scott, J. (1973) *Behind the Urals: An American Worker in Russia's City of Steel*, Indiana University Press.

Service, R. (1979) *The Bolshevik Party in Revolution 1917–23*, Macmillan.

Shafarevich, I. (1974) in Solzhenitsyn, A. (ed) *From Under the Rubble*, Collins Harvill.

Shatz, M. (1980) *Soviet Dissent in Historical Perspective*, Cambridge University Press.

Shevchenko, A. (1985) *Breaking with Moscow*, Knopf.

Shragin, B. (1978) *The Challenge of the Spirit*, Knopf.

Skilling, H. G. and Griffiths, F. (1971) *Interest Groups in Soviet Politics*, Princeton University Press.

Smith, G. (ed) (1980) *Public Policy and Administration in the Soviet Union*, Praeger.

Solzhenitsyn, A. (1974) 'A Letter to the Soviet Leaders', *Sunday Times* (London), 3 March 1974, pp. 33–6.

Solzhenitsyn, A. (1975) *The Gulag Archipelago*, vol. II, Collins-Harvill.

Taafe, R. (1980) in Cohen, S., Rabinowitch, A. and Sharlet, R. (eds) *The Soviet Union since Stalin*, Macmillan.

Tatu, M. (1969) *Power in the Kremlin*, Viking.

Thornton, J. (1986) 'Chernobyl and Soviet Energy, *Problems of Communism*, Nov.–Dec., pp. 1–16.

Trotsky, L. (1959) *The Russian Revolution: The Overthrow of Tsarism and the Triumph of the Soviets*, Doubleday.

Tucker, R. C. (1973) *Stalin as Revolutionary 1879–1929*, Norton.

Tucker, R. C. (1987) *Political Culture and Leadership in Soviet Russia: From Lenin to Gorbachev*, Wheatsheaf.

Voinovich, V. (1977) in *Kontinent 2: The Alternative Voice of Russia and Eastern Europe*, Coronet.

Von Laue, T. H. (1981) 'Stalin Among the Moral and Political Imperatives, or How to Judge Stalin?', *Soviet Union*, vol. 8, pp. 1–37.

Voslensky, M. (1984) *Nomenklatura*, Bodley Head.

Walker, M. (1988) *The Waking Giant: The Soviet Union under Gorbachev*, Abacus.

Wells, A. and Northedge, F. (1982) *Britain and Soviet Communism*, Macmillan.

Wheatcroft, S. G., Davies, R. W. and Cooper, J. (1986) 'Soviet Industrialisation Reconsidered', *Economic History Review*, vol. 39, pp. 264–94.

White, S. (1979) *Political Culture and Soviet Politics*, Macmillan.

White, S. and Pravda, A. (eds) (1988) *Ideology and Soviet Politics*, Macmillan.

Wimbush, S. Enders (1985) *Soviet Nationalities in Strategic Perspective*, Croom Helm.

Yanov, A. (1977) *Détente After Brezhnev*, University of California Press.

Yanov, A. (1978) *The Russian New Right*, University of California Press.

Yanowitch, M. (1977) *Social and Economic Inequality in the Soviet Union*, M. E. Sharpe, White Plains, New York.

Yanowitch, M. (1986) *The Social Structure of the USSR: Recent Soviet Studies*, M. E. Sharpe, White Plains, New York.

Zaslavsky, V. (1982) *The Neo-Stalinist State: Class, Ethnicity and Consensus in Soviet Society*, Harvester.

Zaslavsky, V. and Brym, R. (1983) in Jacobs, E. M. (ed) *Soviet Local Politics and Government*, Allen and Unwin.

Zaslavskaya, T. (1984) 'The Novosibirsk Report', *Survey* 28 (120), pp. 80–108.

Ziegler, C. (1987) *Environmental Policy in the USSR*, Pinter.

Zinoviev, A. (1978) *The Yawning Heights*, Bodley Head.

Index

Abuladze, 164
Afghanistan, 56, 85, 99, 103, 127,
    130, 137
Aganbegyan, 180, 189, 200
agriculture, 6, 27–8, 39, 44, 57
    under Gorbachev, 144–9, 190
Aitmatov, 161, 164
Akhmatova, 69, 163
Aksyonov, 159
alcoholism, 58, 60
Alexander II, 5, 7, 64, 69
Aliev, 136
Alliluyeva, 210
Amalrik, 88
Andropov, 58–60, 63, 79, 134, 216
Armenia, *see* Caucasus
Astafyev, 147
Azerbaidzhan, *see* Caucasus

Baikal, 195–7
Baikal–Amur Railway, 54, 110,
    122, 201
Bakunin, 87
Baltic States, 2, 96, 146–7, 165–7
Belinsky, 157
Belorussia, 2, 169
Belov, 147
Beria, 38
Biryukova, 133
Bolsheviks, *see* Communist Party
Bondarev, 147, 165
Brest Litovsk, 17, 21
Brezhnev:
    Brezhnev doctrine, 50
    criticisms of, under Gorbachev,

56, 66, 79, 86
détente and political ascendancy,
    51–6, 118
dissidents under, 94–7, 159–62
early career, 47–50, 84
ideology under, 78–9
succession crisis, 58–61
Brodsky, 163
Bukharin, 17, 18, 24, 27, 41–2, 69,
    190
Bukovsky, 83, 95, 102
Bulgakov, 158, 163
Burlatsky, 184, 221
Bykov, 164
Byzantine Empire, 1

Catherine the Great, 2
Catholicism, 172
Caucasus, 2, 133–4, 147, 165–177
censorship, 68–9, 157
Central Asia, 2, 46, 48, 57, 68, 137,
    146–8, 161, 164–77
Central Asians, 3, 109–10, 123,
    187, 197–202
Chekhov, 148, 161
Chernenko, 58–61, 79
Chernobyl, 69, 119, 165, 192–5
China, relations with, 39–41, 51,
    127
civil society, 92–3, 217
Civil War, 17–20, 91
Communist Party:
    and revolution, 11, 14–20, 30
    apparat, 110, 120–4, 137
    Central Committee, 139

241

Communist Party: *continued*
  1988 Conference, 66, 113, 121
  Congresses, 20, 34, 40–1, 43, 56,
    65–7, 113, 129
  democratic centralism, 118–24
  General Secretary, 117–18
  membership, 91, 107–12
  perestroika under Gorbachev,
    66, 137–41, 217
  Politburo, 115–17, 131–7
  Secretariat, 116–17
  'stability of cadres' under
    Brezhnev, 48, 60
Constituent Assembly, 16
Council of Ministers, 119–20
Crimea, 2, 5, 96
Cuban crisis, 41, 65
Czechoslovakia and 1968, 50, 69,
  95, 97, 116, 127

Daniel, 49, 94–5
Decembrists, 8
dissidents:
  under Brezhnev, 93–100
  under Gorbachev, 100–3
Djilas, 117, 206
Dostoevsky, 100, 175
Duma, 7
Dudintsev, 159

Economy:
  under Lenin and the Tsars, 4–8,
    21–2
  under Stalin, 22–8
  under Brezhnev, 180–5
  reform debates, 49, 65–7, 185–
    91
Ehrenburg, 42
Eisenhower, 40–1
Engels, 17, 22, 75, 85
Estonia, *see* Baltic States
Etkind, 108

Finland, 2
First World War, 7, 12
foreign policy: 'new thinking'
  under Gorbachev, 67–8, 205
Furtseva, 133

Gagarin, 39
Galanskov, 95
Georgia, *see* Caucasus
Ginsberg, 95
Gladkov, 158
glasnost:
  the strategy, 65, 69, 92–3, 103
  the consequences, 162–5, 218,
    221–2
Gogol, 33, 80, 157
Gorki, 158
Gorshkov, 129
gosplan, 26, 120, 188–91
Gorbachev:
  and criticisms of Brezhnev, 56,
    66, 79, 86
  as cult figure, 89
  early career, 4, 62–4
  and economy, 187–91, 220–2
  and foreign policy, 67–8, 205
  ideology and *perestroika*, 79–82,
    151–4
  and military, 129–30
  and nationalities, 175–7
  and Politburo, 115, 118, 131–7
  as President, 66
  reform programme, 64–9, 138–
    41, 215–22
  reformer before 1985, 63–4
  and writers, 162–5, 215
Granin, 121
Grechko, 133
Gromyko, 62, 133, 135
Grossman, 163
Grishin, 62
Gumilyev, 163

Helsinki, 74
Herzen, 9
Hitler, 27, 30, 32, 218
housing, 150–1, 153
Hungary, 43, 57, 214

Ideology:
  effectiveness of, 83–7
  and political culture, 87–93
  under Brezhnev, 78–9
  under Gorbachev, 79–83

under Lenin and Stalin, 72–5
informal groups under Gorbachev,
102–3, 139
institutional pluralism, 210–11
Ivan the Terrible, 2, 4

Japan, 7, 64
Jews, 7, 96–7, 167, 175

Kadets, 12
Kalinin, 168
Kamenev, 15, 23
Karpov, 121
Katayev, 158
Kazakhstan, *see* Central Asia
Kerensky, 14–15
KGB, 38, 58, 60, 86, 96, 103, 111,
120–1, 125–6
Khrushchev:
  career, 36–8, 114, 117
  de-Stalinisation, 60–3
  and dissidents, 94
  economic and foreign policy, 39–
    45, 190
  fall, 45–7, 116
  and ideology, 44, 64, 77–8, 216
  and writers, 159
Kirov, 28
Kissinger, 51–2
Kolbin, 177
Kopelev, 29
Kornilov, 14
Kosygin, 47–50, 53, 185
Kron, 162
Kulakov, 62–3
Kunaev, 170, 177

Latvia, *see* Baltic States
Lenin:
  banning of factionalism, 20–22
  cult of, 76, 85, 89, 91
  early career, 10, 20
  Last Testament, 20–1, 41
  Politburo under, 115
  responsibility for Stalin, 34
  in Revolution, 14–20
  writings, 11, 76
Ligachev, 135, 216

limitchiki, 146–8
Lithuania, *see* Baltic States
Litvinov, 95
Lukyanov, 137
Lysenko, 155–6

Macmillan, 46
Malenkov, 38, 42
Mandelstam, 88, 155, 157, 163
Mao Tse-Tung, 40, 86, 216
Martov, 10
Marx, 10, 74–5, 85
Marxism–Leninism, 74–7
Medvedev, 83, 96–102, 206
Mensheviks, 10, 14–17, 19–20
Mikoyan, 123
military:
  under Brezhnev, 50, 54
  under Gorbachev, 68
  under Khrushchev, 46
  political role, 125–31
  in war, 12, 30
modernisation, 209–10
Molotov, 38, 42, 61
Morozov, 84
Mzhavanadze, 170

nationalities question, 2, 54, 165–
  77, 217
Neizvestny, 46
neo-traditionalism, 207
NEP under Lenin, 21–5, 67
Nicholas I, 8, 88
Nicholas II, 7, 12
Nixon, 51–2
nomenklatura, 110–11, 137–8

Oblomov, 25
Octobrists, 12
Ogarkov, 127
Orthodox Church, 2, 54, 89, 111,
  172, 175
Orwell, 69, 206
Ostrovsky, 158

Pamyat movement, 175
Pasternak, 69, 159, 163

perestroika:
  and dissidents, 100–3
  and the economy, 65–7, 185–91
  'the human factor', 152–3, 186
  and the military, 130–31
  and the Party, 66, 137–41, 217
  popular support for, 220
Perevedentsev, 200
Peter the Great, 2, 4, 8, 64
Plekhanov, 10
Platonov, 163
Podgorny, 47–8, 51
Poland, 2, 61
  and Solidarity, 53, 56–7, 126–7,
    174, 216
political culture, 91–3
Populists, 7, 9
Preobrazhensky, 18
Prokofiev, 155
Provisional Government, 13–15
Pushkin, 9

Radishchev, 8
Rasputin, 146, 160, 197
Reagan, 68
regional variations in living
    standards, 147–9
religion, 172
renaming of towns, 217–18
Russian historical tradition, 9–13
Russian nationalism, 174–5
Russian Revolution 1905, 7
  1917, 12–17
Russian Social Democratic and
    Labour Party, 10
Rybakov, 163
Ryzhkov, 133–4

Sakharov, 69, 83, 96–102, 137, 206
Semichastny, 55, 116
Shafarevich, 174
Shelepin, 55, 116
Shelest, 53, 116, 170
Shevardnadze, 133–4
Shatrov, 218
Shmelev, 213
Sholokhov, 158, 160
Shostakovitch, 155

Shragin, 88, 155
Shukshin, 160
Shcharansky, 102, 210
Siberian rivers, 197–202
Sinyavsky, 49, 94–5
Slavophile–Westerniser debates,
    8–10
Slyunkov, 134
Socialist Revolutionaries, 9, 12,
    14–16
society, past and present, 144–54
Solomontsev, 136
Solzhenitsyn, 42–4, 47, 92, 96–102,
    119, 160, 183, 218
Soviet patriotism, 90–1
Soviets:
  under Gorbachev, 139–41
  in revolution, 12–17
Stakhanov, 27, 152
Stalin:
  anti-Stalin campaign:
    under Brezhnev, 55
    under Gorbachev, 4, 218
    under Khrushchev, 41–4
  collectivisation and
    industrialisation, 25–42
  and cult, 28
  early career, 4, 20–5, 117
  historical controversies, 31–35,
    77
  and ideology, 76–7
  purges, 28–30, 33
  1941–5 War, 30, 32–3, 40
  and writers, 158–9
state capitalism, 206–7
state corporatism, 212
Stolypin, 6, 21
Suslov, 63

Tadzhikistan, *see* Central Asia
Talyzin, 191
Tatar Mongols, 2
Tolstoy, 87
totalitarianism, 32–3, 204–5
town-versus-country divisions,
    145–9
Trans-Siberian Railway, 6
Trifonov, 160–1

Trotsky, 13, 17–20, 23–4, 42
Tukhachevsky, 127
Tvardovsky, 120

Ukraine, 2, 54, 165–77, 192–5
United States, relations with, 39–41, 51–3, 68–9, 215–6
urbanisation, 143–9
Ustinov, 127, 135
Uzbekistan, *see* Central Asia

Vavilov, 155
Virgin Lands scheme, 39–40, 48, 170
Voinovich, 96, 159, 163
Vorotnikov, 134

wages and differentials, 149–54
War Communism, 30
water resources, 3, 195–202
Witte, 6

women in Soviet Union, 109, 133, 149, 177
World War II, 27, 30, 91, 126
Writers' Union, 156–65

Yakovlev, 133–4
Yazov, 133
Yeltsin, 116, 120
Yevtushenko, 55, 121
Yezhov, 28
youth (Young Communist League), 83, 85, 126, 138
Yugoslavia, 40

Zaikov, 118
Zalygin, 164
Zaslavskaya, 152–3, 186, 189
Zinoviev (the revolutionary), 15, 20, 23
Zinoviev (the dissident), 89, 92, 205
Zhukov, 127